Mercury
COMET
& CYCLONE
Limited Edition Extra
1960-1975

Compiled by R M Clarke

ISBN 1 85520 7133

BROOKLANDS BOOKS LTD.
P.O. BOX 146, COBHAM,
SURREY, KT11 1LG. UK
sales@brooklands-books.com

A-MYCCX2

Printed in China

ACKNOWLEDGEMENTS

Brooklands Books has been publishing automotive works of reference books on a wide range of makes and models for 50 years and today is the world's largest publisher of such material. Like other books in the Brooklands series, this is intended to be a living archive for Mercury Comet and Cyclone enthusiasts. For this the company is grateful to the enthusiast book buyers and to the publishers of the original material used in each book. In the case of the Mercury Comet and Cyclone we would like to express our thanks to the publishers and photographers of *Auto, Automobiles Topics, Car and Driver, Car Craft, Car Facts, Car Life, Cars, Classic American, Hot Rod, Motorcade, Motor Life, Motor Trend, Motor Trend Buyers Guide, New Cars, Performance Cars, Road Test, Sports Car Illustrated, Supercars* and the *World Car Catalogue*.

R.M. Clarke

When Ford introduced the Falcon in 1959 for the 1960 model year as a compact to compete with the Volkswagen Beetle and other European imports, it was only a matter of time before a larger sibling would be released. You see, the American automobile industry did not do small cars—it was ingrained in its psyche that bigger was better.

Sure enough, the Lincoln-Mercury Division of Ford announced the Mercury Comet just four months after the Falcon! Without being too unkind to the Comet, it was a Falcon with a longer wheelbase (all aft of the back seat), a stretched rear end and ugly slanted tail-lights and not much else. Mechanically practically everything was interchangeable.

However, there were bigger plans afoot as soon became apparent a year later when the Comet S-22 V8 was announced as a 1963½ model. Boasting the 260-cid V8 engine, 164 bhp, 4-speed manual gearbox and 10-inch drum(!) brakes all round, it was quite a performance machine for the time. It zipped from 0-60 mph in 11.5 seconds and would run to 94 mph. Stopping it was always an interesting experience.

In the context of what was happening in the US automobile industry at the time, the progression from compact to super-compact to mid-sized was inexorable; it was a time when too much of a good thing was still not enough!

It was not long before the Lincoln-Mercury Division was fielding ever-larger "compacts" that could trace their lineage back to the Falcon and original Comet. By 1964 there was the Comet Cyclone with an even larger 289-cid V8 and in the following year a complete redesign also brought more sheet metal and the added option of a massive 390-cid V8 engine. Would you believe that disc front brakes were an option, even with the biggest engine? Shows how times were then….

By 1967 it was no longer a compact but a proper mid-sized car line that was a Mercury first, Comet second. It went head-to-head with the Pontiac Le Mans chasing the sports sedan buyer in the US market. By 1968 there was the Cyclone GT fastback coupe that was considered by Ford enthusiasts as the epitome of style and performance— the top of the line model could be equipped with every conceivable luxury item and the 355 bhp 428-cid V8 engine. Top speed was only 117 mph but the 0-60 sprint took just 6.0 seconds, very good for a 4000 lb coupe in 1968.

There was a model hiatus in 1970, the Comet name returning in '71 as a rebadged Maverick--*deja vu*. By now the excitement in the model had gone and it was little more than a price-leader for the Mercury range. As the decade passed the inevitable growth of the lineup meant that within five years the roots of the model had vanished as the marketeers took over and expanded the range to market segments never before seen as Lincoln-Mercury territory. In the ever-changing world of the automobile nothing stands still for fear of being overtaken by so-called progress. And that is what happened to the Comet—it lost its identity and was soon a spent force within the Ford Motor Company.

Gavin Farmer

CONTENTS

THE COMET

A penetrating technical analysis of Fo-Mo-Co's new "not-big-not-small" car

FORD'S NEW COMPACT, the Falcon, had been on the market but four months when a still newer, slightly enlarged version was announced—the Comet. Technically, the Falcon's wheelbase of just .5 in. under the recognized limit of 110 in. makes it a true compact, yet the Comet, though very similar, does not qualify because its wheelbase is 114 in. Just how Ford could produce a car so similar to the Falcon, yet so different in appearance and dimensions is a part of the story to follow.

The Concept

The Falcon project was inaugurated in July of 1957 and since it was conceived as a "small" or compact car, it represented a drastic about-face from the thinking which brought the huge 1957 Ford Fairlane into being. In the earliest planning stages the goal was not merely to produce a compact car. More correctly, the basic idea was to see how much the overall dimensions of a car could be reduced and still retain comparable and competitive "full-6-seater" interior roominess. The final result, as seen in the Falcon and Comet, is an interior with just a little less hip room and rear-seat knee room than is found in the so-called big cars.

One interesting point is found in the overall height: 54.5 in. Cars can be built even lower (the Thunderbird is 52 in. high), but the extra inches allow higher seats and this increases the available leg room without the need for a longer wheelbase. A further advantage of extra height is found in the entrance/exit provisions. Ford package designers felt that it should be made easy to get in and out of a utility car of this type. A high roof helps with this problem, and by making the roof contour flatter and thinner than usual, they found it possible to get the upper horizontal edge of the door openings even higher than normal, for the o.a. height selected. Thus, the Falcon (and Comet) have a higher door than any of the new competitive cars.

Once a seating package has been settled, it becomes a simple matter to locate the mechanical components. Since the front toe boards and dash line were right up against front wheels, it was possible to locate the powerplant at either end of the vehicle. Ford chose the front end location for the engine for technical reasons which will be explained later. This also gives a not-incidental advantage of tremendous luggage space without excessive rear end overhang.

Long before the Falcon was ever in production, a more de luxe version of the car was being tooled-up. The Comet is essentially the Falcon with all principal components interchangeable, but with the following exceptions:
1 New front-end sheet metal
2 New rear-end sheet metal
3 New rear-quarter roof sections
4 Wheelbase lengthened 4.5 in.

The increase in wheelbase was accomplished by the simple expedient of relocating the Falcon's 50-in. rear springs, with the axle centerline moved 4.5 in. aft. The new rear-end sheet metal panels cover up this change, but it can readily be observed by noting the wider area just forward of the rear wheel—the area under the rear door wheel cut-out. Cowl, front doors and all body structure are identical. Rear doors are identical, except for the window framing.

Interestingly enough, the Comet station wagon has the shorter Falcon wheelbase and all wagon sheet metal is interchangeable with Falcon from the cowl on back.

From the above it is easy to see that Comet interior dimensions are identical with those of the Falcon, except for the fact that a larger rear-end overhang gives the Comet sedans 2 extra cu ft for luggage. The Comet's wheelbase of 114 in., accompanied by an overall length of 194.9 in., gives it the rather dubious advantage of being very nearly as large as "full-sized" cars of only a few years ago. However, at 2518 lb, curbside, it is much lighter and its appearance is certainly very good by American standards.

To summarize, here's how the actual package dimension's compare, on the 4-door sedans:

	Falcon	Comet
Wheelbase	109.5	114.0
Front overhang	29.4	30.8
Rear overhang	42.2	50.1
Length o.a.	181.1	194.9
Curb weight	2425	2518

Unitized Construction

As is well known, Ford pioneered unit construction in this country in 1935, with the Lincoln-Zephyr (Chrysler Air-Flows had a vestigial, but separate, frame in 1934). Thus it is not surprising to find the Falcon/Comet body shell and structure designed to perform the duties of a frame. Such a design virtually precludes any possibility of future convertible-type bodies being offered, but it gives a notably rigid structure with a worthwhile saving in weight. Entirely different assembly line procedures are required, of course, but ultimately this method of construction and assembly should also produce some cost savings.

An unusual feature of the Falcon/Comet structure is the employment of zinc-coated structural members. This reduces weight by allowing thinner gauge metals with a durability equivalent to the older body-on-frame designs. The problem was the difficulty of welding zinc-coated steel to uncoated steel. This was solved by Ford research engineers via electric welding with special electrodes. Zinc coated parts are located under the car and include rocker panels, floor pan channels and rear body framing, the latter being roughly equivalent to the old-style "kick-ups" of a frame.

Fenders are bolted on, which obviously makes the Falcon/Comet concept of different styling at each end rather convenient, for them. Of course this feature has other advantages too, such as ease of replacement, with resultant lower insurance costs. Ford also points out that better hood fits are possible, because the fenders can be adjusted during assembly.

Suspension

The Falcon and Comet have identical suspension systems, front and rear. At the front, pressed steel wishbones are used with ball joints to serve as steering pivots.

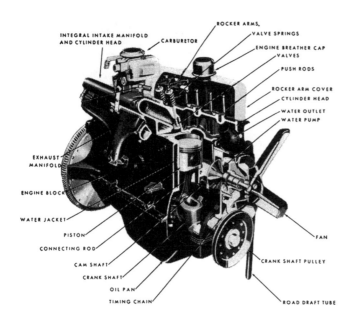

Both cars have 50 in. leaf springs at the rear, though the mounting points and brackets are necessarily different, because of the longer wheelbase of the Comet. The Falcon's rear ride rate is stiffer than the Comet's—the Falcon being 90 lb/in., while the Comet is only 80 lb/in., despite its slightly higher load. All this means that the Comet will ride exceptionally "soft," but its cornering roll will be more noticeable than that of the Falcon. Rear suspension geometry gives 5.5% understeer: a modest amount.

Steering on both cars is identical, with conventional dual pitman arms. The overall steering ratio, including linkage, is 27:1, giving 4.6 turns lock to lock. The Falcon's turning circle is 37.7 ft, but the longer wheelbase Comet requires 39.3 ft.

Ford engineers gave us the following comparison of steering effort, which shows why power steering is not needed on either the Falcon or Comet.

	Weight at front	Rim Pull
Conventional	2097	46
Comet	1580	26
Power Steering	2125	11

Brakes

All brakes are Bendix duo-servo type in 9 in. drums. The front linings are 2.25 in. wide, the rears are 1.50 in. and total effective lining area is 114.3 sq in. The hydraulic system puts 63% of the total braking effort on the front wheels, via a 1-in. master cylinder and a pedal travel of 6.5 in. The small drums are said to be particularly fade-resistant, because a 9 in. drum at 600° F expands less than an 11 in. drum at the same temperature. No automatic adjustment feature is provided, nor is one optional (as is the case on at least one competitor).

Engine and Transmission

While Crosley pioneered the over-square engine with 2.50 x 2.25 dimensions, Ford's new Falcon/Comet powerplant goes about as far as any yet, with dimensions of 3.5 x 2.5 for a stroke/bore ratio of only 0.715. The reasons for going to this extreme are somewhat obscure, but overall engine length was no problem and the short stroke

The coil spring encloses the damper and both are located above the upper wishbone. The original design specified a roll center 5 in. above the ground to eliminate the need for an anti-roll bar. However, the final design has the roll center dropped to 2.5 in. and an anti-roll bar is fitted. Suspension geometry gives 35% anti-dive; and the ride rate is 80 lb/in. on the Falcon, and slightly softer on the Comet. The Comet's ride is described as "60 per minute" which means that the frequency is one of the lowest in the industry.

In this connection, the forward location of the engine is of considerable value. The resultant forward weight bias gives a car basic understeer and good high-speed directional stability. In addition, the ride engineer had an "easier" problem to solve because a slightly heavy front end gave a "slow" ride motion with relatively stiff springs, and shorter bump and rebound travel.

Mechanical components of the Comet are almost entirely Falcon too.

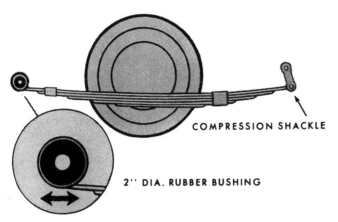

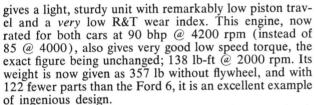

COMPRESSION SHACKLE

2" DIA. RUBBER BUSHING

Front bushing of rear spring allows some movement.

Comet wagon is Falcon shell with changed sheet metal.

gives a light, sturdy unit with remarkably low piston travel and a *very* low R&T wear index. This engine, now rated for both cars at 90 bhp @ 4200 rpm (instead of 85 @ 4000), also gives very good low speed torque, the exact figure being unchanged; 138 lb-ft @ 2000 rpm. Its weight is now given as 357 lb without flywheel, and with 122 fewer parts than the Ford 6, it is an excellent example of ingenious design.

Noteworthy features of this engine include no aluminum (except pistons), centerline-split crankcase, in-line valves with wedge chambers, an intake manifold cast integral with the head and a 4-main-bearing cast crankshaft with cored holes to save weight. The main bearings are very large (2.248 in.) and the rods are very short at 4.855 in., center to center. In all, this is a very sound powerplant, one that will prove to be long-lived, yet obviously designed to be produced at the lowest cost.

Both cars use an entirely new 3-speed manual transmission and a conventional (non-centrifugal) clutch. The clutch-driven disc measures 8.5 in. and is inset into the flywheel, the latter being described as the "pot-type." This moves the aluminum clutch housing, the cast-iron trans-

mission case and attendant parts slightly forward for a smaller, less bulky floor cover in the front compartment. An automatic transmission is optional at extra cost and it has only 2 speeds forward, aided by a torque converter with a stall speed multiplication factor of 2.4.

The new rear axle is very light and utilizes the high-offset type hypoid gears pioneered by Ford a few years ago. The Falcon employs an axle ratio of only 3.10:1, but the he vier (by 93 lb) Comet will have a ratio of 3.56:1 in all models. This will give the Comet a definite performance advantage, with a 15% better performance factor to offset its 4% weight disadvantage.

Conclusion

The Falcon is definitely the lowest production-cost design of any compact, and the car is priced accordingly. It probably should have the 3.56 axle ratio of the Comet to give it a little more performance, but Ford obviously wants the Falcon to be as economical as possible (which it is), and wants to reserve the plushier Comet as a better performer and an easier rider, for those who will pay the modest additional cost. ◉

Unitized body shell is becoming more prevalent with U.S. manufacturers each year.

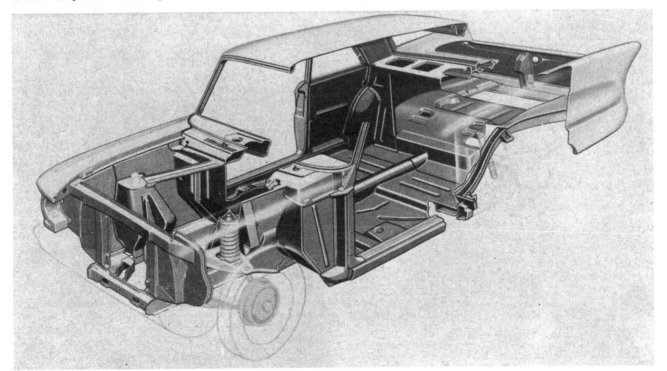

ROAD TEST

RESTYLED Falcon shell carries a grille not unlike the '60 Merc. The test proved that these exterior changes are the main points of difference between the Comet and Falcon.

COMET power at present is the 144-cubic Falcon inline six. Greater weight of Mercury compact caused it to take nine seconds longer than Falcon in 0-60 test runs.

The newest name among the compact cars now on the road is "Comet," the smaller car being handled by Mercury dealers—although the car is not officially designated as a Mercury by the Ford Motor company.

There may be some question whether or not the car is actually a compact. Mercury has thus far avoided attaching any label of size. Like the standard Rambler, the Comet falls somewhere midway between the dimensions of larger cars and true compacts.

The Comet reported upon here was a production prototype and it was tested as long ago as early last December. In order to reduce exposure of the then-unseen car to the public, the testing was conducted chiefly at night on relatively remote public roads in Arizona, California and Nevada. Distances covered, of course, were considerable and the car was fully evaluated on both flat and mountainous terrain.

The Comet, in size, is 195 inches overall length on a wheelbase of 114 inches. Most compacts are 180 inches long and about 108 inches from wheel to wheel. Since standard-sized low-priced cars average 211 inches in length and have wheelbases about 118 inches, the Comet apparently is a compromise between the two categories.

COMET

Mercury's small car adds pounds but loses POWER

It is only in these overall dimensions, however, that the Comet occupies middle ground. In all other respects it is a compact car. The reason, of course, is that the Comet is based upon the Ford Falcon design, which has turned out to be especially successful. That fact gives the Comet a good start.

Since the Comet's power train, running gear and other major mechanical components are identical to the Falcon's, it is natural that the two cars perform in much the same manner. The Comet, as a result of its 160 lbs. greater weight, is slower in accelerating ability. Its fuel economy is from two to four mpg less than the Falcon. With these disadvantages, in comparison to the Falcon, the Comet carries a slightly higher price tag, between $100 and $200 more.

One of the Comet's points of superiority over other cars in the compact class is a more comfortable, smoother ride. The five inches of increased wheelbase iron out more rough spots in the road, which are more noticeable in cars with shorter distances between front and rear wheels. On long trips over poor roads, this is a benefit that can be very noticeable.

Yet the Comet is not a really big car, so it does not present a problem in maneuverability. On the open road it tracks very well and handles nicely in high winds, which were often encountered in the winter desert rain storms. Visibility is good and both front fenders are within range of the driver's vision line. The seating position and cushioning are also adequate.

There are no significant differences between the Falcon and Comet engines. Displacement is 144 cubic inches and the initial rated output is 90 hp, although it is probably that some options may soon be available to increase it. The greater weight of the Comet causes it to take nine seconds longer than the Falcon to reach 60 mph despite the fact that it has a 3.56 rear axle ratio, compared with the Falcon's standard ratio of 3.10.

At full throttle on straight flat roads, the Comet ran to approximately 80 mph for maximum speeds. This is adequate, of course, but the car does not reach top speed quickly. Passing ability and reserve power on hills is limited. The Comet's automatic transmission has a second gear that goes in and out repeatedly during higher normal speeds in order to accelerate around slower vehicles or up grades.

Gas mileage obtained in the testing was 21 to 23 mpg, nearly all at high highway speeds and in very little city traffic. These figures are very good by big-car standards and compare favorably with the average for the compact-car class. They would be significantly surpassed only by the Falcon itself or the Rambler

1960 COMET

Test Car

TEST CAR: Comet
BODY TYPE: four-door sedan
BASIC PRICE: $2,053

Maneuverability Factors

OVERALL LENGTH: 194.9 inches
OVERALL WIDTH: 70.4 inches
OVERALL HEIGHT: 54.5 inches
WHEELBASE: 114 inches
TREAD FRONT/REAR: 55 and 55 inches
TEST WEIGHT: 2733 lbs.
WEIGHT DISTRIBUTION: 52.8 per cent on front
wheels
STEERING: 4.6 turns lock-to-lock
TURNING CIRCLE: not available
GROUND CLEARANCE: 6.1 inches

Interior Room

SEATING CAPACITY: 4 to 5
FRONT SEAT—
HEADROOM: 38.9 inches
WIDTH: 55.2 inches
LEGROOM: 44.6 inches
TRUNK CAPACITY: 26 cubic feet

Engine & Drive Train

TYPE: ohv 6
DISPLACEMENT: 144.3 cubic inches
BORE & STROKE: 3.5 x 2.5 inches
COMPRESSION RATIO: 8.7-to-1
CARBURETION: single barrel
HORSEPOWER: 90 @ 4200 rpm
TORQUE: 132 ft.-lb. @ 2000 rpm
TRANSMISSION: two-speed automatic
REAR AXLE RATIO: 3.56

Performance

GAS MILEAGE: 21/23 mpg
ACCELERATION: 0-30 mph in 7 seconds, 45 mph in
14.2 seconds and 0-60 mph in 27.5 seconds
SPEEDOMETER ERROR: Indicated 30, 45 and 60
mph are actual 29, 41 and 55 mph respectively
POWER-WEIGHT RATIO: 30.4 lbs. per horsepower
HORSEPOWER PER CUBIC INCH: .625

COMET ROAD TEST

American among the current compact crop.

In passenger compartment dimensions, the Comet is identical to the Falcon. All the lengthening of the car has taken place aft of the rear axle. Trunk area, however, is somewhat larger than the Falcon and therefore will hold another suitcase or two more.

Since the Comet is so much like the Falcon, comparison between the two is inevitable and the obvious question is what does it have to offer to justify its extra cost and slightly lesser performance and economy.

It may be conceded that the Comet is more stylish. Detailed examination discloses many fine points where differences exist. The Comet has some sculpturing of body panels, additional chrome and probably more impressive lines, particularly at the rear.

No doubt the fact that the Comet is closely associated with Mercury will give it greater prestige in the eyes of one segment of owners. The increased length of the Comet, about 14 inches overall, undoubtedly will have the same effect. The interior finish also is a notch better than the Falcon.

On the functional side, the Comet's only discernible advantage is its ride. This is not to be discounted but how much worth can be applied to a factor such as this is debatable. From a practical viewpoint, the shorter wheelbase and overall length of the Falcon is more desirable than the Comet's slightly better ride.

The Comet, it must then be concluded, belongs in that category of prestige cars that share body and chassis components with cheaper and better performing cars and, for the increased cost, offer styling, size and modest improvement in comfort.

It must not be overlooked, however, that the foregoing comparison remarks apply only to the Comet in relation to the Falcon. It should be kept in mind that the Falcon, in the present stage of compact car development, is the best car in that class. And the very fact that the Comet is nearly identical also means it is nearly as good, by some standards, and a little better by others. ●

STORAGE capacity of the Comet is one area truly helped by its extra 13 inches in length. The added six inches in the wheelbase department has an advantage that was found on long trips.

Comet

A bit more styling, a few more horses

LINCOLN-MERCURY'S COMET, like the Falcon, continues into the new season without any fundamental changes except a bigger engine as an option and a smoother suspension system.

The new 170-cubic-inch powerplant, available at extra cost, is essentially an enlarged version of the familiar 144-cubic-inch Comet Six. Both units have the same bore, 3.50 inches, but the 170's stroke has been increased to 2.94 inches from the 144's 2.50 inches.

The change was accomplished with a re-designed crankshaft, new connecting rods and special pistons. Because of careful attention to the weights of these components, the 170 is only two per cent heavier than the 144, despite having nearly 18 per cent more displacement.

Other differences in the power option include enlargement of the single-barrel carburetor, intake system and intake valves, reshaping the cylinder head to maintain the standard 8.7-to-1 compression ratio, heavier main bearings and recalibration of the carburetor and distributor. Finally, the radiator and driveline are beefed up to accommodate the higher-output engine.

Actual ratings of the 170 are 101 hp at 4400 rpm and 156 lbs.ft. of torque at 2400 rpm. By way of comparison, the 144 develops 85 hp at 4200 rpm and 138 lbs.-ft. at 2000 rpm. A three-speed manual transmission is standard with either unit and a two-speed automatic optional.

The Comet has become known for its comfortable riding qualities because of its longer-than-compact wheelbase. Now, with the same type of front coil springs and rear semi-elliptics as the Falcon, the 1961 Comet has the same refinements for an even smoother, quieter ride.

Key to the change is a pre-lubricated, threaded metal bushing in each upper A-arm of the front suspension, replacing a rubber component formerly used. The new bushing provides a slower rebound action to reduce any jarring sensation. This, in turn, has forced the use of a lower rear spring rate for consistent overall spring behavior. Also smoothing the system is a smaller-diameter stabilizer bar.

The unit body-and-frame of the new Comet has no changes other than a re-styled grille and chrome trim.

Following the policy established with the 1960 model, the car is available as a two- or four-door sedan with a 114-inch wheelbase and 194.8-inch length, or as a two- or four-door wagon that shares the Falcon's 109.5-inch wheelbase and measures 191.8 inches overall. Standard or deluxe interior trim is offered for all four body types. ●

MORE HORSEPOWER for the Comet is optionally available with stroked version of the regular Comet Six.

REDESIGNED grille and chrome hash marks are main styling changes for Comet. Front coil springs from Falcon and new A-arm bushing improves ride, handling.

DISTINCTIVE slant-eye tail lights are retained, but semi-elliptic rear springs, also borrowed from Falcon, give the 114-inch-wheelbase Comet better riding comfort.

COMET WAGON

Simple front end of the Comet is in the rapidly-building U. S. compact car tradition. New wagon shares body parts with the less-costly Falcon.

The Comet wagon boasts 76.2 cubic feet of cargo room. Usable space is 27 inches high and 106 inches long—with back seat and tailgate down.

▶ Ford Motor Company's Lincoln-Mercury Division has a winner in the Comet. In the first six weeks' retail selling, about 28,500 Comets were delivered to customers. In industry history, this success is second only to FoMoCo's Ford Falcon.

The Comet at mid-spring was rapidly catching up to the Valiant, which in turn was breathing down Corvair's neck. Ford Division's Falcon was still way out in front but at the expense of the regular-sized Ford line, while long-suffering L-M dealers gleefully reported that the Comet was drawing into their showrooms customers who *could* be upgraded to Mercurys and Lincolns.

What is the Comet's appeal? Comet advertising claims "big car styling," "longer wheelbase" and "luxury appointments," all at compact car price and economy. Long lines of Comet customers would seem to testify to the accuracy of the market researchers' pin-pointing.

SIBLING STATUS
We found the design integration of the Comet and Falcon

very like the examples set by our English cousins at Rootes and BMC. Let's face it: the Comet is a mechanical twin to the Ford Falcon. The looks of the Comet, you might say, are only skin deep. The Comet sedan wheelbase is 4½ inches greater, providing more trunk room but equal legroom. Overall weight and length are up accordingly and bumpers, grille, front and rear quarter panels, hood, deck, trunk, instrument panel and greenhouse are different. The like and the unlike blend remarkably.

The Comet station wagon is even more like the Falcon, sharing its 109½-inch wheelbase and rear fender contours. In fact, its rear end differs only in tail-lights and bumpers.

As the Comet matures, it is developing its own character mechanically. First change was an automatic choke as standard equipment (the Falcon has a manual one). Reportedly, the engine's stroke will be lengthened slightly to obtain 170 cubic inches (the Falcon's 144). This move is not expected before the 1961 models and otherwise the engines will be identical, with cast-iron block, integral head and manifold with overhead valves and six still-oversquare cylinders, despite the stroked crankshaft.

In the November, 1959 issue, SCI presented a road test of a Falcon four-door sedan with automatic transmission. For the Comet test, we therefore chose a two-door station wagon with manual transmission. With the exception of the trim and sheet metal variations, what we say about the Comet wagon applies equally to the Falcon wagon.

THE COMET COUP
The secret of the Comet's success is its price. The four-door Comet sedan and station wagon at $2053 and $2365 retail are priced identically to the basic Valiant V-100 models, and only $85 more than stripped Falcon models. But the Comet comes with deluxe trim that's extra on the others.

Lincoln-Mercury Division makes no bones about the fact that it offers little more than a dressed-up Falcon. Why should it? Since the war, dressed-up, deluxe models have taken over the lion's share of the market. The consuming public may be rebelling against size, but there's no sign they're down on prestige or luxury.

Here's what the Comet offers as standard equipment: dual horns, dual sun visors, four headlights, front and rear armrests, cigarette lighter, deluxe steering wheel and horn ring, automatic courtesy lights, automatic choke, foam rubber seat pads in front, vinyl (rather than cloth) headliner, and more brightwork inside and out. To get a Falcon, Lark or Corvair so equipped, you'd have to pay $65 to $150 more than the "basic." So, if you want such "extras," the Comet's a good buy.

The Comet we tested, a stripped-to-the-bone, fire-engine-red, two-door wagon, carried a suggested retail price of $2310, plus transportation. Its only extras were a $74.30 heater, windshield washers for $13.70 and an outside rear view mirror.

AN EARLY EXAMPLE
Brand spanking new when we picked it up, SCI's Red Demon was one of the first Comets or small wagons off the line in February. As a result, it had some shortcomings which we hope will not appear generally on later ones.

The first thing you notice about the Comet — as with the Falcon — is that it is attractively and simply styled and carefully assembled, inside and out. Door fittings and trim are neat, welds are clean and the sheet metal shows no ripples. Even more than on the Falcon, the upholstery is very luxurious-looking.

Like most new cars, the Comet was quite stiff when we started out — particularly the clutch and the column-mounted shift lever. After 500 miles of urban, suburban, expressway and back-country-road driving, everything was nicely loosened up — to the extent that annoying squeaks had developed in the instrument panel around the glove box door and between the chromed instrument cluster housing and the dashboard, not to mention the expected tailgate and window torture strains so usual in station wagons.

Examination of the glove box door showed the red paint wearing through where it had rubbed against the panel. There was no evidence of primer. When we asked a top Ford manufacturing executive about this oversight, he expressed surprise, gave a dirty look to an assistant, and insisted this wasn't within specifications. We suspect glove box doors in Comets are now *all* primed.

ROOM FOR ROAMIN'

The Comet wagon's 76.2 cubic feet of cargo space is, according to Lincoln-Mercury public relations, more than that of the 1956 Ford wagon. It is also more than the Valiant wagon's 72 feet, but considerably less than the Studebaker Lark or the Peugeot. Don't forget, though, that the latter two have a good portion of that volume up high, where it may restrict vision. The crank-down window in the tailgate has finally been accepted by Ford in the Comet and Falcon, an improvement over the split, lift type. Door handles and window cranks, placed so they won't catch clothes, work with easy, positive action.

For those who care, we measured the Comet cargo space. Width is 45½ inches at tailgate bottom, 43½ at tailgate top, 47½ at spare wheel, 42 at rear wheel wells, and 56½ at front door. Height is 27 inches at tailgate, 31½ inches inside. Length is 106 inches with gate and rear seat down, 84 with gate up and 50½ with seat up too. That seems like plenty of room, but if it isn't, a roof-rack is available for $35.10.

HANDLING

The Comet wagon is a pleasant vehicle to drive as long as you are on good road surfaces. It's typically American, soft, comfy and not for sporting types at all. For the suburban set, this is quite all right. But on uneven, badly potted, winding trails, it speaks defiance with body squeaks and groans. It shakes, twists and bumps, trying bronco-like to throw the driver. Since Ford pioneered the station wagon, it's disappointing that one of their latest should be so lacking in the traditional go-anywhere utility of its predecessors.

The drive train is noisy, which seems typical of the Falcon-Comet series. The best improvement Ford Motor Co. could make for 1961 is rigid attention to noise suppression.

We thought the wagon inferior to the Comet sedan in both ride and control over rough surfaces. While part of this may be due to the sedan's longer wheelbase and softer spring rate, neither explains strong road shocks which were transmitted through the steering wheel of the wagon tested.

PERFORMANCE WITH DIGNITY

Acceleration is indifferent, though better than the poorly-tuned Falcon tested previously. Since the oversquare engine on this car would not lug well, judicious use of the gears was called for. Only very gentle nursing will keep the Comet from bucking and vibrating if you try to accelerate in high gear under 20 mph. We found the best shift points for ordinary driving were at 15 and 30. For maximum pick-up, it seemed best to shift at 28 and 40, which in both cases is before the power peak (4200 rpm).

RESPECTABLE ECONOMY

On a hard-driving, cross-state excursion over a variety of roads and driving conditions, the Comet gave 24 miles per gallon. After the engine is broken in, and with an "easier" driving technique, the advertised claim of 28 mpg should not be difficult to attain at moderate highway speeds. Indicated traffic mileage is around 19.

The Comet (and Falcon) wagon presents a good buy as a family utility car. It is well appointed, comfortable, roomy, and handles well on civilized roads. A reasonable compromise is reached in performance, economy and size. Shortcomings in noise control and rough roadholding should be corrected by the manufacturer.

—*Mike Davis*

ROAD TEST

COMET WAGON

Price as tested: $2384

Manufacturer: Lincoln-Mercury Division
Ford Motor Company
Dearborn, Michigan

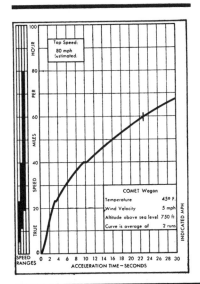

ENGINE:

Displacement	144.3 cu in, 2365 cc
Dimensions	Six cyl, 3.50 x 2.50 in
Compression Ratio	8.7 to one
Power (SAE)	90 bhp @ 4200 rpm
Torque	138 lb-ft @ 2000 rpm
Usable rpm Range	1000-4200 rpm
Piston Speed $\div \sqrt{s/b}$ @ rated power	2070 ft/min
Fuel Recommended	Regular
Mileage	19-28 mpg
Range	265-390 miles

CHASSIS:

Wheelbase	109½ in
Tread, F, R	55, 54½ in
Length	192 in
Suspension:	F, ind., coil, wishbone, lower arm, anti-roll bar; R, rigid axle, leaf springs.
Turns to Full Lock	2.3
Tire Size	6.00 x 13
Swept Braking Area	212 sq in
Curb Weight (full tank)	2655 lbs
Percentage on Driving Wheels	51%
Test Weight	2860 lbs

DRIVE TRAIN:

Gear	Synchro?	Ratio	Step	Overall	Mph per 1000 rpm
Rev	No	4.46		15.88	4.2
1st	No	3.29		11.71	5.7
			88%		
2nd	Yes	1.75		6.23	10.8
			75%		
3rd	Yes	1.00		3.56	18.8

Final Drive Ratios: 3.56 to one std, 3.89 optional.

[Acceleration graph]

Top Speed: 80 mph (estimated)

COMET Wagon
Temperature .... 45° F.
Wind Velocity .... 5 mph
Altitude above sea level ... 750 ft
Curve is average of ...... 2 runs

SPEED RANGES

ACCELERATION TIME—SECONDS

COMET 170

A minor facelift and a larger engine for 1961

MERCURY'S COMET HAS ENJOYED tremendous public acceptance, as we all know, even though it was introduced some six months after the Ford Division's very successful Falcon. Equally well known is the fact that the Comet is, essentially, a Falcon in all mechanical details. However, it does offer much better appearance, a longer wheelbase (by 4.5 in.) and a larger trunk capacity.

Outwardly, the changes for 1961 are very minor indeed—a new aluminum grille and a few minor trim details. But there *are* many important mechanical refinements, plus a significant new option: a larger engine. In our test of the 1960 Comet (August 1960) we said that "the Comet needs about 30 more cu in. of displacement and another 10-20 bhp. What it's getting is just that in 1961."

The new 170-cu-in. engine costs $45 extra and in our opinion is well worth it—for most drivers. The extra zip is noticeable the instant the car moves off and passing ability is much better, particularly above 60 mph. Top speed, though not particularly important any more, is also raised from around 82 mph to very nearly an honest 90.

Our test experience last year covered about 1000 miles of driving, but the 1961 "170" model was not available to us long enough to get any conclusive data on fuel consumption. An average-conservative driver can expect identical mileage from either the standard 144 engine or the 170 unit. In heavy traffic, particularly with the automatic transmission, the big engine will lose about 2 mpg. A heavy foot, where the extra performance is being used, will also cause a drop of one or 2 mpg.

For purposes of comparison with our previous test, we elected to test the automatic transmission version, and the extra performance is not an illusion. Last year's test showed a high gear pull reading of 200 lb/ton (our data panel said 280, a typographical error). The 1961 "144" was also tried briefly and the pull readings were identical to 1960. The Tapley pull reading with the 1961 "170" engine show a gain of approximately 12% and this is reflected in the acceleration times—0 to 60 for example comes up nearly 2 sec earlier, with the more powerful engine. However, we have never been mush-o-matic enthusiasts and it is pertinent to mention that this Comet, as tested (2-speed automatic, 170-cu-in. engine, 3.50:1 axle), will not quite "stay" with a standard 144-cu in.

COMET 170 SEDAN

SCALE:
10" DIVISIONS

DIMENSIONS

Wheelbase, in	114.0
Tread, f and r	55/54.5
Over-all length, in	194.8
width	70.4
height	54.5
equivalent vol, cu ft	432
Frontal area, sq ft	21.3
Ground clearance, in	7.5
Steering ratio, o/a	27.0
turns, lock to lock	4.6
turning circle, ft	39.9
Hip room, front	57.1
Hip room, rear	57.0
Pedal to seat back	42
Floor to ground	11

CALCULATED DATA

Lb/hp (test wt)	28.7
Cu ft/ton mile	106
Mph/1000 rpm (2nd)	19.1
Engine revs/mile	3140
Piston travel, ft/mile	1535
Rpm @ 2500 ft/min	5110
equivalent mph	97.6
R&T wear index	48.2

SPECIFICATIONS

List price	$2053
Curb weight, lb	2550
Test weight	2900
distribution, %	54/46
Tire size	6.00–13
Brake lining area	114.3
Engine type	6 cyl, ohv
Bore & stroke	3.50x2.94
Displacement, cc	2780
cu in	169.6
Compression ratio	8.70
Bhp @ rpm	101 @ 4400
equivalent mph	84.0
Torque, lb-ft	156 @ 2400
equivalent mph	47.8

GEAR RATIOS

2nd (1.00)	3.50
1st (1.75)	6.13
1st (1.75x2.4)	14.7

SPEEDOMETER ERROR

30 mph	actual,	29.0
60 mph		57.5
90 mph		86.0

PERFORMANCE

Top speed (2nd), mph	89
best timed run	90
3rd ( )	
2nd ( )	
1st (5050)	55

FUEL CONSUMPTION

Normal range, mpg	18/23

ACCELERATION

0-30 mph, sec	5.5
0-40	8.6
0-50	13.2
0-60	19.2
0-70	29.0
0-80	48.0
0-100	
Standing ¼ mile	20.7
speed at end	62

TAPLEY DATA

3rd, lb/ton @ mph	@
2nd	225 @ 39
1st	540 @ 12
Total drag at 60 mph, lb	160

ENGINE SPEED IN GEARS

2-SPEED AUTOMATIC

2nd

1st

ENGINE SPEED IN RPM
2000 3000 4000 5000

ACCELERATION & COASTING

90
80
70
60
50
40
30
20
10

SS¼

2nd

1st

MPH

ELAPSED TIME IN SECONDS
5 10 15 20 25 30 35 40 45

Falcon having a stick shift and 3.10 axle ratio. Nevertheless, the Comet offers that extra something that many people seem to want—and are willing to pay for.

Last year we commented somewhat adversely on a Comet trait which could best be described as a slight tendency to wander at high speed. For 1961, the Comet ride, which was excellent before, has been softened by 10%. The front anti-roll bar is reduced in diameter (from 0.72 to 0.65 in.) and these changes, plus a slight revision in steering geometry (Ackermann effect) all contribute to an improved feel on the road. The steering is still much too slow and the turning circle is abominable (see data panel), but the car is very easy and relaxing to drive, even at 70/75 mph. Above that speed the engine begins to buzz and seems to feel as if it's working hard. However, the longer stroke engine is still oversquare and the theoretical cruising speed of 97.6 mph indicates that this car should stand up to anything you care to give it, even down a long hill.

Mechanically, the larger displacement has been achieved by lengthening the stroke from 2.50 to 2.9375 in. The cylinder block is the same, but there are new pistons, rods, main bearings, crankshaft, cylinder head and carburetor. The 170 heads have intake valves and ports which are larger than those used on the 144 engine. When this powerplant is specified, one also gets a larger fan (15 in.), a different radiator, a heavy duty clutch (with manual transmission) and a rear axle with slightly larger gears. The manual transmission supplied with either engine is identical and it has been redesigned with revised synchromesh details, new thrust washers, coarser pitch gears and the 2nd gear ratio raised from 1.75 to 1.83:1. (First gear is unchanged at 3.29:1.)

The automatic transmission has also been changed; in particular, the torque converter has been reworked inside to give a faster break-away from the stop lights. This applies to either engine. Ford engineers also tell us that this transmission is, in effect, better matched to the engine and a number of minor calibration changes in the carburetor and spark advance also contribute extra zip with either engine. This improved calibration would also account for the fact that fuel consumption with the 170 powerplant appears to be virtually the same as in last year's test with the 144-cu-in. engine. The rear axle ratio is also changed; from 3.56 to 3.50:1—not very significant, but a change nevertheless. (This drops the engine revs per mile from 3190 to 3140.)

Equipment-wise, the Comet comes with a large number of extras which are optional at extra cost on the Falcon. Thus, when you add in automatic choke, de luxe trim, etc., the Falcon costs very little less than its "brother" in the Ford family. While we question the need for, or benefits of, the extra wheelbase, there is no denying the fact that some people think it makes for a better ride. The Comet does ride more softly than the Falcon—by design, due to a lower frequency suspension system— and not because the rear springs (and axle) are moved aft. And, of course, the longer wheelbase, plus 10 in. more trunk overhang, gives 28.5 cu ft of luggage space.

As we said last year, the Comet is amazingly close to the over-all dimension of the radical, all new, Ford of 1949. Maybe, if they had left that car alone, or at least had made only minor refinements, we wouldn't have the current compact revolution. But the Comet certainly isn't a compact by any definition, which is their business, not ours. At any rate, the 1961 Comet, particularly with the 170 engine, is a very neat, practical and sturdy automobile and one that offers an excellent combination of performance, ride and economy. ▼

PHOTOS BY BOB D'OLIVO

3 from MERCURY

- COMET
- METEOR
- MONTEREY

MT Road Test by Jim Wright, Technical Editor

a complete check-out
of the full Mercury lineup,
from compact to conventional

WHEN A MANUFACTURER offers more than one type of car (as most of them do), we always welcome the chance to test them as a group. Unfortunately, this is very seldom possible. To get really conclusive results, the test car should be lived with for at least two weeks, and no less (preferably more) than 1000 miles should be recorded on it. Work loads and scheduling (theirs and ours) or unavailability of certain test cars usually restrict us to one car from any one manufacturer at a time. This month everything fell into place, and we were able to grab off all three of the cars that Mercury is offering for 1962.

The MOTOR TREND test group consisted of the 114-inch-wheelbase luxury compact, Comet S-22; the 116.5-inch-wheelbase "in-between"-sized Meteor; and the 120-inch-wheelbase

top-of-the-line Monterey Custom. The Comet and Meteor were both two-door sedans, while the Monterey was a convertible.

The Comet and Monterey have undergone the face-lifting route to update them from the '61 models, but the Meteor is an all-new addition to the line this year. It shares the same basic shell as the Ford Fairlane but has an inch-longer wheelbase, is 6.8 inches longer overall, and has 14-inch wheels in place of the Fairlane's 13. The same engines, drive components and suspension are used in both cars.

All three of the Mercs bear a strong family resemblance when viewed from the front, and all three feature styling that is clean and smooth-lined (see MT, November and December, 1961, for the complete Mercury styling story). All three also

share the same basic purpose, that of a medium-priced (in their respective size groups), family-type transportation vehicle that offers the buyer a bit more luxury and quality than can be had in the low-price field.

The Comet test car came equipped with the optional 170-cubic-inch, 101-hp, ohv in-line Six engine, two-speed automatic transmission with 4-to-1 rear axle and air conditioning, but no power accessories. Standard engine for the Comet is a 144-cubic-inch Six, but even with the big engine, performance is so lacking that we would hesitate to recommend this setup to anyone. The Comet's 0-30, 0-45 and 0-60 mph times were 6.5, 11.9 and 22.2 seconds. It took 24.1 seconds to get to 61 mph at the end of the quarter-mile. On the top end it

was breathing hard at 75 mph, but if the long Riverside Raceway's back stretch had been longer, the car would probably reach 80 or more. Taking into consideration the fact that the 170-cubic-inch engine was originally designed for the smaller, much lighter Ford Falcon, we don't see how one could expect any better performance than this.

Our Meteor had the optional 221-cubic-inch, 145-hp, ohv V-8, two-speed automatic transmission with 3.5-to-1 performance rear axle and power brakes and steering. Our acceleration figures show that the Meteor's performance is about average for its class. We made the 0-30, 0-45 and 0-60 mph runs in 5.0, 8.7 and 15.2 seconds. The quarter-mile was run at 70 mph and 21.5 seconds, and at the end of the Riverside straight

3 from Mercury

the Meteor was flat out at 95 mph. Standard engine for this car is the same 170-incher used in the Falcon and Comet — 'nuff said.

All the power goodies, including seat and windows, were on the Monterey. This definitely dictated the choice of the 390-cubic-inch, 300-hp (four-barrel carburetor) ohv Marauder V-8 that was installed. Power was transmitted through a dual-range, three-speed Merc-O-Matic and 3-to-1 rear axle. Performance on this one would fall somewhere near the upper end of average for the class. Our 0-30, 0-45 and 0-60 mph averages were a respectable 4.1, 6.7 and 10.5 seconds. The end of the quarter-mile was reached in 18.9 seconds, with a terminal speed of 81 mph. At the end of the Riverside straight our Weston electric speedometer was recording an actual 110 mph, while the tach was reading 4300 rpm. The big Merc didn't seem to be laboring at this point and no doubt had a few more mph left.

In summing up the performance figures, we can only draw the rather obvious conclusion that both of the smaller Mercs are hampered by an overweight, underpowered condition that isn't helped a bit by the power-wasting two-speed automatic transmission. Several other manufacturers are also using this device, but we hope that more aren't considering it. The installation of the three-speed manual in both cars would improve performance greatly.

Two-ton-plus Monterey is surprisingly sure-footed on all types of surface. Lean is almost non-existent.

The Holley four-barrel installed on the big Marauder V-8 uses air velocity to actuate the secondary throttles. Mixture heat is supplied by water instead of exhaust.

Meteor's 221-cubic-inch V-8 has its weight set back from the front wheels, which results in better balance and eliminates any hint of nose-heaviness in the car.

Comet's 170-cubic-inch, 101-hp Six is out of its league in a car this size. The car would be a much more appealing package if it came with the Meteor's engine.

Prospective Meteor buyers will be happy to note that a more powerful, 260-cubic-inch version of the V-8 will soon be available. Too bad the factory hasn't decided to put the 221-incher in the Comet. The Monterey is also an overweight car (two tons plus), but the factory has crammed enough horse-power into it to overcome this. Also available is the big 406-inch, 405-hp high-performance mill with four-speed manual gearbox and a variety of rear axle ratios. But as we stated before, these cars were designed for family-type transportation and with the exception of the Comet, their performance is adequate for this.

If you're an avid reader of advertising claims, our fuel consumption figures are less than you'd expect — especially for the Comet and Meteor. These two are being touted as economy cars and by rights they should be, but again, the weight and two-speed transmission problems combine to produce results that say otherwise.

City and freeway driving in the Comet produced figures in the 15.7-to-16.3-mpg range, with an overall average of 16.2 mpg for 1000 miles under all conditions. The Meteor was driven in excess of 1100 miles, with city driving consumption in the 11.3-to-14.8-mpg range. Freeway and open-road speeds pushed the figure up to 17.7 mpg, and the overall average was 14.8 mpg. The Monterey is a big car with a big engine and an appetite to match. A rundown of our figures compiled for everyday city driving shows the range to be 8.9 to 11.3 mpg. Out on the road at cruising speeds with short passing spurts up to 75 mph, we found that the 3-to-1 rear axle allows the big mill to loaf a bit and we were getting a consistent 15.5 mpg. Overall average for 1000 miles was 10.9 mpg.

Some of the Monterey's low around-town figures can be attributed to the four-barrel carburetor. The secondary throttles are actuated by the velocity of the air-fuel mixture through the primary barrels and are consequently open more than they would be if a mechanical progressive system were used. It will also be noted that the Meteor delivered a better figure at

Usable trunk area should be adequate for the needs of most everyone. The lip on all three could be lower.

cruising speeds than did the Comet. This is because at 65 mph the bigger V-8, with bigger tires and a 3.5 axle, is still fairly loafing at 3000 rpm, while the smaller Six in the Comet is almost straining at 3750 rpm to pull the smaller tires and 4-to-1 axle.

The Comet does weight 400 pounds less than the Meteor, but at the same time, its weight-to-power ratio is greater than the Meteor's (24.68 to 1 against 20.75 to 1 — National Hot Rod Association Stock Car Classification Guide). Standard axle for the Comet is 3.20 to 1 and *should* produce better mileage figures but *probably won't* because the throttle would be floorboarded constantly in an effort to keep up with the normal traffic flow.

We hate to keep picking at the Comet, but we also found it to be lacking in stopping power. Before we ran the braking tests, the nine-inch units seemed adequate for normal, everyday use. In the test area they survived several hard stops from 30 mph but about halfway through the first brake-down from 60 mph we could feel the pedal pressure rapidly increasing and our rate of deceleration rapidly decreasing. After this, the brakes never were quite the same. The pedal pressure was abnormally high, and the deceleration rate was much slower.

The ten-inch brakes on the Meteor were power assisted and operated much better. We didn't have the trouble with fade and pressure build-up with these, but they did have a tendency to lock up suddenly and without warning, which necessitated fast and constant steering corrections on our part to keep the car in a straight line. There was some fade apparent after the tests, but as the brakes cooled they came back to normal.

The Monterey had the best-behaving brakes of the three. These were 11-inch, power-actuated units that pulled the big car down to quick, straight-line stops with no sudden lockups. Several panic stops produced a slight amount of fade and pedal hardness but this was negligible and things returned quickly to normal as the brakes cooled.

METEOR USES THE SAME BASIC BODY SHELL, ENGINE AND SUSPENSION COMPONENTS AS THE FORD FAIRLANE, BUT ON A LONGER WHEELBASE.

3 from Mercury

Seating position on the Monterey was the most comfortable. Electric window buttons and door handle could have been placed differently — we kept banging both with our left knee.

Meteor steering wheel (right) was a little close for comfort, but not nearly as bad as the Comet's. Leg-, hip- and headroom are adequate in all three cars.

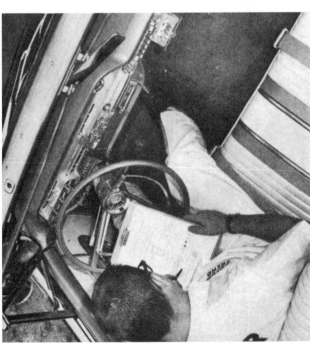

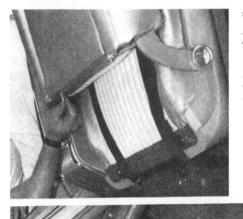

We couldn't get the seat back far enough to suit us in the Comet. Steering wheel's diameter is excessive for the room available. We did like the catches on the front seatbacks that kept them from slamming forward when brakes were applied.

3 from Mercury

We couldn't find a thing to argue about in the ride and handling departments. The suspension on all three cars is firmer than any we've encountered on any of the other '62s, and all three incorporate a stabilizer bar at the front end. As a result, they corner with much less lean than any of the current domestic cars (with the exception of the Fords, which are set up the same way). Even with the firm suspension, the ride is as comfortable as anyone would want it to be. Both the Meteor and the Monterey use Mercury's "Cushion-Link" suspension, introduced last year. This allows both the front and rear wheels to move rearward as well as up and down under road shocks, and as a result, the harshness is taken out of severe bumps and jolts.

On rough, secondary-type roads the three Mercs are well behaved. The suspension doesn't bottom easily but when it does, the cars recover immediately. On the open road all three have good directional stability and are little affected by cross-winds. Thanks to the excellent selection and use of sound-deadening materials, the Mercs are among the quietest-riding cars on the road. Engine noise level is a trifle high in the Comet, but road noise is almost non-existent in all three at cruising speeds.

Traction is very good on loose, wet surfaces or in frame-high mud. We spent the better part of two days, and several hundred miles, up in the mountains on some very tight, wet, twisty roads. As a result, we have a new respect for the cornering power of the Mercurys. They are basic understeerers but not excessively so. They will plough slightly on tight corners but a little fast work with the throttle will bring the rear end around. On wider-radiused turns the Mercs can be pushed hard. We usually shudder at even the thought of putting a stock domestic through any kind of a corner at a velocity even slightly close to the limit of adhesion. Because they do corner so flat that the weight remains over the tires where it belongs, we found that the Mercs could be put into a neat, easily controlled, four-wheel drift with very little effort. We don't recommend that, of course, but it is nice to know it can be done in a pinch.

The Meteor and the Monterey had power-assisted steering, which helped out nicely for in-town driving in heavy traffic. By comparison, the Comet steering at 4.64 turns lock-to-lock and no power assist was sluggish and tiring. Standard lock-to-lock turns on the Meteor and Monterey are 4.68 and 5.25, but with power are 4.34 and 3.75, respectively.

Exterior and interior quality and workmanship are excellent throughout the Mercury line. All panels, doors and trim were flush fit and well aligned.

For our personal configuration (5-11½, 180 pounds), we found that the Monterey offered the best seating position. In the Meteor we were slightly close to the steering wheel and in the Comet we were right on top of it. The Comet's 17-inch steering wheel is also too large for the space available. All three offered plenty of hip-, leg-, and headroom for both driver and passengers (front and rear), but we kept opening the power windows on the Monterey with our left knee.

All three feature well-laid-out instrument panels with all instruments (the Meteor is the only one of the three with *real* gauges) and controls in easy sight or reach. Do-it-yourself tuners and tinkerers will be happy with the accessibility of everything in the engine compartment.

Total trunk volume on all three should be adequate for the average family. The Meteor, with 31.5 cubic feet, has the largest, followed by the Monterey with 30.7 and the Comet with 29.8.

In summing up, we might add that performance is not, and never has been, synonymous with quality. What the Mercs might lack in the first, they more than make up in the latter. Last year they were a solid sixth in total sales, which shows that there's still a big market for a quality product. /MT

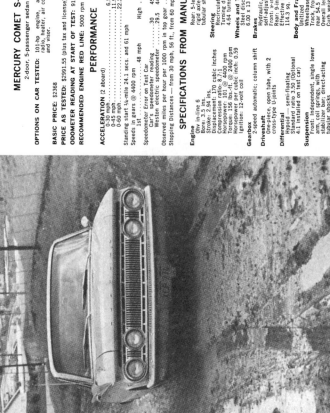

We gave all three a bath in frame-deep goo, and they all charged through without bogging down. Good weight distribution and firm suspension mean good control anywhere.

MERCURY COMET S-22
2-door, 5-passenger sedan

OPTIONS ON CAR TESTED: 101-hp engine, automatic transmission, radio, heater, air conditioning, padded dash and visor.

BASIC PRICE: $2368
PRICE AS TESTED: $2991.55 (plus tax and license)
ODOMETER READING AT START OF TEST: 91 miles
RECOMMENDED ENGINE RED LINE: 5000 rpm

PERFORMANCE
ACCELERATION (2 aboard)
0-30 mph .... 6.5 secs
0-45 mph 11.9
0-60 mph 22.2
Standing start ¼-mile 24.1 secs. and 61 mph
Speeds in gears @ 4400 rpm
1st .... 48 mph   High .... 81 mph (est.)

Speedometer Error on Test Car

Car's speedometer reading	30	45	50	60	70
Weston electric speedometer	29.5	44.5	49.5	59.5	69.5

Observed miles per hour per 1000 rpm in top gear .... 17 mph
Stopping Distances — from 30 mph, 56 ft., from 60 mph, 173 ft.

SPECIFICATIONS FROM MANUFACTURER
Engine
Ohv in-line 6
Bore: 3.5 ins.
Stroke: 2.94 ins.
Displacement: 170 cubic inches
Compression ratio: 8.7:1
Horsepower: 101 @ 4400 rpm
Torque: 156 lbs.-ft. @ 2400 rpm
Horsepower per cubic inch: 0.59
Ignition: 12-volt coil
Gearbox
2-speed automatic; column shift
Driveshaft
One-piece, open tube, with 2 cross-type U-joints
Differential
Hypoid — semi-floating
Standard ratio 3.50 (Optional 4:1 installed on test car)
Suspension
Front: Independent, single lower arm with high-mounted coil, stabilizer bar; direct-acting tubular shocks
Rear: 5-leaf semi-elliptic springs, direct-acting tubular shocks
Steering
Recirculating ball and nut
Turning diameter: 39.9 ft.
4.64 turns lock-to-lock
Wheels and Tires
Steel disc — 4 lugs
6.00 x 13 4-ply tubeless tires
Brakes
Hydraulic, dual-servo; self-adjusting
Front: 9-in. dia. x 2.25 in. wide
Rear: 9-in. dia. x 1.50 in. wide
Effective lining area: 114.3 sq. ins.
Body and Frame
Unitized
Wheelbase 114.0 ins.
Track, front 55.0 ins., rear 54 ins.
Overall length 194.8 ins.
Curb weight 2711 lbs.

MERCURY METEOR
2-door, 6-passenger sedan

OPTIONS ON CAR TESTED: 145-hp engine, automatic transmission, radio, heater, power brakes, power steering.

BASIC PRICE: $2469
PRICE AS TESTED: $2952.30 (plus tax and license)
ODOMETER READING AT START OF TEST: 2778 miles
RECOMMENDED ENGINE RED LINE: 5000 rpm

PERFORMANCE
ACCELERATION (2 aboard)
0-30 mph .... 5.9 secs.
0-45 mph 8.7
0-60 mph 15.2
Standing start ¼-mile 21.5 secs. and 70 mph
Speeds in gears @ 4500 rpm
1st .... 52 mph   High .... 95 mph (est.)

Speedometer Error on Test Car

Car's speedometer reading	30	45	50	60	70
Weston electric speedometer	30	45	50	60	70

Observed miles per hour per 1000 rpm in top gear .... 21 mph
Stopping Distances — from 30 mph, 50 ft., from 60 mph, 166 ft.

SPECIFICATIONS FROM MANUFACTURER
Engine
Ohv V-8
Bore: 3.50 ins.
Stroke: 2.87 ins.
Displacement: 221 cubic inches
Compression ratio: 8.5:1
Horsepower: 145 @ 4500 rpm
Torque: 217 lbs.-ft. @ 2200 rpm
Horsepower per cubic inch: 0.64
Ignition: 12-volt coil
Gearbox
2-speed automatic; column shift
Driveshaft
One-piece, open tube, with 2 cross-type U-joints
Differential
Hypoid — semi-floating
Standard ratio 3.50
(Optional 3.5:1 installed on test car)
Suspension
Front: Independent, single lower arm, coil springs, stabilizer bar; double-acting tubular shocks
Rear: Rigid axle, 5-leaf semi-elliptic springs; direct, double-acting tubular shocks
Steering
Recirculating ball and nut, with power assist
Turning diameter: 39.5 ft.
4.3 turns lock-to-lock
Wheels and Tires
Steel disc — 5 lugs
6.50 x 14 4-ply tubeless tires
Brakes
Hydraulic, duo-servo. Single anchor, internal expanding; self-adjusting
Front: 10-in. dia. x 2.25 in. wide
Rear: 10-in. dia. x 1.75 in. wide
Effective lining area: 120.5 sq. ins.
Body and Frame
Unitized
Wheelbase 116.5 ins.
Track, front 57.0 ins., rear 56.0 ins.
Overall length 203.8 ins.
Curb weight 3224 lbs.

MERCURY MONTEREY CUSTOM
2-door, 6-passenger convertible

OPTIONS ON CAR TESTED: 300-hp engine, dual-range Merc-O-Matic transmission, radio, heater, power windows, power seat, power brakes, power steering, padded dash and visor

BASIC PRICE: $3222
PRICE AS TESTED: $4086.95 (plus tax and license)
ODOMETER READING AT START OF TEST: 3908 miles
RECOMMENDED ENGINE RED LINE: 5200 rpm

PERFORMANCE
ACCELERATION (2 aboard)
0-30 mph .... 4.1 secs.
0-45 mph 6.7
0-60 mph 10.5
Standing start ¼-mile 18.9 secs. and 81 mph
Speeds in gears @ 4500 rpm
1st .... 47 mph   High .... 114 mph (est.)
2nd .... 79 mph

Speedometer Error on Test Car

Car's speedometer reading	30	45	50	60	70	80
Weston electric speedometer	32	50	65	76	86	

Observed miles per hour per 1000 rpm in top gear .... 25.5 mph
Stopping Distances — from 30 mph, 58.5 ft.; from 60 mph, 158.5 ft.

SPECIFICATIONS FROM MANUFACTURER
Engine
Ohv V-8
Bore: 4.05 ins.
Stroke: 3.78 ins.
Displacement: 390 cubic inches
Compression ratio: 9.6:1
Horsepower: 300 @ 4600 rpm
Torque: 427 lbs.-ft. @ 2800 rpm
Horsepower per cubic inch: 0.77
Ignition: 12-volt coil
Gearbox
3-speed automatic; column shift
Driveshaft
One-piece, open tube, with 2 cross-type U-joints
Differential
Hypoid — semi-floating
Standard ratio 3.00:1
Suspension
Front: Independent, single lower control arm with cushion-link coils, stabilizer bar; double-acting tubular shocks
Rear: 5-leaf semi-elliptic springs, with double-acting tubular shocks
Steering
Recirculating ball and nut, with power assist
Turning diameter: 41.6 ft.
3.9 turns lock-to-lock
Wheels and Tires
Steel disc — 5 lugs
8.00 x 14 4-ply tubeless tires
Brakes
Hydraulic, internal expanding; self-adjusting
Front and rear:
11-in. dia. x 2.5 in. wide
Effective lining area: 180 sq. ins.
Body and Frame
Separate "X"-type frame
Wheelbase 120 ins.
Track, front 61 ins., rear 60 ins.
Overall length 215.5 ins.
Curb weight 4550 lbs.

One of the 12 models available is this Mercury Comet custom four-door sedan for 1963.

Mercury Comet Stresses Low Upkeep

TWO convertibles and numerous cost-reducing maintenance improvements have been added to the 1963 Mercury Comet model offerings. The convertibles, with power operated tops, are available in the custom series and the S-22 series, which is the bucket seat version of the Comet.

Engineering advances developed originally for the big car field have been incorporated into the new Comet and substantially reduce the time and cost of auto maintenance.

Service-saving maintenance features include: an increase in the major lubrication cycle from 1,000 miles to 36,000 miles with minor lube intervals of 6,000 miles; a replaceable fuel filter element sufficient for 36,000 miles; new front wheel bearings that require cleaning and packing only after 24,000 miles, compared to 12,000 miles in 1962; and new self-adjusting brakes that are designed to last longer.

A new high detergent engine oil, factory installed oil filter and adjustments to the transmission, engine and electrical system have eliminated the need for the 1,000 mile checkup. The 1963 Comet will not require its initial servicing until six months or 6,000 miles have elapsed.

Ben D. Mills, Ford Motor Company vice president and general manager of Lincoln-Mercury Division, said: "The Comet should attract even greater acceptance among sports-minded buyers while continuing to improve on low cost, dependable transportation. The Comet consistently has ranked among the leaders in the industry in low dollar depreciation. We expect the new convertibles and engineering refinements on the 1963 models to strengthen our hand in this respect."

Over-all styling theme of the Comet has been maintained with appearance changes in grille treatment, rear ornamentation and taillamps.

Two six-cylinder engines which have been improved to run more quietly and efficiently, are offered on the Comet. They are the standard 144-cubic-inch and the optional higher performance 170-cubic-inch engines. An improved carburetor is designed to make both Comet engines attain new levels of smoothness and dependability. The engines are equipped with a smog reducing "blow-by" device.

The sporty trend in Comet is supported by the addition of an optional new four-speed floor mounted manual transmission, which gives greater performance and fuel economy. The two-speed Merc-O-Matic transmission also is available.

A tachometer kit will be optional on all Comet models. The tachometer operates with less than one percent error, about twice the accuracy of most commercial tachometers.

Other electronic options include a rear-seat reverberator radio speaker which lends a simulated stereo effect

to music, a Raytel two-way citizens band radio, and an all-transistorized AM radio.

The Comet comes in 12 models: two and four-door sedans and station wagons in both standard and custom series; two convertibles in custom and S-22 series; S-22 two-door sedan and the Villager station wagon. The Villager four-door wagon features simulated wood-grain paneling and rails, and bucket seats are optional.

Redesigned bucket seats on the S-22 models contain an additional ½ inch of foam padding for a more comfortable ride. The S-22 also features distinctive exterior ornamentation on the rear metal applique and special, tri-color wheel covers. Back-up lights and plush carpeting are standard on this luxury model. ★

YOUTH'S CONTRACT VOIDED

INDIANAPOLIS—A car purchase contract executed by a 16-year-old boy was voided by the Indiana Appellate Court. Judge Walter Myers, Jr., ruled that the car was not "necessary" for a minor. Had it been, the minor's contract could have been ruled binding. Myers, in his ruling, quoted a decision handed down in 1878, which said: "It has been pithily and happily said that necessaries do not include 'horses, saddles, bridles, liquors, pistols, powder, whips and fiddles.'"

FORD EXPANDS GLASS LINE

NASHVILLE, Tenn. — Commercial sheet glass in 500 dimensions in thicknesses of three-sixteenth and seven-thirty seconds of an inch is now being produced in Ford Motor Company's glass plant here. Commercial sheet glass has been added to the line of Car Lite automotive replacement and Ford architectural plate glass currently marketed by the company's Glass and Paint Products sales division.

Down, down, down goes a 1963 Chrysler Corporation car into a tank of water reducible primer. This is the final dip of an intensive process which involves six external spray operations and seven internal and external immersions to beat the problem of corrosion.

University of Cincinnati students about to tour the campus in a 1914 Model T Ford.

WE HAD OUR FIRST RIDE in a new Comet V-8 a few months ago at Ford's Pico Rivera, California, assembly plant, when we attended a preview of Mercury's 1963½ offerings along with most other automotive writers from Southern California. So popular was it that we had to stand in line to take the S-22 Comet hardtop out on Ford's banked test track (although there were 18 big Mercs and Lincolns on hand for testing).

The combination of the 260-cubic-inch V-8 and four-speed box gives this car a vast improvement in performance over the six-cylinder Comet we tested last year, so we asked for a similar model for our road test.

Our test S-22 turned out to be a bright red hardtop, with every extra except air conditioning and power brakes. No major changes have been made in styling except for the roof, and the V-8-equipped car uses basically the same body shell with a greatly improved chassis under it. And herein lies a real story.

Since the Meteor was already using the same basic V-8 engine, Mercury engineers knew just which components would need beefing up when they put 65 more horses and about 200 more pounds into the Comet. And beef it up they did, stiffening 14 places in the integral body/chassis by increasing the thickness of existing members or by additional struts. Most of the stiffening is in front of the cowl. One example is

Not only a new engine but a vastly improved chassis as well are all part of the new 1963½...

S-22 *Comet* V-8

A 260-inch V-8 engine under the hood doesn't leave much room for routine maintenance. Additional struts from cowl to the fender-mounted spring housings increase rigidity.

in the struts from the cowl to the front spring housings: an additional member increases stiffness 150 per cent.

All V-8 cars use five-bolt wheels, with a wider rim base and 7.00 x 13-inch tires (Sixes have four-bolt wheels and 6.00 x 13 tires), larger wheel bearings, tie-rod ends, and drag links. Comet front spindles are made from Meteor forgings (Meteors weigh 430 pounds more model for model), and they use bigger brakes with 10-inch drums as compared with the nine-inch units on the Sixes.

Axle shafts are the same beefy items found on Econoline trucks. Shocks and springs are stiffer all around, with an additional leaf added in the rear, bringing the number to six. Of special interest is the rear axle. It's of the straddle-mounted pinion variety, styled after that of a heavy-duty truck. Owners pulling trailers or hauling heavy loads will appreciate this.

Both manual and power steering units have been suitably beefed up, along with the other components. So Mercury hasn't just dropped a bigger engine into an existing car — they've made the chassis strong enough to take the added strains and, in addition, they've come up with a very roadable car — one that offers a very good package of performance, handling, and braking.

The big news — that which can be seen and felt — lies under the hood. Our S-22 shares the 260-cubic-inch V-8 engine with the Falcon, Meteor, and the Cobra sports/racing car. In the Comet, the tuning is mild, stressing long life, economy and adequate rather than flashing performance. Rated at a modest 164 hp, the Cyclone engine has a bore and stroke of 3.80 and 2.87 inches respectively. Compression ratio is only 8.70 to 1, and it burns a modest amount of regular gasoline. The only thing available is the two-throat carburetor, which restricts engine breathing along with the single exhaust system.

Our S-22 Sportster was all wound out at 5000 rpm in any of the lower three gears. Top speed down Riverside Raceway's back straight was a strained 94 mph at 4200 rpm. With a longer run and a few more break-in miles, the car should come close to the century mark.

We enjoyed the smooth four-speed gearbox. Throws from second to third are a bit long, but after six runs we finally turned in acceleration figures of zero to 30, 45, and 60 in 3.7, 7.4, and 11.5 seconds respectively. On our best run, we whizzed through the quarter-mile traps at 75 mph, with the clocks stopped at 19 seconds flat. During our

speed runs, the normal 2956-pound weight of the car was increased to over 3400 pounds with two men and test equipment on board.

Even though the Comet's brakes were used hard after each run, they always came back for more and proved better than average. Panic stops were made from 30 and 60 mph in 32 feet and 146 feet respectively. The combination of good weight distribution, big 10-inch drums, and good lining material gave us straight-line stops, with a minimum of wheel lockup and swerving. Our Comet hardtop offered a good all-around balance of performance in both the go and stop departments. Normal everyday use found the brakes up to every occasion. They weren't power-assisted, so pedal pressures were fairly high, but not objectionable.

Another big plus for Comet is its firm yet comfortable suspension system. The V-8's heavier shocks and springs make it a road car that can take sharp or sweeping curves at speeds that would find more softly sprung cars all over the road. With the smooth four-speed lever in the proper gear, our S-22 could be pushed through turns at a very rapid rate in perfect safety. There's very little body lean.

Mounted on the center transmission hump is the chrome-plated shift lever, topped with a man-sized plastic handle. Fast shifts are possible, and we could choose between blazing, wheel-spinning starts in low or slower starts in second. For normal traffic conditions, where top acceleration isn't necessary or desirable, only two gears are really necessary: first and fourth. Second, third, and fourth can be used quite easily, and even third-gear starts are possible — so flexible is the 260-inch engine. It puts out 258 pounds-feet of torque at a low 2200 rpm and proved a real lugger in any gear.

COMET S-22 V-8

Reverse can't be engaged until you pull a finger-operated lever on the gearshift.

Our V-8 gave us better mileage on the highway than last year's Six, with a top figure of 17 mpg at a steady 65 mph (the Six gave 16.3 mpg). Hard driving took the figure down to a low of 10 mpg, while traffic and freeway driving found the Comet giving 14.6. Our average for nearly 1000 miles figured out at 14.2 mpg.

Now that we've mentioned many of the car's good points, there's one glaring fault that everyone who drove the car noticed: The steering wheel's too big and too close to the driver. Even the Falcon Sprint uses a 16-inch wheel, but the Comet still has a 17-incher that's not only hard to see over but makes exit and entry a chore.

The bigger members of our staff didn't have enough seat travel for a comfortable driving position. Certainly with power steering, a 16-inch wheel would be big enough. And even without power assist, we'd appreciate more elbow room, because the 4.6 turns lock to lock do require a bit of wheel spinning during fast driving and quick maneuvering. One less turn would be a great advantage.

Driver vision's good from inside the S-22. We found the bucket seats to be among the most comfortable we've used (they're not nearly so hard as the big Ford's seats), but the back seat was too low for an adult to be comfortable for any length of time.

Definitely a luxury compact, the S-22 Sportster includes carpets, vinyl upholstery, and a padded dash. A center console's located between the seats and gives usable space for odds and ends. Gauges are used for gasoline level and engine temperature, while warning lights give oil pressure and generator warnings. The speedometer proved dead accurate at all speeds and is easy to read. A pull-out hand brake operates the rear brakes and is located just to the left of the wheel post. It's easy to pull out and release and proved handy for starts on steep hills.

Equipped as it was for our test, the Comet S-22 hardtop had a dealer-suggested price tag of $3356 (including $128 freight). With the addition of an air conditioner at $231.70, the price would go up to $3588 and change, and the shift lever would have to be bent a little to get the cooling unit in. The S-22 series is the top of the Comet line. Our hardtop had a base price of $2594, including heater. Standard on Comets is the all-synchromesh three-speed column shift. The four-speed box for the V-8 costs an additional $188. Ford's English-made four-speed box for the Six goes for $90 — a bargain with the smaller engine.

The plain-Jane Comet series offers two- and four-door sedans and station wagons. The Comet Custom series has a deluxe version of these same models plus a two-door hardtop and a convertible. Next up the line is the S-22 series, with a two-door sedan, a convertible, and the two-door hardtop like the car we tested. Last is the Villager four-door station wagon. Only two engines are offered now: the 260-inch V-8 and a 170-cubic-inch Six. Any model can be ordered with

COMET'S WIDE DOORS AFFORD EASY ENTRY AND EXIT. BACK SEAT, HOWEVER, LACKS LEG ROOM AND IS TOO LOW FOR COMFORT ON LONG HAULS.

either engine. All V-8 cars will have a 3.25 axle ratio, while six-cylinder cars can be ordered with either a 3.50 or a 3.20 ratio.

We liked the new 1963½ Comet and felt it was a real man's car — one a man will enjoy driving. It's not the hottest number in the Ford-Mercury garage by a long shot, but it does offer a good balance of performance, braking, and economy — and when it comes to handling, few other Detroit sedans can match it. The real story is underneath where it's hard to see, but it can be felt.

With the 24-month/24,000-mile warranty and the quality built in at the factory, the Comet V-8 should provide its owner with reliable transportation, luxury, plus economy for quite a few years. It's a good, solid car, with emphasis on handling and safety rather than a soft ride. It's also a whale of an improvement over the Six. **/MT**

GOOD WEIGHT DISTRIBUTION GIVES COMET VERY SOLID TRACTION ON LOOSE DIRT. NEW V-8 SUPPLIES PLENTY OF WHEEL-SPINNING POWER.

Sportster's big 10-inch brake drums were always up to their job. They gave straight-line stops, always came back for more.

Hardtop trunk is large but has a high lip. Spare is easy to get at, yet takes up space that could be used for luggage.

COMET S-22 SPORTSTER

2-door, 5-passenger hardtop

OPTIONS ON CAR TESTED: 4-speed gearbox, power steering, radio, heater, electric tachometer, console, tinted glass, padded dash and visors, seat belts, whitewalls
BASIC PRICE: $2594
PRICE AS TESTED: $3356.95 (plus tax and license)
ODOMETER READING AT START OF TEST: 550 miles
RECOMMENDED ENGINE RED LINE: 5200 rpm

PERFORMANCE

ACCELERATION (2 aboard)
0-30 mph............................. 3.7 secs.
0-45 mph............................. 7.0
0-60 mph.............................11.5

Standing start ¼-mile 19.0 secs. and 75 mph
Speeds in gears @ 5200 rpm

1st ....40 mph	3rd ....76 mph
2nd ....56 mph	4th ....94 mph
	(@ 4200 rpm)

Speedometer Error on Test Car
Car's speedometer reading 30 45 50 60 70 80
Weston electric speedometer .. 30 45 50 60 70 80

Observed miles per hour per 1000 rpm in top gear ....22.0 mph
Stopping Distances — from 30 mph, 32 ft.; from 60 mph, 146 ft.

SPECIFICATIONS FROM MANUFACTURER

Engine
90-degree, ohv V-8
Bore: 3.80 ins.
Stroke: 2.87 ins.
Displacement: 260 cu. ins.
Compression ratio: 8.70:1
Horsepower: 164 @ 4400 rpm
Torque: 258 lbs.-ft. @ 2200 rpm
Horsepower per cubic inch: 0.63
Ignition: 12-volt coil
Gearbox
4-speed manual, all-synchro;
floor shift
Driveshaft
One-piece — open tube
Differential
Hypoid — semi-floating
Standard ratio: 3.25:1 (3.50 installed on test car)
Suspension
Front: Independent ball joint, with coil springs mounted on upper A-arm, direct-acting tubular shocks
Rear: Rigid axle; rubber-mounted 6-leaf semi-elliptic springs, direct-acting tubular shocks; torque taken through rear springs

Steering
Recirculating ball and nut; power assist
Turning diameter: 39.9 ft.
Turns: 4.64 lock to lock

Wheels and Tires
5-lug, stamped steel disc wheels
7.00 x 13 2-ply nylon tubeless tires

Brakes
Hydraulic, duo-servo; self-adjusting; cast-iron drums
Front: 10-in. dia. x 2.25 ins. wide
Rear: 10-in. dia. x 1.75 ins. wide
Effective lining area: 127.8 sq. ins.

Body and Frame
Unitized construction
Wheelbase: 114.0 ins.
Track: front, 55.0 ins.; rear, 54.5 ins.
Overall length: 194.8 ins.
Test weight: 2956 lbs. (with full tank of gas)

COMET CALIE

A Finer Filly For Track Or Touring Is Posted For Mid-Range Sweepstakes

BECAUSE THE METEOR burned out before it could set fire to the car-buying world, Lincoln-Mercury Division has turned to the Comet to brighten the automotive sky. It is a curious area, one in which GM has fielded four lines for 1964 even though Ford Motor Co. has found sales for the Fairlane/ Meteor size car anything but stimulating. Economics and internecine competition being what they are, FoMoCo product planners determined that an upgraded Comet could best fill the Meteor void at less cost in dollars and inter-divisional sales.

The move is like a basketballer's shift from man-to-man to zone defense. It was accomplished basically by giving a new personality to the Comet with the installation of the 289-cu. in.

V-8. This Mercury is called the Caliente, to conjure up images of hot Latin blood, race tracks and thoroughbreds. That this would be the direction of Comet evolution was obvious last year when the mid-year Sportster was introduced with the 260-cu. in. engine (CL, July 1963).

Our test Caliente, finished in screaming scarlet inside and out, was equipped with a 289-cu. in. engine rated at 210 bhp at 4400 rpm, the newly available 3-speed Merc-O-Matic transmission, power brakes, power steering and air conditioning. In addition, we sampled several other similarly equipped Calientes at Daytona Beach (see p. 13) to further check the characteristics of the car.

When L-M engineers started install-

ing the V-8 in the Comet, several significant changes were made in the body/chassis structure for additional strength. These changes have been incorporated throughout the line for 1964, regardless of what engine, V-8 or 6-cyl., is ordered. Most important is the addition of integral torque boxes, welded up to tie together the front side rails and the body side members for additional rigidity and strength in the underbody and to help absorb body twist.

Other structural beefing up includes box-section reinforcements running from dash to spring towers, sturdier fender aprons, additional reinforcements between the front end structure and rocker panels, reinforced radiator support, and heavier gauge steel for

RALPH POOLE PHOTOS

the rocker rail and rocker rail extension. All underbody structural pieces, incidentally, are galvanized steel to resist rust. Since these and other underbody strengthening details were thoroughly discussed in our test of the Sportster 260, there is little need to go into them further.

The lightweight 289 engine more than doubles the power output over what had been available with the 6-cyl. Comets and it produces a decided—almost startling—increase in performance over the 260 V-8. It has a 9.0:1 compression ratio, a single 4-barrel carburetor with 1.562-in. venturis and intake valves of 1.74 in. diameter (over the 260's 1.64 in. intakes). Exhaust valves are 1.42 in., as on the 260, and self-adjusting hydraulic lifters are used. Camshaft duration for intake is a mild 266° with 256° for exhaust, and lift is 0.38 in. In such tune, the Caliente is motivated quite briskly amidst the traffic flow.

But if that isn't enough, it is possible to special order the Comet with the HP version of the thinwall 289, which develops 271 bhp at 6000 rpm by utilizing mechanical lifters, 10.5:1 compression ratio, single 4-barrel carburetor and wilder valve timing. The HP has 306° intake and exhaust durations and 0.477-in. valve lifts, using heavier springs with auxiliary damping springs. This engine, however, comes only with the 3- or 4-speed manual transmission.

A 3-element torque converter couples the 3-speed automatic transmission to the engine. This transmission, identical to Ford's Cruise-O-Matic, uses two planetary gear sets for the

forward and reverse ratios. Two clutches and two bands, along with a roller type one-way clutch, are used to hold or to drive the planetary elements as necessary for gear changes. Shift control is maintained by a vacuum servo unit actuating the manual valve in the control assembly. Pattern on the column-mounted lever is P-R-N-D2-D1-L. The torque converter's maximum ratio at stall is 2.02:1 and gear ratios are 2.46 first, 1.46 second, and 1.00 third, with an overall torque multiplication of 5.04:1.

Final drive, with a ratio of 3.25:1 (optional; 3.00:1 is standard with automatic), is taken through the Meteor differential which uses a straddle-mounted pinion gear with semi-floating axle shafts. Track has been widened at the rear by 1.5 in. to 56 in., adding a slight bit of stability. Tires on the test car(s) were 7.00-14s, the optional larger size which are fitted when air conditioning is specified.

The air conditioner, slung under the center of the dashboard even in the factory installation, proved a boon on one occasion. At Riverside Raceway for the *Times* Grand Prix, where cars with our Comet's engine swept the field (Carroll Shelby's AC-Ford Cobra and his Cooper-Ford "King Cobra"), the

ALL-VINYL interior is long-wearing, comfortable with textured panels in an oblong design.

COMPRESSOR FOR air conditioner atop 289 engine with 4-barrel carburetor makes for an overflowing engine compartment.

COMET CALIENTE

heat and dust became much more bearable with our Caliente's fast-chilled interior as a refuge. But this creature comfort had a discomforting price. A great many of the performance ills which the test car suffered were chargeable directly to that air conditioner.

Automatic gear changes, in particular, were an uncertain thing. The necessity to increase idle rpm settings with the cooler installation in turn made it necessary to alter the vacuum servo shift mechanism; the result was anything but happy. It took a fairly long interval, once shifting speed was reached, for the transmission control to decide to change gears. It was the same with all the other Calientes we drove at Daytona, also equipped with the 3-speed automatics and air conditioners; because of that our observation in the 260 road test that the 3-speed automatic would be a better transmission than the 2-speed might not stand up. Without the cooler, however, we believe this problem with the 3-speed would not exist—since our test Ford in this issue, with the same transmission, proved a great deal smoother with a flexibility that would please all but the most discriminating enthusiast.

As it was, we had two choices: either drive around with the engine roaring away while the little black box decided to shift gears, or forcefully take over the shift function by manually overriding the shift control. The latter course, although frowned upon by the

factory, was the one we took and, indeed, had to be used to secure optimum acceleration figures for our data panel. Why bother with a manual transmission when an automatic can be worked the same way? Still, in all fairness, this problem existed only because the air conditioner was installed (and which, by the way, isn't available with the 4-speed manual transmissions).

Full fuel tank (now 20 gal. instead of 14) notwithstanding, the rear end was lightly loaded enough to make wheelspin off the line a problem. This was largely overcome by a throttle

feathering technique during maximum acceleration tests. But once mastered, the Caliente turned in surprising times. It performs almost as well as the 383-cu. in. Dodge tested last month and right with the F-85 Cutlass, both heavier cars with stronger engines. The 260 Sportster returned a 5-sec. 0-30, 14.5-sec. 0-60, and a 19.3-sec. standing quarter, making the improvement with the 289 engine substantial.

As improved as the straight line performance is with the 289, it still is only a minor part of the Caliente story. More important, in our estimation, is the improved handling and roadability of the car over Comets which have gone before. This is all the more unexpected because of the great number of changes made by L-M chassis en-

NEW GRILLE has unmistakable Lincoln Continental stamp, an aid in upgrading the image of the more powerful Caliente.

gineers to give a softer ride and reduce harshness.

The Hotchkiss drive rear suspension, common to Ford products, uses 4-leaf semi-elliptic springs 55 in. long and 2.5 in. wide. Rate at the wheel is a nominal 93 lb./in., although heavy-duty springs are available with rates up to 117 lb./in. Full length butyl liners between leaves reduce friction and harshness is reduced by the use of rubber iso-clamp insulators at the axle attachment. Front eye bushings for the spring hanger are high resilient rubber of 2-in. diameter with a wider shackle to accommodate the wider spring. Rubber has also been lavished on the front suspension, where lower shock absorber insulators have doubled in thickness, larger bushings have been installed at the strut mounting, a new rubber bushing is used at the spring seat pivot and idler arm bushings now have rubber sliding within a steel shell. Combined with a more tilted arrangement for the ball joint and altered pivot bushings, the changes add up to less friction and more precise handling. The Autolite telescopic shock absorbers using a new constant viscosity fluid also add significantly to the ride and handling.

Under normal driving conditions, the Caliente is basically a somewhat nose-heavy understeerer, tracking quite truly down the pike. When pushed hard, there is enough power and the balance is just about right for the car to take on a neutral inclination. There is enough power to break loose the rear wheels, promoting a fleeting oversteer condition when conditions warrant. It will plow off the outside of a corner, when entered too fast and the throttle is backed off, but judicious use of the throttle will get the Comet around that same corner at speed once the proper slip angles have been set

WOOD GRAIN effect is carried on plastic wheel, across dashboard and in door inserts. Driver's position has been slightly altered.

up. This we found out at Daytona, on the varied-radius east turn of the infield road course. Flinging the car about with more abandon, we came to the conclusion that here indeed was a car with excellent handling characteristics, ranking closely behind the Dodge Dart in this respect.

The power steering, a linkage assist type of unit, has virtually no effect on directional control other than to reduce effort. Turns remain at 4.6 between locks and the overall ratio is still 27:1. It is, however, a much improved installation over that which was fitted to our 260 Sportster and the problems then encountered have been eliminated.

Although available only with the automatic transmission, the power as-

sisted brakes proved adequate for normal use. With the 289 engine, drums are 10-in. dia., fully cast on front and composite steel disc and cast at the rear. Gross lining area is 154.2 sq. in. with the 2.25-in. wide front drums, 1.50-in. wide rear drums, but use of 2.25-in. drums and shoes on the rear (as on the station wagons and convertibles) would increase that to 193.6 with a total swept area of 314.2 sq. in.

We are not sure whether the bigger rear brakes would have corrected the problem we encountered in making our usual pair of crash stops from 80 mph, however. During both of these tests, a terrific shudder set up in the car as the brakes on all four wheels alternately locked and released, slewing the car first one direction, then the other.

REAR SECTION, though still overly busy, shows more restraint than Comet stylists formerly used.

LARGE TRUNK would be more than adequate for most touring, despite space-robbing spare location.

COMET CALIENTE

This was such an old-fashioned phenomenon that we were fascinated and tried a few more such stops after the brakes cooled—with the same result. Hopefully, the situation might be corrected by better brake adjustment and better balancing of the wheels, which proved badly in need of it. Despite all the hop-skipping about, the brakes recorded a notable 22 ft./sec./sec. deceleration rate.

Our test car was one of the first off the production line and as such was afflicted with a couple of bodywork bothers (poor panel fit, balky door latch) that should be sorted out once the assembly line crews get the routine mastered. Exterior sheet metal—hood, rear deck, front and rear quarter panels, door panels, bumpers and grille—are all new for 1964 and the result is

fairly pleasing. Though there remains a faint trace of Falcon ancestry, the Caliente's appearance now more strongly suggests a Lincoln Continental lineage, particularly in the grille and front fender line. Somewhat surprisingly, however, Comet stylists still believe that gingerbread is in vogue at a time when other car makers are on a clean-up kick.

There has been some juggling of space in the driver's position, pedals and steering wheel and seat relationships altered an inch here and there, and the result is a more comfortable command post. The backs of the bucket seats, however, still should be adjustable for rake (via a pair of stop screws at the bottom) to suit the individual driver. One good feature was the stiff foam cover for the 'tween

seats knick-knack bin, which would be less lethal than the sharp-edged metal plates used in other cars. The instrument panel, with a dash-wide strip of plastic simulating wood veneer trim, shows real improvement where improvement was due.

Though the Comet's dimensions remain unchanged with the new sheet metal, the diet of beans it has been fed moves it as smartly away from the intermediate class image as it does from the traffic signals. Perhaps, like good wine, it was necessary to spend some time as grape juice.

There's just one further step to take, and L-M engineers undoubtedly will take it. That is to take Ford's 427, destroked to something like 396 cu. in. for the new NASCAR limit, and stuff it into the Caliente. With a wheelbase right at NASCAR's new minimum, Dearborn could have something even more potent for Daytona, Darlington, and other points south. ∎

CAR LIFE ROAD TEST

1964 COMET
Caliente Hardtop

SPECIFICATIONS

List price	$2472
Price, as tested	3377
Curb weight, lb	3170
Test weight	3500
distribution, %	56.6/43.4
Tire size	7.00-14
Tire capacity, lb	3900
Brake swept area	251.3
Engine type	V-8, ohv
Bore & stroke	4.00 x 2.87
Displacement, cu in	289
Compression ratio	9.0:1
Carburetion	1 x 4
Bhp @ rpm	210 @ 4400
equivalent mph	109
Torque, lb-ft	300 @ 2800
equivalent mph	69.5

EXTRA-COST OPTIONS

Auto. trans., 289 engine, power steering, power brakes, wsw tires, air conditioner, radio, tinted glass, seat belts. remote-control outside mirror.

DIMENSIONS

Wheelbase, in	114.0
Tread, f and r	55.6/56.0
Over-all length, in	195.1
width	71.4
height	53.6
equivalent vol, cu ft	432
Frontal area, sq ft	21.3
Ground clearance, in	5.5
Steering ratio, o/a (power)	27.0
turns, lock to lock	4.6
turning circle, ft	40.0
Hip room, front	2 x 22
Hip room, rear	56.5
Pedal to seat back, max	43
Floor to ground	11.5
Luggage vol, cu ft	15.5
Fuel tank capacity, gal	20.0

GEAR RATIOS

3rd (1.00), overall	3.25
2nd (1.46)	4.74
1st (2.46)	7.99
1st (2.46 x 2.02)	16.15

PERFORMANCE

Top speed (4400), mph	109
Shifts, @ mph (auto., forced)	
3rd ( )	
2nd (4300)	73
1st (4300)	43

ACCELERATION

0-30 mph, sec	3.8
0-40	6.5
0-50	9.1
0-60	11.8
0-70	15.0
0-80	19.7
0-100	41.6
Standing ¼ mile, sec	16.5
speed at end, mph	73.8

FUEL CONSUMPTION

Normal range, mpg	12-15

SPEEDOMETER ERROR

30 mph, actual	28.5
60 mph	58.0
90 mph	88.2

CALCULATED DATA

Lb/hp (test wt)	16.6
Cu ft/ton mile	115
Mph/1000 rpm	24.8
Engine revs/mile	2420
Piston travel, ft/mile	1158
Car Life wear index	28.0

PULLING POWER

70 mph, (3rd) max. gradient, %	10.8
50 (2nd)	18.4
30 (1st)	31.2
Total drag at 60 mph, lb	155

ACCELERATION & COASTING

ELAPSED TIME IN SECONDS

Comet

Only the 114-inch wheelbase and upper body are essentially unchanged. Everything else, including 'hot' 289-inch V8 option, is new

WHEN COMET first hit the market back in 1960 it was a stretchout, slightly styled up version of Falcon. It was an economy car with a slightly better ride than Falcon's due to an extra five inches of wheelbase.

The '64 Comets still have that 115-inch wheelbase and the unit construction underbodies, plus the basic over-all length of 194 inches, but from here on it really lives up to its billing as "all new."

Out on the road the '64 Comet feels like a much bigger, solider car than the '63 although weight of comparable six-cylinder sedans

is up 122 and the optional V8s add approximately 290 pounds more as a complete package.

That 122 pounds comes from additional metal in the unit body such as torque boxes which tie together the front side rails and the body side members. There's a more durable spring tower and fender apron design to provide greater strength in the engine and front suspension area. Heavier gauge galvanized steel is used in body sills and rocker panels.

The ride and handling are noticeably improved. Rear tread is 1½ inches wider for greater sta-

IMPROVEMENTS IN THE SUSPENSION SYSTEM have made Comet for '64 both comfortable to ride in and stable to handle.

ELEGANT IS THE WORD for the plush two-door Caliente hardtop in Lincoln-Mercury's Comet line.

THE CALIENTE'S CLUSTER shows off with attractive wood trim and a full set of instruments.

EVEN IN SMALLEST MODELS, rear compartment knee room is adequate in the Comet sedan.

A NEW THREE-SPEED automatic transmission is available to buyers of V8-equipped Comet models.

HOT WATER HOSE is routed to warm up the Comet's choke control for improved economy.

YOU LIFT LUGGAGE high to get it over Comet's trunk sill, but the trunk itself is quite roomy.

	202	404	Caliente
Wheelbase	114	114	114
Over-all length	195.1	195.1	195.1
width	71.4	71.4	71.4
height	55.3	55.3	55.3
Weight	2721	2729	2809
Minimum road clearance	5.5	5.5	5.5
Wheel and tire size	6.50x14	6.50x14	6.50x14
Chassis:			
Front suspension	Independent; short & long control arms torque strut, coil spring above upper arm		
Rear suspension	Hotchkiss; solid axle leaf springs		
Hydraulic brakes	Duo-Servo	Duo-Servo	Duo-Servo
Power brakes	Standard	Standard	Standard
Drum diameter/lining area	9/114.3	9/114.3	9/114.3
Steering ratio (mech./power)	27:1/27:1	27:1/27:1	27:1/27:1
Wheel turns (mech./power)	4.6/4.6	4.6/4.6	4.6/4.6
Power steering, std. or opt.	Optional	Optional	Optional
Turning circle	40	40	40
Gear type	Recirculating Ball and Nut		
Interior:			
Headroom f/r	38.8/36.7	38.8/36.7	38.8/36.7
Seat height f/r	9/11.4	9/11.4	9/11.4
Steering wheel leg clearance	4.3	4.3	4.3
Legroom f/r	42/35.5	42/35.5	42/35.5
Hiproom f/r	57.1/56.8	57.1/56.8	57.1/56.8
Compartment room f/r	43.8/27.7	43.8/27.7	43.8/27.7
Trunk volume	12.8	12.8	12.8
Body types available:			
2-door hardtop		X	X
2-door sedan (coupe)	X	X	
2-door convertible			X
4-door sedan	X	X	X
4-door hardtop			X
4-door, 6-pass. wagon	X	X	
4-door, 9-pass. wagon		X	

Engine:	170 Six	260 V8	
Bore and stroke	3.50x2.94	3.80x2.87	
Displacement	170	260	
Compression ratio	8.4:1 nom. 8.7:1 max.	8.4:1 nom. 8.8 max.	
Horsepower	101 @ 4400	164 @ 4400	
Torque	156 @ 2400	258 @ 2200	
Carburetor type	1, 1V downdraft	1, 2V downdraft	
Oil capacity	4.5 qts.	5 qts.	
Water capacity	9.5 qts.	14.5 qts.	
Fuel capacity	20 gal.	20 gal.	
Grade recommended	Regular	Regular	
Rear axle ratio, manual	3.20:1	3:1	
auto	NA	2.80:1	
overdrive	NA	NA	
Automatic trans. type	Torque Converter w/planetary gears		
Forward ratios, manual	3.29:1	2.79:1	2.74:1
	1.83:1	1.70:1	2.04:1
	1.00:1	1.00:1	1.51:1
auto	1.82:1	2.46:1	1.00:1
	1.00:1	1.46:1	
	1.73:1	1.00:1	

Basic dimensions are for 4-door sedans unless otherwise noted.

bility. Rear springs have only four leaves instead of five for a lower rate, but have ½-inch wider leaves and are four inches longer.

Up front, more and larger (softer) rubber bushings are used in the moving joints of the suspension and to reduce the effort of steering, needle bearings have been added to the steering gear cross shaft.

Driving is much happier too, thanks to a smaller (16-inch) steering wheel and moving it an inch ahead.

There are two V8s, a 260 cubic inch displacement job of 164 horsepower and a 289 cubic incher rated at 195. Either of these engines may be teamed with three-speed manual column shift of four speeds on the floor, as well as with Ford Motor Co.'s new lightweight three-speed automatic, a much more efficient transmission. Unfortunuately this one is not available on the Sixes as yet (where it's needed most). All four engines operate on regular grade fuel.

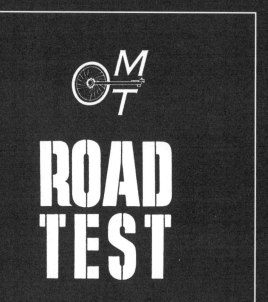

ROAD TEST

by Jim Wright, *Technical Editor*

THE CYCLONE WAS BORN when it became clear that Comet buyers were going in heavily for luxury and performance options. By bringing out a model that has many of these items as standard equipment, Mercury is now able to give buyers a better break on prices. This kind of car will also give Mercury a little more ammunition to stave off the mid-year Ford Mustang attack.

Standard Cyclone equipment includes a dash-mounted tachometer, individual front bucket seats and center console, padded dash, three-spoke rally steering wheel, and special chrome wheel covers. With the reliable, lightweight 289-cubic-inch V-8 and three-speed, all-synchromesh manual transmission, it makes an attractive car for the sports-minded.

The Cyclone will be immediately recognized in any crowd of Comets by the absence of excess trim, side spears, and other shiny gimcracks so prevalent on the others. In our opinion, it's one of the most tasteful renderings to come out of the Mercury styling studios in many a moon.

If you feel the need to tailor your Cyclone more to your particular tastes or needs, there are still plenty of options not included as standard equipment. Our test car had a minimum of extras. Right after the initial production run, Mercury decided to replace the Warner Gear four-speed transmission with one that Ford now builds. So we specified the four-speed instead of the standard three-speed. Also specified was the 3.50-to-1 performance rear axle, offered at no extra cost. A 3.25-to-1 gearset comes standard with any manual transmission. Also available is the new three-speed automatic, which comes with a 3.00-to-1 rear axle. The Cyclone isn't exactly a heavy car, but we feel that the manual steering in this line is slightly on the sluggish side, so we asked for power steering in the test car. Seat belts, padded sun visors, AM-FM radio, vinyl roof, and larger 7.00 x 14 tires (6.50s are standard) completed the extras.

A good balance of usable and reserve power came by way of the 210-hp engine. This version of the Fairlane V-8 uses a four-barrel carburetor, hydraulic lifters, and 9.0-to-1 compression ratio. Peak horsepower is reached at 4400 rpm, with 300 pounds-feet of torque at 2800 rpm. If you want even more go, the Cyclone can also be had with the "289" engine in Cobra tune. This one's rated at 271 hp at

COMET CYCLONE

COMET CYCLONE

6000 rpm and 314 pounds-feet of torque at 3400 rpm. Stronger cam timing and 11.6-to-1 compression ratio produce the increase.

With the standard engine and performance axle, the Cyclone can break 10 seconds during 0-60-mph runs. Ford's new four-speed has ratios more compatible with the engine's power and torque curves than the ratios in the Warner Gear transmission. Overall ratios with the 3.50 axle are 9.73, 6.75, and 4.76, with direct fourth. The old ratios of 9.56, 7.25, and 5.29 had too much gap between third and fourth, which made third a bit impractical for passing. For example, if you were cruising along in fourth at 60 mph, the engine would be turning 3150 rpm. Dropping into third with the old unit would raise engine speed to 4200 rpm, a difference of 1050 rpm and very close to the power peak of 4400 rpm. Dropping down into third in the new trans-

mission raises engine speed to 3900 revs, a difference of only 750 rpm and still far enough below the power peak so the engine can pull strongly enough to keep passing times to a minimum.

The standard 3.25-to-1 rear axle would drop performance slightly, but it'd still be adequate. This would be the case even if the automatic's 3.00-to-1 unit were installed. For the best all-around combination, we'd choose the standard 3.25 gearset; for economy, the 3.00-to-1 axle; for performance only, the 3.50 axle.

The Ford-built transmission seems strong enough and operates without much noise. During our acceleration tests, we made full-throttle shifts without outsmarting the synchromesh. We did have trouble with the shift linkage (also built by Ford). After about the fourth run, the linkage bent, and quick shifts were no longer possible. For normal use, the standard linkage should be more than adequate. Its tubular lever is strong though a bit short — we had to stretch to make third gear. A sliding collar under the shift knob prevents accidental engagement of reverse.

For those who prefer not to shift for themselves, the

LOCKING DIFFERENTIAL WOULD HELP CONTROL WHEELSPIN ON HARD ACCELERATION; H-D SPRINGS AND SHOCKS COULD CURE SPRING WIND-UP.

Sporting flair comes through by way of the three-spoke rally steering wheel. Dashboard houses a full complement of gauges.

Shift lever for Ford's new four-speed is strong, doesn't flex when used hard. To be really effective, it should be longer.

Multi-Drive (three-speed) Merc-O-Matic is available for an extra $189.60. The overall ratios in first and second (with 3.00-to-1 rear axle) are 6.37 and 4.38. The torque converter has a stall ratio of 2.02 to 1, which combines with first gear for an overall ratio of 14.9 to 1 for quick initial get-aways. Upshifts are set at about 37 (1-2) and 65 mph (2-3). Second gear is available as a passing gear below 63.5 mph.

Even with the oversized 7.00 x 14 tires, wheelspin's a problem with the 3.50 rear axle. A locking differential would help some and should definitely be considered if you're ordering the performance axle. Wheelspin also increases by the fact that the Cyclone is rather light on its rear. This was a problem on certain types of corners — mainly slow, tight ones. The inside rear wheel lifted easily and broke traction.

The five-leaf rear springs use an asymmetrical mounting for squat control during acceleration, and thereby they're also supposed to restrict spring wind-up. But we were bothered by a slight amount of rear-wheel judder — during both hard acceleration and hard braking. Convertibles and wagons use a six-leaf spring, which is also the optional heavy-duty offering for Cyclones. These springs, along with heavy-duty shock absorbers (also available), would be wise choices for all but completely normal use.

The owner's manual recommends regular gasoline for the 289-inch, 210-hp engine. We found, though, that the 9-to-1 compression ratio is critical enough to balk at regular unless it's absolutely top-grade. Even though we always gas up at reputable stations, we've found that the quality of the gas varies slightly from tank to tank. We could get a tankful from a certain station on one day that'd perform all right and then go back after a few days and get another tankful from the same pump that would cause engine ping. Toward the end of the test, we were burning nothing but premium fuel and were having no problems.

Fuel consumption around town varied from 11.5 mpg up to 13.5. It depended mainly on how we drove the Cyclone and what traffic conditions we encountered — not on the grade of fuel. Out on the highway, several hundred miles of non-stop steady cruising gave a top average of 17.5 mpg. From an economy angle, either the 3.00 or 3.25 rear axle would've given better mileage. The Cyclone has a 20-gallon

Tasteful interior uses all one color except for headliner. The bucket seats would be more comfortable if they weren't so soft.

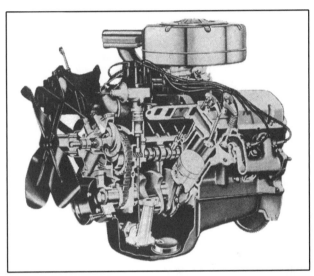

Heart of Cyclone package, the lightweight Fairlane V-8, pumps out 210 hp at 4400 rpm in test version, gives good performance.

Six-thousand-rpm tachometer comes standard in Cyclone. Driver gets good view of it, but loose mounting let it wobble around.

AS PHOTO SHOWS, REAR WHEELS LOCKED EASILY ON BRAKING TESTS. UNEVEN BRAKING PRESSURES FROM WHEEL TO WHEEL CAUSED SWERVING.

PHOTOS BY PAT BROLLIER

There's plenty of trunk space for size of car. High lip may offer a loading obstacle for shorter drivers, especially for women. Spare occupies usable space, but it's easy to reach.

Look again! What seems to be a chromed wheel is actually a snap-on cover. Chromed lugs are for real, though. Detroit stylists have surely reached their nadir with simulated wheels.

COMET CYCLONE

fuel tank, which gives a cruising range of roughly 350 miles on highway trips.

We weren't too happy with the brakes on our test car. While they're larger than those used on the six-cylinder Comets, they didn't seem to be quite large enough to handle the Cyclone's weight. Factory specifications show that Comet convertibles and wagons get brakes that offer 21 per cent more effective lining area and 25 per cent more swept-drum area. These brakes installed on the Cyclone would do a lot to cure the overheating and fade problems we ran into.

The standard brakes heated very rapidly, and we were barely able to complete two 60-mph panic stops before they faded completely. A car this size shouldn't need power brakes, but we would've welcomed them to cope with the high pedal effort needed after the brakes were used hard. The rear wheels locked up easily, due to the fact that the rear end is light and gets even lighter as the rear-to-front weight shifts on hard stops. A certain amount of steering wheel correction was necessary to keep the car in a straight line during these panic stops.

The heavy-duty suspension mentioned previously would improve the overall handling to a point where it'd be more in keeping with the Cyclone's sporting character. As it was, we felt the car was badly under-shocked. The slightest ripple or roughness in the road caused front- and rear-wheel judder. Very little bounce and rebound control was avail-

able, and even a slight dip would cause the car to oscillate three and four times before straightening out. Cornering characteristics were completely predictable once we got used to how easily the inside rear wheel would lift. We could then compensate for it. Crosswinds caused a slight amount of wander but not enough to be annoying.

In the overall analysis, the Cyclone was put together very well. Everything fit as designed. The only complaint here was that the tachometer was always loose on its mounting. This seems a problem with every Comet or Falcon we've seen that uses the factory tach.

Interiors are color-keyed, and the combinations of materials offer both elegance and durability. The bucket seats were fairly comfortable, although we felt they were a bit too soft. Given a little firmer padding, they'd offer better support. For our particular height (five feet, 11½), the steering wheel felt too high and too close. More seat travel would've been welcome, but the wheel would still have been too high.

Full instrumentation is offered, and the layout's convenient and readable. Most controls, knobs, and switches are also within easy reach of most drivers. Padding is provided on the top of the dash, while the face of it is finished in a pebble-grained vinyl similar to that used on cameras. The overall effect is one of function and good looks.

We felt that the Cyclone's a good basic car and that by judiciously scanning the options list, the buyer can put together a package that'll satisfactorily meet his needs. The 24-month/24,000-mile warranty applies. /MT

CYCLONE'S UNUSUALLY HIGH POSITION ON ITS SUSPENSION MAKES IT SEEM TO BE LEANING, BUT ACTUALLY IT TOOK CORNERS FAIRLY FLAT.

COMET CYCLONE

2-door, 5-passenger hardtop

OPTIONS ON CAR TESTED: 4-speed transmission, power steering, vinyl roof, padded visors, AM-FM radio, whitewall tires, seat belts

BASE PRICE: $2655
PRICE AS TESTED: $3299.25 (plus tax and license)
ODOMETER READING AT START OF TEST: 3967 miles
RECOMMENDED ENGINE RED LINE: 5200 rpm

PERFORMANCE

ACCELERATION (2 aboard)
    0-30 mph............................3.1 secs.
    0-45 mph............................5.9
    0-60 mph............................9.7
PASSING TIMES AND DISTANCES
    40-60 mph..........................5.1 secs.
                    372 ft.
    50-70 mph..........................6.1 secs.
                    536 ft.
Standing start ¼-mile 16.2 secs. and 80 mph
Speeds in gears @ 5200 rpm
    1st ....39 mph   3rd 80
    2nd 56   4th ....103 mph (actual
                              top speed @ 4800 rpm)
Speedometer Error on Test Car

Car's speedometer reading	36	55	60	74	86	98
Weston electric speedometer	30	45	50	60	70	80

Observed miles per hour per 1000 rpm in top gear ....20.5 mph
Stopping Distances — from 30 mph, 33 ft.; from 60 mph, 169.5 ft.

SPECIFICATIONS FROM MANUFACTURER

Engine
  Ohv V-8
  Bore: 4.00 ins.
  Stroke: 2.87 ins.
  Displacement: 289 cu. ins.
  Compression ratio: 9.0:1
  Horsepower: 210 @ 4400 rpm
  Torque: 300 lbs.-ft. @ 2800 rpm
  Horsepower per cubic inch: 0.73
  Carburetion: 1 4-bbl.
  Ignition: 12-volt coil

Gearbox
  4-speed manual, all synchro;
  floorshift

Driveshaft
  1-piece, open tube

Differential
  Hypoid, semi-floating
  Installed ratio: 3.50:1

Suspension
  Front: Independent, single lower
  arm, with stabilizing strut, coil
  springs, direct-acting tubular
  shocks, and anti-roll bar
  Rear: Rigid axle, with 5-leaf,
  semi-elliptic springs, direct-
  acting tubular shocks

Steering
  Recirculating ball and nut,
  with linkage-type power assist
  Turning diameter: 40.0 ft.
  Turns lock to lock: 4.6

Wheels and Tires
  5-lug, steel disc wheels
  7.00 x 14 2-ply nylon
  tubeless tires

Brakes
  Hydraulic, duo-servo; self-
  adjusting; cast-iron drums
  Front: 10-in. dia. x 2.25 ins. wide
  Rear: 10-in. dia. x 1.75 ins. wide
  Effective lining area:
  127.8 sq. ins.
  Swept drum area: 251.3 sq. ins.

Body and Frame
  Unitized
  Wheelbase: 114.0 ins.
  Track: front, 55.6 ins.;
  rear, 56.0 ins.
  Overall length: 195.1 ins.
  Overall width: 71.4 ins.
  Curb weight: 3160 lbs.

■ 2 COMETS:

by John Ethridge
Technical Editor

IT'S NOT OFTEN that we get a chance to compare two cars that are so much alike (except for engine and gearbox) as this month's test Comets. Much of our reader mail comes from people who ask what differences in performance, gas mileage, etc., they can expect if they order manual gearboxes and hotter

engines in their new cars. Of course, the results we got with the Comets won't apply directly to *any* two cars, but they should at least make our readers better guessers.

When we say cars are alike, we mean they're alike in those respects that affect performance. As for role and purpose, the cars are quite different. The Caliente is Comet's top-line offering. It's available as a four-door sedan, two-door convertible, or as a two-door hardtop (our test car). Thus it can be anything from

a family sedan to a personal car. On the other hand, the Cyclone's available only as a two-door hardtop with bucket seats. This one's tailored for the performance-minded buyer.

Our test Caliente had a bench front seat, but it's also available with buckets. The Caliente's optional bucket seats, though, are somewhat different from those of the Cyclone.

One source of certain confusion is the names of Comet's engines. Our Caliente was equipped with the 200-hp V-8 with

HOT & COOL

two-barrel carb. This engine is referred to as the "Comet Cyclone 289 V-8." The only engine offered in the Cyclone is the 225-hp, four-barrel-carb power-plant called the "Comet Cyclone Super 289 V-8." But *this* engine's optional on the Caliente — so you see what we mean.

The Cyclone's 225-hp engine had what you'd consider a healthy feeling at any speed between idle and 3000 rpm. Then it felt like four more cylinders were suddenly added and came on *very* strongly. This exhilarating burst of

torque and power continued until 5000 rpm, when everything came to an untimely end due to valve float (this engine uses hydraulic lifters). It was within this short, happy rpm span that we got our acceleration times. They wouldn't have been possible without the test car's four-speed, close-ratio transmission.

Unfortunately for Comet, there's no engine option like the 271-hp "289" solid-lifter V-8 offered for the Mustang. We feel the Cyclone's 225-hp engine, with some changes in the valve gear to

let it rev to 6000 rpm, would result in a sizable performance improvement.

Another drawback to good acceleration times with the Cyclone was severe rear-axle hop, even with its optional performance handling kit. The Caliente didn't have this kit. Once we broke a rear wheel loose, the Cyclone would churn out huge clouds of tire smoke and wouldn't regain traction until we backed off completely. It took a good deal of experimenting to find the right combination of throttle and clutch to

2 COMETS

avoid breaking the rear end loose or bogging down the engine. Here again is a place where correction of the defect would improve performance, even with the power the car now has.

Particularly noticeable was the exceptional tracking ability of both our test Comets. (Tracking ability means the ability of the car to maintain a given direction without steering correction.) We tried some hands-off driving over uneven ground. Here the steering wheel turned back and forth, but the car kept on in a straight line. This calls for a generous amount of front wheel toe-in (specs call for $\frac{5}{16}$-inch) plus well designed suspension geometry.

The Caliente had optional power steering, which was quicker than the Cyclone's manual steering. But at all times except when parking, the Cyclone's steering felt as quick or quicker, because the handling kit gave a faster steering response. The Cyclone was more fun to drive for this reason. All things considered, both cars cornered pretty well and didn't need a lot of sawing on the wheel to keep control. But

Cyclone wheelspin was hard to control getting off line. Automatic-transmissioned Caliente would often get jump on hot car.

Results were always same at end of quarter, though. Here Cyclone leads Caliente across line in one of the closer finishes.

We check out a pair of the brightest Comets in a side-by-side, point-by-point evaluation of their merits

UNDER-HOOD APPEARANCES WERE SAME EXCEPT FOR AIR CLEANER MARKINGS, CARBS. CYCLONE (RIGHT) HAS ITS OWN DISTINCTIVE GRILLE.

PHOTOS BY DARRYL NORENBERG, BOB MCVAY

STOPPING DISTANCES WERE REASONABLY SHORT WHEN WE STARTED WITH COOL BRAKES. MUCH COAXING WITH STEERING KEPT COMETS STRAIGHT.

here again the Cyclone had a decided edge because of the handling kit.

You might expect the Cyclone to be quite a bit noisier inside than the Caliente, but it wasn't. Panel vibration and drive-line noises were about the same in both cars. The Cyclone's gearshift linkage was the source of a fair amount of noise.

Both test Comets had the optional "interval selector" windshield wipers. This features a basic improvement on wipers. You can adjust the wiper so it'll flick the moisture off the windshield at whatever interval you select, up to one sweep every 10-12 seconds. This

works fine in a drizzle or when following cars on a wet road after the rain has stopped.

There was something rather special about our test Cyclone. It had the prototype fiberglass hood with simulated airscoops — optional on a limited basis for the Cyclone. It borrows from the image of the experimental supercharged Cyclones that have been burning up the drag strips lately. The hood had an aluminum screen on the underside to prevent radio interference from the ignition system. This was only partially effective. When passing under bridges, etc., noise from our own ignition would

drown out the radio. Better electrical contact between the screen and the rest of the body will undoubtedly help the situation.

The new hood does what it's intended to do, though. It proved an eye-catcher and attention-getter wherever we went. With this ominous-looking accessory, only you and your mechanic know for sure whether something wild and powerful lurks underneath.

The two Comets gave nearly identical average gas mileages for the test. The Cyclone got 13.8 mpg, and the Caliente got slightly less, 13.2 The Cyclone's fuel consumption varied from 11.2 to 16.8

2 COMETS

mpg and was more sensitive to the way the car was driven. The spread for the Caliente was 10.7 to 15.2 mpg. The Caliente's still the more economical in spite of the lower miles-per-gallon figure, because its 200-hp engine takes regular while Cyclone's 225-hp V-8 requires premium gasoline.

In the case of the Caliente, the speed we recorded for top gear was near the maximum — the engine felt wound out. This wasn't true of the Cyclone. Its speed was still creeping up when pre-

vious experience with the brakes told us to shut off in plenty of time for Riverside's Turn Nine. The brakes on both cars faded after a few stops at the end of acceleration runs. They required considerable time to cool before we could do our panic stopping tests.

Both Comets were good for general driving. Their excellent all-around visibility was a big help when driving on multi-lane freeways. The four fender corners are high and visible. They're as much help in parking as the compact

Cyclone's bucket seat backs fold well forward, allowing easy access to rear seat. Room's adequate for four adults on trips.

Caliente's bench seat with divided back was comfortable in a more forward position and gives rear occupants more knee room.

Remote trunk lid release can be reached from driver's seat. Tach, clock, and vacuum gauge atop dash are small but readable.

Caliente's air conditioner interfered with driver's right leg. Relocation toward passenger side would be a great improvement.

CYCLONE'S PERFORMANCE HANDLING KIT WAS EFFECTIVE AID TO CORNERING. CAR WAS STABLE, CONTROLLABLE, AND RAPID AROUND BENDS.

dimensions of the car. The Caliente's power steering had a good feel and no idiosyncrasies. The Cyclone's manual steering was commendably light, even when parking. In our opinion, power steering isn't an absolute necessity on either car.

The Caliente had power brakes, and the Cyclone didn't. The standard brakes seemed heavy when we first used them after driving a power-braked car, but we quickly got used to them. Comet's power brakes aren't over-powered as

some are, and they're therefore very controllable. It's hard to say, in the case of these cars, which of the braking systems is better. We've always felt that, provided the driver has enough leg power, standard brakes are less prone to lock up under panic conditions. On the other hand, when tendency to fade is a problem (as it is with these cars), power brakes are mighty handy for coping with the higher pedal pressure required.

Our test Comets, in car dealer's

language, were fully equipped, but the accessory lists were by no means exhausted. Three-speed manual transmissions are standard for both cars. The Merc-O-Matic and the four-speed manual (V-8s only) are optional. The Cyclone has no engine options, but the Caliente's available with any of the Comet engines, including the 120-hp Six.

Simulated chrome wheel covers with real chrome lug nuts are standard on the Cyclone, with simulated wire wheels (just as deceiving) optional. The Cyclone

CALIENTE DIDN'T HAVE KIT AND WAS FOUR TO FIVE MPH SLOWER FOR SAME DEGREE OF CONTROL IN TURNS LIKE THIS. LEAN WAS MODERATE.

comes with a tachometer, but you can order one for the Caliente — or clocks for both cars. A long list of comfort and convenience items complete the bill.

Besides the inevitable horsepower escalation, Comet changes for 1965 include a 38-ampere alternator and low-silhouette tires. But the biggest change is a restyling of the front end, which in our personal opinion is an improvement.

Mercury emphasizes durability for their Comet. As far as major components are concerned, there's no reason to doubt this — all of them have been around several years and are thoroughly proven, both in customer use and factory durability runs. **/MT**

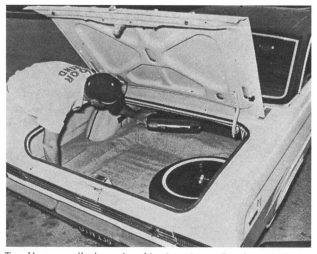

Trunk's unusually large for this size of car. Depth extends well past rear axle center line: width exceeds that of wheel wells.

COMET CALIENTE
2-door, 5-passenger hardtop

OPTIONS ON TEST CAR: Merc-O-Matic transmission, air conditioner, power steering, AM-FM radio, tinted glass, whitewalls, misc. access.
BASE PRICE: $2511
PRICE AS TESTED: $3559.90 (plus tax and license)
ODOMETER READING AT START OF TEST: 5029 miles
RECOMMENDED ENGINE RED LINE: 5200 rpm

PERFORMANCE
ACCELERATION (2 aboard)
0-30 mph..........................3.7 secs.
0-45 mph..........................6.5
0-60 mph..........................11.0
PASSING TIMES AND DISTANCES
40-60 mph.....................6.8 secs., 498 ft.
50-70 mph.....................6.3 secs., 557 ft.
Standing start ¼-mile 18.1 secs. and 76 mph
Speeds in gears @ shift points
1st .....42 mph @ 4200 rpm   3rd ....96 mph @ 3700
2nd .....76 mph @ 4000 rpm   rpm (observed)
Speedometer Error on Test Car
Car's speedometer reading......32 47 53 64 75 86
Weston electric speedometer ..30 45 50 60 70 80
Observed miles per hour per 1000 rpm in top gear ....26 mph
Stopping Distances — from 30 mph, 35 ft; from 60 mph, 158 ft.

SPECIFICATIONS FROM MANUFACTURER

Engine
Ohv V-8
Bore: 4.00 ins.
Stroke: 2.87 ins.
Displacement: 289 cu. ins.
Compression ratio: 9.3:1
Horsepower: 200 @ 4400 rpm
Horsepower per cubic inch: 0.69
Torque: 282 lbs.-ft. @ 2400 rpm
Carburetion: 1 2-bbl.
Ignition: 12-volt coil

Gearbox
3-speed automatic (Merc-O-Matic). column shift

Driveshaft
1-piece, open tube

Differential
Hypoid, semi-floating
Standard ratio: 3.00:1

Suspension
Front: Independent, single lower arm, with stabilizing strut, coil springs, direct-acting, tubular shocks, and anti-roll bar
Rear: Rigid axle, with semi-elliptic springs and tubular shocks

Steering
Recirculating ball and nut, power assisted
Turning diameter: 41.2 ft.
Turns lock to lock: 3.5

Wheels and Tires
5-lug, steel disc wheels
7.35 x 14 2-ply whitewall tires

Brakes
Hydraulic, duo-servo, self-adjusting; cast-iron drums
Front: 10-in. dia. x 2.25 ins. wide
Rear: 10-in. dia. x 1.75 ins. wide
Effective lining area: 126.0 sq. ins.
Swept drum area: 251.3 sq. ins.

Body and Frame
Unitized
Wheelbase: 114.0 ins.
Track: front, 55.6 ins.; rear, 56.0 ins.
Overall length: 195.3 ins.
Overall width: 72.9 ins.
Overall height: 53.5 ins.
Curb weight: 3140 lbs.

COMET CYCLONE
2-door, 5-passenger hardtop

OPTIONS ON TEST CAR: 4-speed manual transmission, AM-FM radio, handling package, vinyl roof, special fiberglass hood, whitewalls, seat belts, tinted glass, misc. access.
BASE PRICE: $2683
PRICE AS TESTED: $3544.40 (plus tax and license)
ODOMETER READING AT START OF TEST: 5600 miles
RECOMMENDED ENGINE RED LINE: 5200 rpm

PERFORMANCE
ACCELERATION (2 aboard)
0-30 mph..........................3.2 secs.
0-45 mph..........................5.5
0-60 mph..........................8.8
PASSING TIMES AND DISTANCES
40-60 mph.....................3.9 secs., 286 ft.
50-70 mph.....................5.4 secs., 475 ft.
Standing start ¼-mile 17.1 secs. and 82 mph
Speeds in gears @ 5000 rpm
1st ....48 mph   3rd ....86 mph
2nd ....65 mph   4th ....108 mph
                                  @ 4200 rpm (observed)
Speedometer Error on Test Car
Car's speedometer reading 33 46 53 64 75 86
Weston electric speedometer ...30 45 50 60 70 80
Observed miles per hour per 1000 rpm in top gear................26 mph
Stopping Distances — from 30 mph, 34 ft.; from 60 mph, 161 ft.

SPECIFICATIONS FROM MANUFACTURER

Engine
Ohv V-8
Bore: 4.00 ins.
Stroke: 2.87 ins.
Displacement: 289 cu. ins.
Compression ratio: 10.0:1
Horsepower: 225 @ 4800 rpm
Horsepower per cubic inch: 0.78
Torque: 305 lbs.-ft. @ 3200 rpm
Carburetion: 1 4-bbl.
Ignition: 12-volt coil

Gearbox
4-speed manual, all-synchro; floorshift

Driveshaft
1-piece, open tube

Differential
Hypoid, semi-floating
Standard ratio: 3.00:1

Suspension
Front: Independent, single lower arm, with stabilizing strut, coil springs, direct-acting tubular shocks, and anti-roll bar
Rear: Rigid axle, with semi-elliptic springs, tubular shocks

Steering
Recirculating ball and nut
Turning diameter: 41.2 ft.
Turns lock to lock: 4.6

Wheels and Tires
5-lug, steel disc wheels
7.35 x 14 2-ply whitewall tires

Brakes
Hydraulic, duo-servo, self-adjusting; cast-iron drums
Front: 10-in. dia. x 2.25 ins. wide
Rear: 10-in. dia. x 1.75 ins. wide
Effective lining area: 126.0 sq. ins.
Swept drum area: 251.3 sq. ins.

Body and Frame
Unitized
Wheelbase: 114.0 ins.
Track: front, 55.6 ins.; rear, 56.0 ins.
Overall length: 195.3 ins.
Overall width: 72.9 ins.
Overall height: 53.5 ins.
Curb weight: 3060 lbs.

INSTANT SPECIFICATIONS

COMET:

ENGINES--120 hp 6, 195/220 hp V8

WHEELBASE--114" L.O.A.--195"

WEIGHT--3075 lbs.

COMET

Comet is going in two directions at once in this year's models. The 'Mom and Pop' package, the standard car, has even softer springs and more sound-proofing for a big-car ride and feel. For the brisker motorist, an optional suspension, quick steering and rally instrument group is available on the "Cyclone". This sort of covers the kinds of buyers who might be attracted to Comet with its basic 200 inch seven-main Six or the hot 289 V8 with 10-1 compression and 4-barrel carb. An intermediate 195 hp 289 gets the in-betweeners. Gone are the 170 Six and 220 V8. A three-speed transmission -- automatic that is-- is stock throughout, with a four speed on the floor optional. The instrument panel is new, with all round bezels for the dials, even though not all of them are filled with needles, and numerous ignition improvementa have been made. Since Comet got its feet wet in competition and rallies, emphasis has been on performance and the 1965 is signifigantly hotter than the 1964. Buy the stiff suspension job. It's far better.

MERCURY COMET

In keeping with the trend of the time five years ago, Ford's Mercury Division introduced a compact model for the changing automobile market. At introduction, the Comet was a small car designed to appeal to the economy-minded buyer and to get a share of the then rapidly expanding import car business. Now with the introduction of the new '66s, Comet has joined its contemporaries in going full circle and stands firmly in the medium size sedan classification.

The length of the new Comet is actually more than that of the full size 1953 Mercury, and nearly eight inches more than last year's model. Its new appearance is a definite change from last year's boxy look and is a well-integrated design by the present mass interpretation of aesthetics.

One of the few domestic cars with leaf rear springs, Comet this year has new ones heavier and three inches longer to handle the increased weight of the enlarged body. Front suspension also received similar treatment with longer and softer coils.

Lengthening of the wheel base by two inches to 116 in. human comfort is increased generally throughout the car. More shoulder room, hiproom, and leg room are measurable. The luggage area has also been increased from 11% to 26% in the new models. This year the Comet wagon is offering a third seat, which faces to the rear. Which places Comet in the nine passenger wagon business for the first time.

An industry "first" has been achieved by the incorporation of fiberglass hood, bucket seats and console as standard equipment on the Cyclone series and should be a big thing with the drag set.

Power units available are the 200 cu. in. six, 289 V8 and 390 V8 in several horsepower ratings. Transmissions for these are manual 3-speed, 4-speed and the Multi-drive Merc-O-Matic.

The Comet's brakes have undergone no change from those of last year. In the May **Road Test** we rated them rather low, so after the addition of 200 pounds more weight, and more powerful engine options it seems a shame that the discs optional on the big Merc aren't available for this sensible sized car.

With nearly more options than parts in the car, the Comet should be able to provide any degree of luxury the owner is able to pay for. Because of this kind of marketing versatility plus the fact that the average

U.S. buyer seems to be more concerned about "Sporty" appearance than ever, **Road Test** predicts a good sales year ahead for Mercury's now grown up "compact."

DIMENSIONS	4-DR.	2-DR.	CONV.	WAGON
Wheelbase	116	116	116	113
Tread, F & R	58	58	58	58
Over-all length....	203	203	203	200
Height	55	54	54	56
Width	74	74	74	74

CHASSIS		6-CYL.	V-8 MOD'S
Type		unit	unit
Brake swept area, sq. in....		212	251
Turning circle, ft.........		41.5	41.5
Tire size		6.95 x 14	7.35 x 14
Ground clearance, in.		6.0	6.0
Fuel cap., gals............		20	20
Diff. ratio ....3.25:1, 2.80:1 & 3.00:1			

ENGINE	6-CYL.	V-8	V-8	V-8
Disp., cu. in. 200	289	390	390
Carb s ....1 bbl.	2 bbl.	2 bbl.	4 bbl.
Comp. ratio 9.2	9.3	9.5	10.5
Bore 3.68	4.00	4.05	4.05
Stroke 3.13	2.87	3.78	3.78
BHP 120	200	265	315
Torque 190	282	397	427

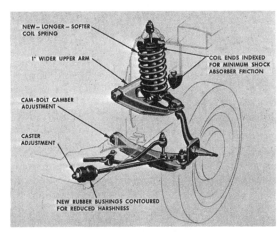

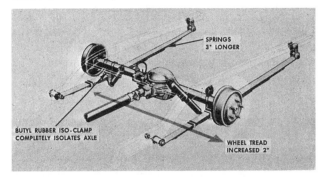

1966 Comet is larger, heavier car, has revised suspension, front and rear. Brakes, however, remain same size as on previous models.

Comet Caliente convertible is typical of "sporty" cars which Mercury Division will push. Market analysis has resulted in decision to take Comet out of "Economy" category. Family four-door has also been dressed up.

MERC MAKES THE MUSCLECAR SCENE

with a striped and scooped Comet Cyclone GT that doubles in durability

BY MARTYN L. SCHORR

IMAGE, IMAGE, who's got the image? That's the big question around the Motor City these days. Pontiac originated the image or supercar with its GTO and the other divisions and competitive manufacturers followed right behind. Pontiac has been a leader in this unpredictable market which started out as a haven for hot rodders who wanted to buy ready-built hot machinery and has expanded to encompass young and old alike who are just interested in a head-turning, super-jazzy stocker.

This year Pontiac's position is being threatened by Chevy with its Chevelle 396 and to a lesser degree by all the other manufacturers. Detroit has learned a lot since 1964 when Pontiac made the big plunge. They discovered that the average buyer of a car such as the GTO doesn't give a row of beans about the high rev hydraulic lifter cams or the tuned headers and excellent porting layout. They really dig the racing stripes, hood and side panel scoops and the image ornamentation. Of course, they also want

a respectable sounding and performing engine to back up the show features.

Lincoln-Mercury's entry in the image car sweepstakes is the super racy Comet Cyclone GT. In stock showroom trim it's every bit as showy as the accepted leaders in the field and has the potential to become a class winner at the strip. It's not as popular as the GTO or the Chevelle Super Sport, but that's mainly because Lincoln-Mercury up until now has not spent that much for image merchandising. They have been putting

Bold frontal styling and stacked quads give the sleek Cyclone that "big car" look. Fiberglass hood on test car was poorly fitted. Potent 335 hp mill boasts big Holley quad, reworked sparker and 5000 rpm cam. Auto trans engine is shown here.

Clutch-type slip fan cuts down on hp drain. Fiberglass radiator shroud is standard on GT. Beefy leaf-spring rear carries 3.90 limited slip gears, by axles. HD suspension and handling package is standard on 390 models. Hidden by the simulated chrome wheel-type covers are 10-inch finned brake drums. Test car was shod with high speed 7.75 x 14-inch Firestone 500's.

the emphasis on the bread and butter models such as the full-size Mercs and standard model Comets.

The product planning boys at Lincoln-Mercury have just finished an all-out campaign to put the Cyclone GT on the map, and it won't be long before C and D/Stock competition at strips all over the country feel the sting of special Cyclone models. As of this writing you can actually purchase a ready-to-race, 100-percent legal NHRA-AHRA stock Cyclone with either automatic or four-speed manual transmissions from any authorized dealer. This manuever makes it that much easier for the average guy to go racing for the least amount of cash output.

Instead of testing a Cyclone as soon as one was available in New York, we decided to wait until the Press test model had been flogged by every *would be* performance buff before putting it through its paces. This is somewhat less than desirable as there is a better than average chance that by the time you recover one of these has-been test cars it's ready for the glue factory, not street or strip! Being gamblers at heart we waited until everyone from *Better Homes and Garages* to *Sandbaggers Illustrated* had finished their so-called testing before taking over.

Waiting for us at the Ford Motor Company garage in New York was a bright red, rallye-striped Cyclone GT with more than 8000 *rough* miles on its odometer. Except for spanking new Firestone 500 high speed shoes the GT was 8000 miles old. Before going on we should clarify the term "Press mileage." The 8000 miles on the Cyclone GT was equal to 15,000-plus miles registered by the average owner of a performance-type automobile. Press cars are passed from one driver to another and the cars receive a minimum of dealer servicing. It's not at all unusual to find these cars with badly worn clutches, an engine running on six cylinders or a front end that's ready to fall apart. Any Press car

1966 MERCURY COMET CYCLONE GT SPECIFICATIONS

ENGINE

Type	OHV V-8
Displacement	390 cubic inches
Compression Ratio	10.50 to 1
Carburetion	Holley 600 CFM quad
Camshaft	5200 rpm Hydraulic,
Horsepower	335 @ 4800 rpm
Torque	427 foot/pounds @ 3200 rpm
Exhaust	Dual headers, dual pipes
Ignition	Dual points, special curve

TRANSMISSION

Make	Reverse lockout, floor mounted
Ratios	2.32, 1.69, 1.29, 1.00

REAR END

Type	Locking differential, 9-inch ring gear
Ratio	3.89-to-1

BRAKES

Type	10-inch finned drums, metallic linings
Area	282.6 square inches

SUSPENSION

Front	Independent high rate coil springs, HD shocks
Rear	High rate leaf springs, HD shocks
Steering	Power assisted
Overall Ratio	20-to-1

GENERAL

List Price	$2890
Price As Tested	$3490
Weight	3580 pounds
Wheelbase	116 inches
Overall Length	195 inches
Tire Size	7.75 x 14-inch Firestone 500

PERFORMANCE

0 to 30 mph	3.2 seconds
0 to 60 mph	7.0 seconds
Standing ¼ mile	98 mph
Elapsed Time	14.95 seconds
Top Speed	118 mph
Fuel Consumption	13.6 mpg (Sunoco 260)

that reaches 8000 miles and is still in the pool is in our eyes a durability champion!

We were most impressed with our *slightly used* test car, as there was plenty of meat left on the clutch, the body and running gear were pretty tight and the engine proved to be quite responsive. As we tooled through rush hour traffic on our way out of

1966 COMET Optional Axle Ratios — 9" Ring Gear	
	Part No.
4.33:1	C4AZ-4209-C
4.44:1	C3AZ-4209-F
4.57:1	C3UZ-4209-A
4.71:1	C4AZ-4209-E
4.86:1	C4AZ-4209-F
5.14:1	C4AZ-4209-G
5.43:1	C4AZ-4209-H
5.67:1	C4AZ-4209-J

Rotunda electric tach was installed on the steering post, as "Mickey Mouse" Comet tach is less than desirable for performance driving. Rear end styling is ultra-smooth with the tail blinkers integrated into the deck lid trim.

the city it was evident that the plugs were caked up, and although the engine was firing on all eight, it didn't have the pizazz that we had expected. We were also quite amazed at the exhaust tone level, as it was only a shade bit noiser than the average V-8 dual setup. The suspension was obviously stiffer than stock, but not to the point where it was objectionable. And that's saying a lot considering the condition of New York City streets!

Before taking any more notes we turned our rallye-striped, Michigan-plated red Cyclone over to Charlie Dodge and George Snizek at Pacers Auto for a basic tune job. Since the engine was packed with hydraulic lifters there was no need to even remove the valve covers. A couple of hours later the car was ready and we packed our gear into the trunk for a 500 mile tour of the New England countryside.

For those of you not familiar with the Cyclone GT super street package, here's a rundown on our test car's nomenclature. With the exception of the steering post-mounted electric tach (car was also equipped with a strictly-for-effect Comet accessory tach high on the dash), chrome wheel-type covers and locking differential, our car was pretty much production stock. The factory GT package includes the 390 four-barrel engine, dual pipes, chrome engine goodies, high speed handling suspension, oversize tires, clutch fan and a twin-scoop fiberglass hood. The phoney scoops can be converted to functional operation, or the car can be ordered with the *special* scooped GT C/Stock competition hood from the factory.

The original GT option had as its top engine a 315 hp four-barrel that was just about useless against GTO, 442 and Chevelle musclecars. Lincoln-Mercury quietly amended the option list after the car had been introduced, upping the output of the top 390 to 335 hp. They accomplished this by adding a new hydraulic lifter cam and kit good for 5200 rpm, a 600 CFM Holley quad and a new dual point distributor with a quick advance curve. For those who purchased the 315 hp model here's the number and price of the hot cam setup: # C6AZ-6A25-A, $59. The 335 hp engine is the one Mercury is running in its limited producion C/Stock Cyclones. *(Continued on page 82)*

COMET CYCLONE GT

IF BIGNESS must always be equated with better, the Comet Cyclone GT ought to be one of the best cars around. It certainly has the bigness of engine in relation to the car's overall size, to make it "better" than most of its roadmates. Unfortunately, or fortunately, depending upon who views it, the Cyclone GT is no better or no worse than the other examples of the current "Supercar" idiom.

The Cyclone GT is a new-for-'66 development of Lincoln-Mercury Division and its basic components are a plushed-up Comet hardtop coupe or convertible and a warmed-up 390-cu. in. Ford/Mercury engine. It follows the pattern of big-engine/little-car established by Pontiac for its '64 Tempest GTO, though the basic idea of stuffing the largest possible engine under the smallest possible hood harks back to the dim beginnings of hotrodding.

Along with the GTO (389 cu. in.), the group includes the Buick Skylark Gran Sport (401 cu. in.), Chevrolet Chevelle Super Sport (396 cu. in.), Ford Fairlane GT (390), Dodge Coronet (383 and 426), Oldsmobile F-85 442 (400), Plymouth Satellite (383 and 426). Certain others of the larger cars, such as Chevrolet Impala and Ford Galaxie, also fall into this category when they are equipped with High Performance 427-cu. in. engines. Su-

Supercar Status
For Lincoln's
Little Brother

SCOTT MALCOLM PHOTOS

CYCLONE GT

percar status (*CL*, May '65) comes with a weight-to-power loading of 12 lb./bhp or less.

Surplus horsepower thus has become a very real marketing entity, just as have automatic transmissions, power windows and electronic headlight dimmers. Every major domestic manufacturer, with the exception of American Motors and Cadillac, is producing its own Supercars to meet the demand. Remember six years back? The automakers couldn't build enough simple, 6-cyl. economy cars. Now the bottom has dropped out of that market and the manufacturers are rushing to fill orders for the overpowered and the overstuffed.

Lincoln-Mercury might have produced its GT a few years earlier, had the division aspired to leadership rather than followership. The Comet has been in its lineup since 1960; the 390-cu. in. V-8 engine has been powering Mercurys and Fords since 1961.

As it should be, after having two years to profit by the other fellows' experience, the L-M product is well dressed for this market place. The Cyclone itself is a slicked-off version of the standard models, thus offering its buyer something a little more exclusive. To further the idea, L-M replaces the normal stamped steel engine compartment hood on the Cyclone GT with one of molded fiberglass which has the added distinction of twin (nonfunctional) air scoops. White racing/rally stripes just above the rocker panels provide instantaneous recognition.

The GT's mechanical equipment can include either a 4-speed manual transmission or the Sport Shift automatic in place of the standard 3-speed all-synchromesh manual unit. Suspension of the GT definitely is firmer than that of the normal Comets and brake linings are of harsher material, to give the GT better resistance to fade. Obviously, planners have followed all the signposts in composing the Cyclone GT package.

THAT 390 CU. IN. will impart outstanding performance to a Comet is a conclusion readily believable on the basis of simple mathematical progression. After all, the standard Comet engine is an economizing 200-cu. in. Six and the first option is a modest little V-8 of 289 cu. in. and 200 bhp.

A true interpretation of the term performance would encompass all of a vehicle's dynamic activities. Performance evaluation should include fuel consumption, braking, handling, riding quality, top speed, and windshield wiper and heater operation, along with acceleration. Unfortunately, performance, in the context of the youth market, equates as straight-line, dragstrip type of acceleration.

So, Lincoln-Mercury has elected the 390 V-8 to do the job that several hot versions of the 289 couldn't do—that is, make a name for Comet at dragstrip and stoplight. There are two versions of the 390 V-8 in the lineup, a 2-barrel carburetor equipped, 275-bhp unit which may be ordered in any Comet, and the pepped-up 4-barrel 335-bhp engine which is available only in the Cyclone GT. The first version should be a good "torquer" for normal highway driving, the second is aimed directly at the enthusiastic, knowledgeable type of driver.

A S A PROPELLER of passenger sedans, the 390 Ford/Mercury engines do a fine, fussless job. They did, and do, a good job as 332- and 352-cu. in. V-8s. Their bigger brothers have had 406 and 427 cu. in., and, in full racing dress, have proved equal to that task, too. However, by strange admixture of mechanical alchemy, the 390/4-barrel has never been much of a top-end performer. It develops plenty of usable torque in the lower reaches and it pumps up more than enough horsepower for its nominal purpose. But, as a performer, it just doesn't deliver.

What is the 390's problem? Enginemen point mainly to the cylinder heads as the basic problem. Restrictive valve passages hinder the engine's "breathing" and hydraulic lifters limit attainable rpm. Maximum engine speed seems to be approximately 5000 rpm, even with an "open" exhaust system, because of the pumping up of the hydraulic lifters.

FIBERGLASS HOOD with twin air scoops heralds Cyclone GT arrival on the drag scene. Some judicious drilling would make the scoops functional.

On the other hand, valve size at 2.022 in. intake, 1.551 in. exhaust, would seem adequate, as would the Holley carburetor's four bores of 1.562 in. each. Compression, at 10.5:1, is also up toward the enthusiastic area. Exhaust should be no restriction, as any performance fan can install a set of tubular headers similar to those which equipped the test car. Basic engine specifications of 4.054 in. bore, 3.78 in. stroke, and 390 cu. in. displacement are certainly husky enough for a car of 3580 lb. curb weight.

Ford Motor Co. engineers have warmed up the 390 for use in the Cyclone GT by increasing valve lift to 0.48 from 0.40 in. although the camshafts appear to remain the same—both the normal passenger car version

and the Cyclone GT cams have 270° duration. No other specifications have been changed except horsepower rating; it jumped from 300 at 4600 rpm to 335 at 4800.

It's just possible that Ford/Mercury haven't gone far enough with this 390. Perhaps some of those high-rev, quick-bleed hydraulic lifters (like those used by Pontiac and Chevrolet to get over 6000 rpm from their HP engines) and a hotter camshaft would give it some excitement.

A visit to the local dragstrip for some of that straight-line performance evaluation gave results that were adequate, but not overwhelming. The 390 does a reasonable job, but promises no more. The Comet times are median for the big-engine/small-car group. At

CYCLONE GT

MISFIT panels—here the decklid and taillight sections—typify Comet assembly.

15.2 sec. elapsed time, 90 mph trap speed for the quarter-mile is good without being outstanding.

Shifts of the controllable Sport Shift 3-speed transmission were made both manually and automatically; the quickest times were achieved by letting the transmission select its own shift points. Several types of starts were tried, to overcome the handicap of highway-type tires; the best were those where not too much static pressure was built up in the torque converter before releasing the brakes, thus keeping wheel-spin at a minimum. A dozen runs were made over the Carlsbad Raceway dragstrip and their average was 15.2 sec., 90 mph.

Readers should keep in mind that this was a normally equipped, highway-geared Comet Cyclone GT. As delivered, this particular specimen had a set of curvaceous, fabricated tubing exhaust headers with removable plates at the ends of the 3-in. dump tubes. Cyclone GT specifications reveal no such option, but, because they were

there, *CL* made runs with blocking plates both on and off. Recorded times reflect the open condition; accelerations over the quarter-mile with the pipes plugged were 0.5-1-sec. slower.

The Comet-sized car lends itself well to dragstrip performance, it being reasonably light in weight and presenting minimal front area. Although a GT-opted Comet gets a bit on the bulky side of the scales, it doesn't come out nearly as porcine as many of its separate-frame competitors.

Unit construction provides structural integrity with lighter weight and benefits from modern torque-box technology, which produces tautness of construction and lowered noise levels. Additional chassis tuning for the '66 version isolated torque boxes to reduce vibration and harshness. Suspension components are heftier, as is steering linkage. Wheelbase and overall length have been increased, 2 in. and 7.7 in., respectively, in the reshaping of the sheet metal. This has added around 100 lb. to the overall mass, but the

shipping (dry) weight of the lightest Comet Six still is under 2800 lb.

Despite the nominally light weight of the car, excess poundage is a problem with the GT version. Adding the first-option 289-cu. in. V-8 increases the weight by 169 lb., while ordering a 390-cu. in. V-8 puts on 433 lb. over the basic Six. The XPL Sport Shift automatic ups the scales by 59 lb. (the 4-speed manual is only 28 lb. over the normal 3-speed) while power steering and power brakes add 38 lb. more.

1966 MERCURY COMET
CYCLONE GT HARDTOP

DIMENSIONS

Wheelbase, in.	116
Track, f/r, in.	58.3
Overall length, in.	203
width	73.8
height	54.3
Front seat hip room, in.	2 x 25
shoulder room	58.0
head room	38.1
pedal-seatback, max.	43.5
Rear seat hip room, in.	58.3
shoulder room	56.7
leg room	34.1
head room	36.7
Door opening width, in.	43.3
Floor to ground height, in.	12.5
Ground clearance, in.	6.5

PRICES

List, fob factory............$2891
Equipped as tested..........3391
Options included: Sport Shift automatic trans., clock, power steering, power brakes, am/fm radio, front and rear seat belts.

CAPACITIES

No. of passengers	5
Luggage space, cu. ft.	17.0
Fuel tank, gal.	20.0
Crankcase, qt.	4.0
Transmission/diff., pt.	13.3/4.5
Coolant radiator, qt.	19.5

CHASSIS/SUSPENSION

Frame type	unit
Front suspension type: Independent by s.l.a., coil springs, telescopic shock absorbers, link-type stabilizer.	
ride rate at wheel, lb./in.	119
anti-roll bar dia., in.	0.85
Rear suspension type: Hotchkiss drive with longitudinal semi-elliptic leaf springs; telescopic shock absorbers.	
ride rate at wheel, lb./in.	146
Steering system: Recirculating ball and nut with power-boosted parallelogram linkage; ball-joint steering knuckles.	
gear ratio	16.0
overall ratio	21.6
turns, lock to lock	3.5
turning circle, ft. curb-curb.	41.5
Curb weight, lb.	3580
Test weight.	3920
Weight distribution, % f/r.	56.4/43.6

BRAKES

Type: Single-line hydraulic with duo-servo shoes in cast-iron drums.

Front drum, dia. x width, in.	10 x 2.5
Rear drum, dia. x width	10 x 2.0
total swept area, sq. in.	282.6
Power assist	integral, vacuum
line psi @ 100 lb. pedal	760

WHEELS/TIRES

Wheel size	14 x 5.5
optional size available	none
bolt no./circle dia., in.	5/4.5
Tire make, brand: Goodyear Power Cushion	
size	7.75-14
recommended inflation, psi	28
capacity rating, total lb.	n.a.

ENGINE

Type, no. cyl.	V-8, ohv
Bore x stroke, in.	4.054 x 3.78
Displacement, cu. in.	390
Compression ratio	10.5
Rated bhp @ rpm	335 @ 4800
equivalent mph	114
Rated torque @ rpm	427 @ 3200
equivalent mph	76
Carburetion	Holley, 1 x 4
barrel dia., pri./sec.	1.562/1.562
Valve operation: Hydraulic lifters, pushrods and rocker arms.	
valve dia., int./exh.	2.03/1.56
lift, int./exh.	0.4809
timing, deg.	18-72, 68-22
duration, int./exh.	270
opening overlap	40
Exhaust system: Headers with dual reverse-flow mufflers.	
pipe dia., exh./tail	2.00/2.00
Lubrication pump type	rotor
normal press. @ rpm	50 @ 2000
Electrical supply	alternator
ampere rating	38
Battery, plates/amp. rating	66/70

DRIVE-TRAIN

Clutch type	
dia., in.	
Transmission type: Automatic with 3-element torque converter and planetary gearbox.	
Gear ratio 4th ( ) overall	
3rd (1.00)	3.25
2nd (1.46)	4.75
1st (2.46)	7.99
1st x t.c. stall (2.10)	16.8
Shift lever location	console
Differential type: Hypoid, straddle-mounted pinion.	
axle ratio	3.25

INSTRUMENT layout put everything in front of driver, but lacked a tachometer.

HEADERS helped improve performance as much as 1 sec. in quarter-mile time.

FUEL filler extension looks vulnerable inside the Cyclone's huge compartment.

Of course, the Cyclone GT is available only as a convertible or hardtop coupe; both of which are heavier models.

It is easily seen, then, why a basic car which ships at 2800 lb. inflates to 3580 lb. when ready to drive. By the same token, the basic Six's good weight balance of 52.8% front, 47.2% rear, deteriorates to 56.4/43.6 with the Cyclone GT equipment. The shift in balance, and the nearly tripled power, only compound the problem of drive-wheel traction.

As would be indicated by such weight distribution, driving the Cyclone GT generates a definite front-heavy feeling. Directional control didn't seem particularly precise, even with the arrowhead out front, and the *CL* test car was wont to lurch and ramble at highway imperfections. The power-assisted steering may have contributed to that feeling as it effectively masked any indication or reaction of the road wheels under a bland, constant steering wheel effort. The standard equipment 7.75-14 Goodyear Power Cushion tires did a good job of putting what traction they could to the road. Only at the dragstrip, where full-throttle starts were permissible, were they inadequate.

Driving the Cyclone GT with automatic can be as delightful in some ways as it is disappointing in others. Freeway traffic, where close-quarter maneuvering and acceleration to flow-speed from on-ramps are everyday necessities, is just its meat. The surplus

CAR LIFE ROAD TEST

ACCELERATION & COASTING

ELAPSED TIME IN SECONDS

CALCULATED DATA

Lb./bhp (test weight)	11.7
Cu. ft./ton mile	146
Mph/1000 rpm (high gear)	23.7
Engine revs/mile (60 mph)	2530
Piston travel, ft./mile	1590
Car Life wear index	40.3
Frontal area, sq. ft.	22.3
Box volume, cu. ft.	472

SPEEDOMETER ERROR

30 mph, actual	28.8
40 mph	37.2
50 mph	46.5
60 mph	57.6
70 mph	67.6
80 mph	73.8
90 mph	84.9

MAINTENANCE INTERVALS

Oil change, engine, miles	6000
transmission/differential	as req.
Oil filter change	6000
Air cleaner service, mo.	12
Chassis lubrication	36,000
Wheelbearing re-packing	30,000
Universal joint service	30,000
Coolant change, mo.	24

TUNE-UP DATA

Spark plugs	Autolite BF-42
gap, in.	0.032
Spark setting, deg./idle rpm.	10/575
cent. max. advance, deg./rpm	24.5/4000
vac. max. adv., deg./in. Hg.	25/20
Breaker gap, in.	0.014
cam dwell angle	26
arm tension, oz.	17
Tappet clearance, int./exh.	0
Fuel pump pressure, psi.	5.0
Radiator cap relief press., psi.	12-15

PERFORMANCE

Top speed (5000), mph	120
Shifts (rpm) @ mph	
3rd to 4th ( )	
2nd to 3rd (4600)	75
1st to 2nd (4800)	46

ACCELERATION

0-30 mph, sec.	2.3
0-40 mph	3.3
0-50 mph	4.8
0-60 mph	6.6
0-70 mph	9.1
0-80 mph	12.1
0-90 mph	15.2
0-100 mph	18.7
Standing ¼-mile, sec.	15.2
speed at end, mph	90
Passing, 30-70 mph, sec.	6.8

BRAKING

(Maximum deceleration rate achieved from 80 mph)

1st stop, ft./sec./sec.	23
fade evident?	yes
2nd stop, ft./sec./sec.	23
fade evident?	yes

FUEL CONSUMPTION

Test conditions, mpg	10.1
Normal cond., mpg	10-13
Cruising range, miles	200-260

GRADABILITY

4th, % grade @ mph	
3rd	19 @ 71
2nd	29 @ 58
1st	36 @ 41

DRAG FACTOR

Total drag @ 60 mph, lb.	175

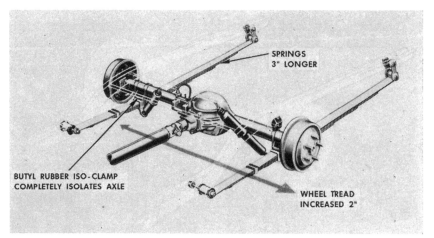

COMET REAR suspension for '66 shows longer springs for softer ride, wider tread for greater stability. Rubber "iso-clamp" is supposed to block drive-line noise.

SPORT SHIFT T-handle allows driver the 1-2-3 selection of automatic's gears.

CYCLONE GT

of power hustles the GT into any available "hole" and the Cyclone's size makes it easily maneuvered. Less-than-straight roads are less pleasing, and here the overbalance of weight makes for a nervous drive. Overall handling is not, then, a highpoint with the Cyclone GT.

In styling, the car has good proportions, but poor detailing. A novel front-end treatment leaves no doubt that it's a Comet. Headlights and their surrounding panels, however, seem to be the work of a committee which couldn't achieve agreement. Mercifully, the flanks and stern are not bela-

bored with excess decoration so the overall effect is at least one of cleanness. The bucket seat interior is contemporary and the ubiquitous console sprouts forth the transmission control lever. Comets, as do others this model year, suffer from gaposis of panels. A walk-around inspection revealed more misalignments than would seem acceptable to a discerning buyer about to sign his name to a $3400 bill. Neither hood nor decklid looked as if they belonged to that particular car; sculpture lines "broke" where they crossed panel joints.

What is there about the Comet Cyclone GT for the enthusiastic driver

to look for? What is there for him to be enthusiastic about?

He might get fired up about the bigness of the engine—if he knows a few ways to extract what potential is there for dragstrip performance. He might be intrigued by the proved durability of Comet cars. Or, he might go for the styling; it doesn't appear to be a carbon copy of another division's car, even though it and the Fairlane GTA share most components.

For the youth market, however, it might behoove Lincoln-Mercury planners to take a longer, harder look at the Cyclone GT and take the step to make it a leader and a standout in the Supercar crowd. What's that? Scrap the 390/4-bore and pop in the Big Daddy of the NASCAR scene—the 427 V-8 with its 7000 rpm potential. Now, that would be a hauler! ∎

HOLLEY 4-BARREL carburetor has 1.562-in. bores, nestles between Cyclone GT's chromium-plated rocker covers and breather cap.

ENGINE SECTION shows wedge-head chambers of big Ford family V-8 design and layout of hydraulic lifter, rocker-shaft valve system.

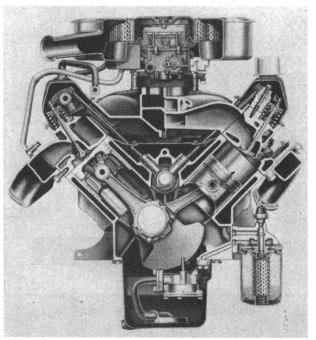

MERCURY

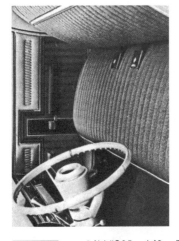

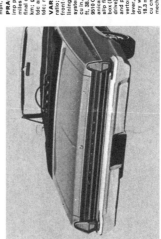

Caliente 4-door Sedan

ENGINE CAPACITY 200 cu in, 3,277.40 cu cm
FUEL CONSUMPTION 20.8 m/imp gal, 17.3 m/US gal, 13.6 l × 100 km
SEATS 6   MAX SPEED 96 mph, 154.6 km/h
PRICE IN USA $ 2,535

ENGINE front, 4 stroke; cylinders: 6, slanted at 4°, in line; bore and stroke: 3.68 × 3.13 in, 93.5 × 79.5 mm; engine capacity: 200 cu in, 3,277.40 cu cm; compression ratio: 9.1; max power (SAE): 120 hp at 4,400 rpm; max torque (SAE): 190 lb ft, 26.2 kg m at 2,400 rpm; max engine rpm: 4,600; specific power: 36.6 hp/l; cylinder block: cast iron; cylinder head: cast iron; crankshaft bearings: 7; valves: 2 per cylinder, overhead, in line, push-rods and rockers, hydraulic tappets; camshafts: 1, side; lubrication: rotary pump, full flow filter; lubricating system capacity: 7.39 imp pt, 8.80 US pt, 4.2 l; carburation: 1 Ford 9510-C60F-AD downdraught single barrel carburettor; fuel feed: mechanical pump; cooling system: water; cooling system capacity: 15.84 imp pt, 19 US pt, 9 l.

TRANSMISSION driving wheels: rear; clutch: single dry plate; gearbox: mechanical; gears: 3 + reverse; synchromesh gears: II and III; gearbox ratios: I 2.760, II 1.690, III 1, rev 3.740; gear lever: steering column; final drive: hypoid bevel; axle ratio: 3.250.

CHASSIS integral; front suspension: independent, wishbones, lower trailing links, coil springs, anti-roll bar, telescopic dampers; rear suspension: rigid axle, semi-elliptic leafsprings, telescopic dampers.

STEERING recirculating ball; turns of steering wheel lock to lock: 5.25.

BRAKES drum; area rubbed by linings: total 251.40 sq in, 1,621.53 sq cm.

ELECTRICAL EQUIPMENT voltage: 12 V; battery: 45 Ah; generator type: alternator, 38 Ah; ignition distributor: Ford; headlamps: 4.

DIMENSIONS AND WEIGHT wheel base: 116 in, 2,946 mm; front track: 58 in, 1,473 mm; rear track: 58 in, 1,473 mm; overall length: 203.50 in, 5,169 mm; overall width: 73.80 in, 1,875 mm; overall height: 55.20 in, 1,402 mm; ground clearance: 5.90 in, 150 mm; dry weight: 3,012 lb, 1,366 kg; distribution of weight: 52.6% front axle, 47.4% rear axle; turning circle (between walls): 44.4 ft, 13.5 m; width of rims: 5"; tyres: 7.35 × 14; fuel tank capacity: 16.7 imp gal, 20 US gal, 76 l.

BODY saloon/sedan; doors: 4; seats: 6; front seats: bench.

PERFORMANCE max speeds: 38 mph, 61.2 km/h in 1st gear; 63 mph, 101.4 km/h in 2nd gear; 96 mph, 154.6 km/h in 3rd gear; power-weight ratio: 25.1 lb/hp, 11.4 kg/hp; carrying capacity: 1,036 lb, 480 kg; speed in direct drive at 1,000 rpm: 23.1 mph, 37.2 km/h.

PRACTICAL INSTRUCTIONS fuel: 95-100 oct petrol; engine sump oil: 5.63 imp pt, 6.80 US pt, 3.2 l, SAE 5W-20 (winter) 10W-30 (summer), change every 6,000 miles, 9,700 km; gearbox oil: 1.58 imp pt, 2 US pt, 0.9 l, SAE 80, change every 32,000 miles, 51,500 km; final drive oil: 3.34 imp pt, 4 US pt, 1.9 l, SAE 90, change every 32,000 miles, 51,500 km; greasing: every 32,000 miles, 51,500 km; valve timing: inlet opens 7° before tdc and closes 65° after bdc, exhaust opens 55° before bdc and closes 21° after tdc; normal tyre pressure: front 24 psi, 1.7 atm, rear 26 psi, 1.8 atm.

VARIATIONS AND OPTIONAL ACCESSORIES limited slip final drive: 3.500 axle ratio; power-assisted steering, 3.50 turns of steering wheel lock to lock; servo brake; front disc brakes, diameter 11.37 in, 289 mm, internal radial fins, total area rubbed by linings 361 sq in, 2,328.45 sq cm, servo brake; 6.50/7.75/8.95 × 14 tyres; cleaner air system; 3-speed heavy-duty mechanical gearbox (I 2.990, II 1.750, III 1, rev 3.170); Merc-o-Matic automatic gearbox, hydraulic torque convertor and planetary gears with 3 ratios (I 2.460, II 1.460, III 1, rev 2.200), max ratio of convertor at stall 2.1, possible manual selection, central or steering column selector lever, 3.250 (limited slip final drive) or 2.800 axle ratio; V8 engine, capacity 289 cu in, 4,735.84 cu cm, 200 hp, dry weight 3.173 lb, 1,439 kg, max speed 109 mph, 175.5 km/h (for further mechanical elements see variations Caliente Convertible); V8 engine, capacity 390 cu in, 6,390.93 cu cm, 270 hp, dry weight 3,439 lb, 1,560 kg, max speed 118 mph, 190 km/h (for further mechanical elements see variations Capri 2-door Hardtop). **Ⓥ** Caliente 2-door Hardtop, overall length 196.40 in, 4,989 mm, overall height 54 in, 1,372 mm.

Caliente Convertible

ENGINE CAPACITY 200 cu in, 3,277.40 cu cm
FUEL CONSUMPTION 20.8 m/imp gal, 17.3 m/US gal, 13.6 l × 100 km
SEATS 5   MAX SPEED 96 mph, 154.6 km/h
PRICE IN USA $ 2,818

ENGINE front, 4 stroke; cylinders: 6, slanted at 4° in line; bore and stroke: 3.68 × 3.13 in, 93.5 × 79.5 mm; engine capacity: 200 cu in, 3,277.40 cu cm; compression ratio: 9.1; max power (SAE): 120 hp at 4,400 rpm; max torque (SAE): 190 lb ft, 26.2 kg m at 2,400 rpm; max engine rpm: 4,600; specific power: 36.6 hp/l; cylinder block: cast iron; cylinder head: cast iron; crankshaft bearings: 7; valves: 2 per cylinder, overhead, in line, push-rods and rockers, hydraulic tappets; camshafts: 1, side; lubrication: rotary pump, full flow filter; lubricating system capacity: 7.39 imp pt, 8.80 US pt, 4.2 l; carburation: 1 Ford 9510-C60F-AD downdraught single barrel carburettor; fuel feed: mechanical pump; cooling system: water; cooling system capacity: 15.84 imp pt, 19 US pt, 9 l.

TRANSMISSION driving wheels: rear; gearbox: Merc-o-Matic automatic, hydraulic torque convertor and planetary gears with 3 ratios + reverse, max ratio of convertor at stall 2.1, possible manual selection; gearbox ratios: I 2.460, II 1.460, III 1, rev 2.200; selector lever: central or steering column; final drive: hypoid bevel; axle ratio: 3.250.

CHASSIS integral; front suspension: independent, wishbones, lower trailing links, coil springs, anti-roll bar, telescopic dampers; rear suspension: rigid axle, semi-elliptic leafsprings, telescopic dampers.

STEERING recirculating ball; turns of steering wheel lock to lock: 5.25.

BRAKES drum; area rubbed by linings: total 282.60 sq in, 1,822.77 sq cm.

ELECTRICAL EQUIPMENT voltage: 12 V; battery: 45 Ah; generator type: alternator, 38 Ah; ignition distributor: Ford; headlamps: 4.

DIMENSIONS AND WEIGHT wheel base: 116 in, 2,946 mm; front track: 58 in, 1,473 mm; rear track: 58 in, 1,473 mm; overall length: 196.40 in, 4,989 mm; overall width: 73.80 in, 1,875 mm; overall height: 54.20 in, 1,377 mm; ground clearance: 5.90 in, 150 mm; dry weight: 3,311 lb, 1,502 kg; distribution of weight: 50.1% front axle, 49.9% rear axle; turning circle (between walls): 44.4 ft, 13.5 m; width of rims: 5"; tyres: 7.35 × 14; fuel tank capacity: 16.7 imp gal, 20 US gal, 76 l.

BODY convertible; doors: 2; seats: 5; front seats: separate.

PERFORMANCE max speeds: 38 mph, 61.2 km/h in 1st gear; 63 mph, 101.4 km/h in 2nd gear; 96 mph, 154.6 km/h in 3rd gear; power-weight ratio: 27.6 lb/hp, 12.5 kg/hp; carrying capacity: 882 lb, 400 kg; speed in direct drive at 1,000 rpm: 23.1 mph, 37.2 km/h.

PRACTICAL INSTRUCTIONS fuel: 95-100 oct petrol; engine sump oil: 5.63 imp pt, 6.80 US pt, 3.2 l, SAE 5W-20 (winter) 10W-30 (summer), change every 6,000 miles, 9,700 km; gearbox oil: 13.02 imp pt, 15.70 US pt, 7.4 l, ATF type A-M2C33D; final drive oil: 3.34 imp pt, 4 US pt, 1.9 l, SAE 90, change every 32,000 miles, 51,500 km; greasing: every 32,000 miles, 51,500 km; valve timing: inlet opens 7° before tdc and closes 65° after bdc, exhaust opens 55° before bdc and closes 21° after tdc; normal tyre pressure: front 24 psi, 1.7 atm, rear 26 psi, 1.8 atm.

VARIATIONS AND OPTIONAL ACCESSORIES limited slip final drive: 3 axle ratio; power-assisted steering, 3.50 turns of steering wheel lock to lock; servo brake; front disc brakes, diameter 11.37 in, 289 mm, internal radial fins, total area rubbed by linings 361 sq in, 2,328.45 sq cm, servo brake; 6.50/7.75/8.95 × 14 tyres; cleaner air system; V8 engine, bore and stroke 4 × 2.87 in, 101.6 × 72.9 mm, engine capacity 289 cu in, 4,735.84 cu cm, max power (SAE) 200 hp at 4,400 rpm, max torque (SAE) 282 lb ft, 38.9 kg m at 2,400 rpm, 9.3 compression ratio, 42.2 hp/l specific power, 1 Ford 9510-C7DF downdraught twin barrel carburettor, 3-speed fully synchronized mechanical gearbox (I 2.990, II 1.750, III 1, rev 3.170), steering column gear lever, 3-speed fully synchronized mechanical gearbox (I 2.780, II 1.360, III 1, rev 2.780), central gear lever, 3.250 (limited slip final drive) or 3 axle ratio, Merc-o-Matic automatic gearbox, hydraulic torque convertor and planetary gears with 3 ratios (I 2.460, II 1.460, III 1, rev 2.200), max ratio of convertor at stall 2.1, possible manual selection, central or steering column selector lever, 3 (limited slip final drive) or 2.800 axle ratio, 55 Ah battery, 42 Ah alternator, dry weight 3,472 lb, 1,575 kg, max speed 109 mph, 175.5 km/h, fuel consumption 18.3 m/imp gal, 15.3 m/US gal, 15.4 l × 100 km; V8 engine, capacity 390 cu in, 6,390.93 cu cm, 270 hp, dry weight 3,738 lb, 1,696 kg, max speed 118 mph, 190 km/h (for further mechanical elements see variations Capri 2-door Hardtop).

MERCURY

Comet 202 2-door Sedan

ENGINE CAPACITY 200 cu in, 3,277.40 cu cm
FUEL CONSUMPTION 20.8 m/imp gal, 17.3 m/US gal, 13.6 l × 100 km
SEATS 6 **MAX SPEED** 96 mph, 154.6 km/h
PRICE IN USA $ 2,284

ENGINE front, 4 stroke; cylinders: 6, slanted at 4°, in line; bore and stroke: 3.68 × 3.13 in, 93.5 × 79.5 mm; engine capacity: 200 cu in, 3,277.40 cu cm; compression ratio: 9.1; max power (SAE): 120 hp at 4,400 rpm; max torque (SAE): 190 lb ft, 26.2 kg m at 2,400 rpm; max engine rpm: 4,600; specific power: 36.6 hp/l; cylinder block: cast iron; cylinder head: cast iron; crankshaft bearings: 7; valves: 2 per cylinder, overhead, in line, push-rods and rockers, hydraulic tappets; camshafts: 1, side; lubrication: rotary pump, full flow filter; lubricating system capacity: 7.39 imp pt, 8.80 US pt, 4.2 l; carburation: 1 Ford 9510-C60F-AD downdraught single barrel carburettor; fuel feed: mechanical pump; cooling system: water; cooling system capacity: 15.84 imp pt, 19 US pt, 9 l.

TRANSMISSION driving wheels: rear; clutch: single dry plate; gearbox: mechanical; gears: 3 + reverse; synchromesh gears: II and III; gearbox ratios: I 2.760, II 1.690, III 1, rev 3.740; gear lever: steering column; final drive: hypoid bevel; axle ratio: 3.250.

CHASSIS integral; front suspension: independent, wishbones, lower trailing links, coil springs, anti-roll bar, telescopic dampers; rear suspension: rigid axle, semi-elliptic leafsprings, telescopic dampers.

STEERING recirculating ball; turns of steering wheel lock to lock: 5.25.

BRAKES drum; area rubbed by linings: total 251.40 sq in, 1,621.53 sq cm.

ELECTRICAL EQUIPMENT voltage: 12 V; battery: 45 Ah; generator type: alternator, 38 Ah; ignition distributor: Ford; headlamps: 4.

DIMENSIONS AND WEIGHT wheel base: 116 in, 2,946 mm; front track: 58 in, 1,473 mm; rear track: 58 in, 1,473 mm; overall length: 196.40 in, 4,989 mm; overall width: 73.80 in, 1,875 mm; overall height: 55.20 in, 1,402 mm; ground clearance: 5.90 in, 150 mm; dry weight: 2,928 lb, 1,328 kg; distribution of weight: 52.9% front axle, 47.1% rear axle; turning circle (between walls): 44.4 ft, 13.5 m; width of rims: 5"; tyres: 7.35 × 14; fuel tank capacity: 16.7 imp gal, 20 US gal, 76 l.

BODY saloon/sedan; doors: 2; seats: 6; front seats: bench.

PERFORMANCE max speeds: 38 mph, 61.2 km/h in 1st gear; 63 mph, 101.4 km/h in 2nd gear; 96 mph, 154.6 km/h in 3rd gear; power-weight ratio: 24.5 lb/hp, 11.1 kg/hp; carrying capacity: 1,058 lb, 480 kg; speed in direct drive at 1,000 rpm: 23.1 mph, 37.2 km/h.

PRACTICAL INSTRUCTIONS fuel: 95 - 100 oct petrol; engine sump oil: 5.63

imp pt, 6.80 US pt, 3.2 l, SAE 5W - 20 (winter) 10W - 30 (summer), change every 6,000 miles, 9,700 km; gearbox oil: 1.58 imp pt, 2 US pt, 0.9 l, SAE 80, change every 32,000 miles, 51,500 km; final drive oil: 3.34 imp pt, 4 US pt, 1.9 l, SAE 90, change every 32,000 miles, 51,500 km; greasing: every 32,000 miles, 51,500 km; valve timing: inlet opens 7° before tdc and closes 55° before bdc, exhaust opens 55° before bdc and closes 21° after tdc; normal tyre pressure: front 24 psi, 1.7 atm, rear 26 psi, 1.8 atm.

VARIATIONS AND OPTIONAL ACCESSORIES limited slip final drive; 3.500 axle ratio; power-assisted steering, 3.50 turns of steering wheel lock to lock; servo brake; front disc brakes, diameter 11.37 in, 289 mm, internal radial fins, total area rubbed by linings 361 sq in, 2,328.45 sq cm, servo brake; 6.50/7.75/8.95 × 14 tyres; cleaner air system; 3-speed heavy-duty mechanical gearbox (I 2.990, II 1.750, III 1, rev 3.170); Merc-o-Matic automatic gearbox, hydraulic torque convertor and planetary gears with 3 ratios (I 2.460, II 1.460, III 1, rev 2.200), max ratio of convertor at stall 2.1, possible manual selection, central or steering column selector lever, 3.250 (limited slip final drive) or 2.800 axle ratio; V8 engine, capacity 289 cu in, 4,735.84 cu cm, 200 hp, dry weight 3,089 lb, 1,401 kg, max speed 109 mph, 175.5 km/h (for further mechanical elements see variations Caliente Convertible); V8 engine, capacity 390 cu in, 6,390.83 cu cm, dry weight 3,355 lb, 1,522 kg, max speed 118 mph, 190 km/h (for further mechanical elements see variations Capri 2-door Hardtop). ◼ Comet 202 4-door Sedan, overall length 203.50 in, 5,169 mm, dry weight 2,966 lb, 1,345 kg, distribution of weight 52.8% front axle, 47.2% rear axle.

Capri 2-door Hardtop

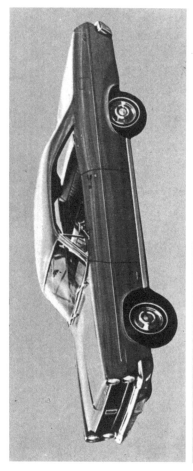

ENGINE CAPACITY 200 cu in, 3,277.40 cu cm
FUEL CONSUMPTION 20.8 m/imp gal, 17.3 m/US gal, 13.6 l × 100 km
SEATS 5 **MAX SPEED** 96 mph, 154.6 km/h
PRICE IN USA $ 2,459

ENGINE front, 4 stroke; cylinders: 6, slanted at 4°, in line; bore and stroke: 3.68 × 3.13 in, 93.5 × 79.5 mm; engine capacity: 200 cu in, 3,277.40 cu cm; compression ratio: 9.1; max power (SAE): 120 hp at 4,400 rpm; max torque (SAE): 190 lb ft, 26.2 kg m at 2,400 rpm; max engine rpm: 4,600; specific power: 36.6 hp/l; cylinder block: cast iron; cylinder head: cast iron; crankshaft bearings: 7; valves: 2 per cylinder, overhead, in line, push-rods and rockers, hydraulic tappets; camshafts: 1, side; lubrication: rotary pump, full flow filter; lubricating system capacity: 7.39 imp pt, 8.80 US pt, 4.2 l; carburation: 1 Ford 9510-C60F-AD downdraught single barrel carburettor; fuel feed: mechanical pump; cooling system: water; cooling system capacity: 15.84 imp pt, 19 US pt, 9 l.

TRANSMISSION driving wheels: rear; clutch: single dry plate; gearbox: mechanical; gears: 3 + reverse; synchromesh gears: II and III; gearbox ratios: I 2.760, II 1.690, III 1, rev 3.740; gear lever: steering column; final drive: hypoid bevel; axle ratio: 3.250.

CHASSIS integral; front suspension: independent, wishbones, lower trailing links, coil springs, anti-roll bar, telescopic dampers; rear suspension: rigid axle, semi-elliptic leafsprings, telescopic dampers.

STEERING recirculating ball; turns of steering wheel lock to lock: 5.25.

BRAKES drum; area rubbed by linings: total 251.40 sq in, 1,621.53 sq cm.

ELECTRICAL EQUIPMENT voltage: 12 V; battery: 45 Ah; generator type: alternator, 38 Ah; ignition distributor: Ford.

DIMENSIONS AND WEIGHT wheel base: 116 in, 2,946 mm; front track: 58 in, 1,473 mm; rear track: 58 in, 1,473 mm; overall length: 196.40 in, 4,989 mm; overall width: 73.80 in, 1,875 mm; overall height: 54 in, 1,372 mm; ground clearance: 5.90 in, 150 mm; dry weight: 3,026 lb, 1,373 kg; distribution of weight: 51.7% front axle, 48.3% rear axle; turning circle (between walls): 44.4 ft, 13.5 m; width of rims: 5"; tyres: 7.35 × 14; fuel tank capacity: 16.7 imp gal, 20 US gal, 76 l.

BODY hardtop; doors: 2; seats: 5; front seats: separate.

PERFORMANCE max speeds: 38 mph, 61.2 km/h in 1st gear; 63 mph, 101.4 km/h in 2nd gear; 96 mph, 154.6 km/h in 3rd gear; power-weight ratio: 25.1 lb/hp, 11.4 kg/hp; carrying capacity: 882 lb, 400 kg; speed in direct drive at 1,000 rpm: 23.1 mph, 37.2 km/h.

PRACTICAL INSTRUCTIONS fuel: 95 - 100 oct petrol; engine sump oil: 5.63 imp pt, 6.80 US pt, 3.2 l, SAE 5W-20 (winter) 10W-30 (summer), change every 6,000 miles, 9,700 km; gearbox oil: 1.58 imp pt, 2 US pt, 0.9 l, SAE 80, change every 32,000 miles, 51,500 km; final drive oil: 3.34 imp pt, 4 US pt, 1.9 l, SAE 90, change every 32,000 miles, 51,500 km; greasing: every 32,000 miles, 51,500 km; valve timing: inlet opens 7° before tdc and closes 55° before bdc, exhaust opens 55° before bdc and closes 21° after tdc; normal tyre pressure: front 24 psi, 1.7 atm, rear 26 psi, 1.8 atm.

VARIATIONS AND OPTIONAL ACCESSORIES see variations Comet 202 2-door Sedan except V8 engines; V8 engine, capacity 289 cu in, 4,735.84 cu cm, 200 hp, dry weight 3,187 lb, 1,446 kg, max speed 109 mph, 175.5 km/h (for further mechanical elements see variations Caliente Convertible); V8 engine, bore and stroke 4.05 × 3.78 in, 102.9 × 96 mm, engine capacity 390 cu in, 6,390.83 cu cm, max power (SAE) 270 hp at 4,400 rpm, max torque (SAE) 403 lb ft, 55.6 kg m at 2,600 rpm, 9.5 compression ratio, 42.2 hp/l specific power, 1 Ford 9510 C70F-Y twin barrel carburettor, 3-speed fully synchronized mechanical gearbox (I 2.420, II 1.610, III 1, rev 2.330), steering column gear lever, 3 (limited slip final drive) or 3.250 axle ratio, 4-speed fully synchronized mechanical gearbox (I 2.320, II 1.690, III 1.290, IV 1, rev 2.320), central gear lever, 3.250 (limited slip final drive) or 3 axle ratio, Merc-o-Matic automatic gearbox, hydraulic torque convertor and planetary gears with 3 ratios (I 2.460, II 1.460, III 1, rev 2.200), max ratio of convertor at stall 2.1, possible manual selection, central or steering column selector lever, 3 (limited slip final drive) or 3.250 axle ratio, total area rubbed by linings 282.60 sq in, 1,822.77 sq cm, 7.75 × 14 tyres, dry weight 3,453 lb, 1,566 kg, valve timing 16° 60° 55° 21°, max speed 118 mph, 190 km/h, fuel consumption 16.5 m/imp gal, 13.7 m/US gal, 17.1 l × 100 km. ◼ Capri 4-door Sedan, overall length 203.50 in, 5,169 mm, overall height 55.20 in, 1,402 mm, dry weight 3,001 lb, 1,361 kg, distribution of weight 52.5% front axle, 47.5% rear axle.

Cyclone Hardtop

MERCURY

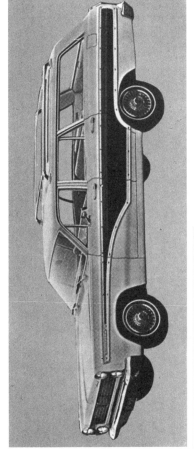

Villager

ENGINE CAPACITY 390 cu in, 6,390.83 cu cm
FUEL CONSUMPTION 14.7 m/imp gal, 12.2 m/US gal, 19.21 × 100 km
SEATS 5   MAX SPEED 122 mph, 196.4 km/h
PRICE IN USA $ 2,779

ENGINE front, 4 stroke; cylinders: 8, Vee-slanted at 90°; bore and stroke: 4.05 × 3.78 in, 102.9 × 96 mm; engine capacity: 390 cu in, 6,390.83 cu cm; compression ratio: 10.5; max power (SAE): 320 hp at 4,800 rpm; max torque (SAE): 427 lb ft, 58.9 kg m at 3,200 rpm; max engine rpm: 5,400; specific power: 50.1 hp/l; cylinder block: cast iron; cylinder head: cast iron; crankshaft bearings: 5; valves: 2 per cylinder, overhead, in line, push-rods and rockers, hydraulic tappets; camshafts: 1, at centre of Vee; lubrication: rotary pump, full flow filter; lubricating system capacity: 8.27 imp pt, 10 US pt, 4.7 l; carburation: 1 Holley C7OF-A downdraught 4-barrel carburettor; fuel feed: mechanical pump; cooling system: water; cooling system capacity: 34.14 imp pt, 41 US pt, 19.4 l.

TRANSMISSION driving wheels: rear; clutch: single dry plate; gearbox: mechanical; gears: 3 + reverse; synchromesh gears: I, II, III; gearbox ratios: I 2,420, II 1,610, III 1, rev 2,330; gear lever: central; final drive: hypoid bevel; axle ratio: 3.250.

CHASSIS integral; front suspension: independent, wishbones, lower trailing links, coil springs, anti-roll bar, telescopic dampers; rear suspension: rigid axle, semi-elliptic leafsprings, telescopic dampers.

STEERING recirculating ball; turns of steering wheel lock to lock: 5.25.

BRAKES front disc (diameter 11.37 in, 289 mm), rear drum, internal radial fins, servo; area rubbed by linings: total 361 sq in, 2,328.45 sq cm.

ELECTRICAL EQUIPMENT voltage: 12 V; battery: 45 Ah; generator type: alternator, 55 Ah; ignition distributor: Ford; headlamps: 4.

DIMENSIONS AND WEIGHT wheel base: 116 in, 2,946 mm; front track: 59 in, 1,499 mm; rear track: 59 in, 1,499 mm; overall length: 203.50 in, 5,169 mm; overall width: 73.80 in, 1,875 mm; overall height: 54.50 in, 1,384 mm; ground clearance: 5.90 in, 150 mm; dry weight: 3,534 lb, 1,603 kg; distribution of weight: 55.3% front axle, 44.7% rear axle; turning circle (between walls): 42.1 ft, 13.5 m; width of rims: 5.5''; tyres: 6.50/8.95 × 14; fuel tank capacity: 16.7 imp gal, 20 US gal, 76 l.

PERFORMANCE max speeds: 53 mph, 85.3 km/h in 1st gear; 80 mph, 128.8 km/h in 2nd gear; 122 mph, 196.4 km/h in 3rd gear; power-weight ratio: 11 lb/hp, 5 kg/hp; carrying capacity: 882 lb, 400 kg; speed in direct drive at 1,000 rpm: 23.9 mph, 38.5 km/h.

PRACTICAL INSTRUCTIONS fuel: 100 oct petrol; engine sump oil: 6.69 imp pt, 8 US pt, 3.8 l, SAE 5W-20 (winter) 10W-30 (summer); change every 6,000 miles, 9,700 km; gearbox oil: 2.99 imp pt, 3.50 US pt, 1.7 l, SAE 80, change every 32,000 miles, 51,500 km; final drive oil: 4.22 imp pt, 5 US pt, 2.4 l, SAE 90, change every 32,000 miles, 51,500 km; greasing: every 32,000 miles, 51,500 km; valve timing: inlet opens 20° before tdc and closes 70° after bdc, exhaust opens 66° before bdc and closes 24° after tdc; normal tyre pressure: front 28 psi, 2 atm, rear 28 psi, 2 atm.

BODY hardtop; doors: 2; seats: 5; front seats: separate.

VARIATIONS AND OPTIONAL ACCESSORIES limited slip final drive; 3 axle ratio; power-assisted steering, 3.50 turns of steering wheel lock to lock; cleaner air system; 4-speed fully synchronized mechanical gearbox (I 2,780, II 1,930, III 1,360, IV 1, rev 2,780), central gear lever; Merc-o-Matic automatic gearbox, hydraulic torque convertor and planetary gears with 3 ratios (I 2,460, II 1,460, III 1, rev 2,000), max ratio of convertor at stall 2.1, possible manual selection, central or steering column selector lever ⓥ Cyclone GT Convertible, overall height 53.2% front axle, 46.8% rear axle ⓥ Cyclone Hardtop, V8 standard engine capacity: 289 sq in, 1,377 cu cm, 200 hp, drum brakes, total area rubbed by linings 280 sq in, 1,830.66 sq cm, drum brakes, 38 Ah alternator, front and rear tracks 58 in, 1,473 mm, dry weight 3,228 lb, 1,464 kg, distribution of weight 53.7% front axle, 46.3% rear axle, 7.35 × 14 or 6.50/7.75/8.95 × 14 tyres, normal tyre pressure front 24 psi, 1.7 atm, rear 26 psi, 1.8 atm, max speed 110 mph, 177 km/h (for further mechanical elements see variations Caliente Convertible), on request V8 engine, capacity 390 cu in, 6,390.93 cu cm, 270 hp, drum brakes, total area rubbed by linings 282.60 sq in, 1,830.66 sq cm, 42 Ah alternator, 7.75 × 14 or 6.50/8.25 × 14 tyres, max speed 119 mph, 151.6 km/h (for further mechanical elements see model mentioned above) ⓥ Cyclone Convertible, overall height 54.20 in, 1,377 mm, dry weight 3,492 lb, 1,584 kg, distribution of weight 51.7% front axle, 48.3% rear axle (for further mechanical elements see model mentioned above).

Cyclone GT Hardtop

ENGINE CAPACITY 200 cu in, 3,277.40 cu cm
FUEL CONSUMPTION 20.8 m/imp gal, 17.3 m/US gal, 13.61 × 100 km
SEATS 6   MAX SPEED 94 mph, 151.3 km/h
PRICE IN USA $ 2,841

ENGINE front, 4 stroke; cylinders: 6, slanted at 4°, in line; bore and stroke: 3.68 × 3.13 in, 93.5 × 79.5 mm; engine capacity: 200 cu in, 3,277.40 cu cm; compression ratio: 9.1; max power (SAE): 120 hp at 4,400 rpm; max torque (SAE): 190 lb ft, 26.2 kg m at 2,400 rpm; max engine rpm: 4,600; specific power: 38.6 hp/l; cylinder block: cast iron; cylinder head: cast iron; crankshaft bearings: 7; valves: 2 per cylinder, overhead, in line, push-rods and rockers, hydraulic tappets; camshafts: 1, side; lubrication: rotary pump, full flow filter; lubricating system capacity: 7.39 imp pt, 8.80 US pt, 4.2 l; carburation: 1 Ford 9510-C66F-AD downdraught single barrel carburettor; fuel feed: mechanical pump; cooling system: water; cooling system capacity: 15.84 imp pt, 19 US pt, 9 l.

TRANSMISSION driving wheels: rear; clutch: single dry plate; gearbox: mechanical; gears: 3 + reverse; synchromesh gears: II and III; gearbox ratios: I 2,760, II 1,690, III 1, rev 3,740; gear lever: steering column; final drive: hypoid bevel; axle ratio: 3.500.

CHASSIS integral; front suspension: independent, wishbones, lower trailing links, coil springs, anti-roll bar, telescopic dampers; rear suspension: rigid axle, semi-elliptic leafsprings, telescopic dampers.

STEERING recirculating ball; turns of steering wheel lock to lock: 5.25.

BRAKES drum; area rubbed by linings: total 282.60 sq in, 1,822.77 sq cm.

ELECTRICAL EQUIPMENT voltage: 12 V; battery: 45 Ah; generator type: alternator, 38 Ah; ignition distributor: Ford; headlamps: 4.

DIMENSIONS AND WEIGHT wheel base: 113 in, 2,870 mm; front track: 58 in, 1,473 mm; rear track: 58 in, 1,473 mm; overall length: 199.90 in, 5,077 mm; overall width: 73.80 in, 1,875 mm; overall height: 56.20 in, 1,427 mm; ground clearance: 5.90 in, 150 mm; dry weight: 3,393 lb, 1,539 kg; distribution of weight: 42.7% front axle, 57.3% rear axle; turning circle (between walls): 44.4 ft, 13.5 m; width of rims: 5''; tyres: 7.35 × 14; fuel tank capacity: 16.7 imp gal, 20 US gal, 76 l.

BODY estate car/station wagon; doors: 4 + 1; seats: 6; front seats: bench.

PERFORMANCE max speeds: 38 mph, 61.2 km/h in 1st gear; 63 mph, 101.4 km/h in 2nd gear; 94 mph, 151.3 km/h in 3rd gear; power-weight ratio: 28.2 lb/hp, 12.8 kg/hp; carrying capacity: 1,058 lb, 480 kg; speed in direct drive at 1,000 rpm: 23.1 mph, 37.2 km/h.

PRACTICAL INSTRUCTIONS fuel: 95-100 oct petrol; engine sump oil: 5.63 imp pt, 6.80 US pt, 3.2 l, SAE 5W-20 (winter) 10W-30 (summer), change every 6,000 miles, 9,700 km; gearbox oil: 1.58 imp pt, 2 US pt, 0.9 l, SAE 80, change every 32,000 miles, 51,500 km; final drive oil: 3.34 imp pt, 4 US pt, 1.9 l, SAE 90, change every 32,000 miles, 51,500 km; greasing: every 32,000 miles, 51,500 km; valve timing: inlet opens 21° before tdc and closes 65° after bdc, exhaust opens 55° before bdc and closes 21° after tdc; normal tyre pressure: front 24 psi, 1.7 atm, rear 26 psi, 1.8 atm.

VARIATIONS AND OPTIONAL ACCESSORIES see variations Comet 202 2-door Sedan except V8 engines; V8 engine, capacity 289 cu in, 4,735.84 cu cm, 200 hp, only with 3-speed fully synchronized mechanical gearbox (3,250 axle ratio) and Merc-o-Matic automatic gearbox (3 axle ratio), dry weight 3,554 lb, 1,612 kg, max speed 107 mph, 172.3 km/h (for further mechanical elements see variations Caliente Convertible); V8 engine, capacity 390 cu in, 6,390.93 cu cm, only with 3-speed fully synchronized mechanical gearbox and Merc-o-Matic automatic gearbox (3,250 or 3 axle ratio), total area rubbed by linings 314 sq in, 2,025.30 sq cm, dry weight 3,820 lb, 1,733 kg, 7.75 × 14 tyres, normal tyre pressure front 22 psi, 1.5 atm, rear 34 psi, 2.4 atm, max speed 116 mph, 186.6 km/h (for further mechanical elements see variations Capri 2-door Hardtop) ⓥ 8-passenger Villager ⓥ 6-passenger Comet Voyager, dry weight 3,371 lb, 1,529 kg, distribution of weight 43.5% front axle, 56.5% rear axle ⓥ 8-passenger Comet Voyager, dry weight 8,371 lb, 1,529 kg, distribution of weight 43.5% front axle, 56.5% rear axle.

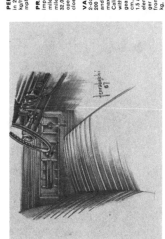

COMET

intermediate on the move — up!

Don't call it a Comet any more! It's now a full-fledged Mercury, with the Comet designation limited to the low-priced 202 series and the Voyager wagon. Other models — the Capri, Caliente, Cyclone and Villager — are Mercs, pure and simple.

But, beneath its minor facelift for '67, it's still essentially the Comet of yesteryear. And that, in our book, is a pretty good thing to be.

A wheelbase of 116 inches is used on conventional passenger body types, while a measurement of 113 inches appears on wagons. The 202 series is 195.9 inches long, the Capri, Caliente and Cyclone are all 203.5 inches and the Voyager and Villager wagons 199.9 inches.

Engine choices range from a little 200-cubic-inch, 120-horsepower 6 to a formidable 427-cubic-inch, 425-horsepower V-8, while manual transmissions include 3- and 4-speed units with a variety of column, console and foot controls.

The Sport Shift introduced successfully in last year's Cyclone GT has now been spread across the board as the automatic transmission option for all models.

The Comet — or whatever it is — is suspended on coils at the front and semi-elliptics at the rear.

Changes in Mercury's intermediate are, then, nothing but nominal. And, happily, they don't include any very noticeable modifications to the handsome body shell introduced last year.

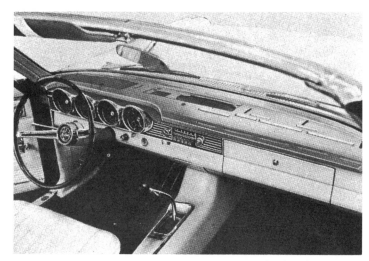

Dash design exemplifies auto industry's renewed concern for safety, has louvers along top surface for emergency absorption under impact. New instruments are more legible.

Taillift for '67 includes little more than new lights, slightly revised bumper. Big news this year is soft-pedalling of Comet name. Except for lowest-priced models, cars are now called Mercs.

Revised top on convertible provides smoother tonneau look when down. Boot with hidden fasteners is neater, cleaner.

Slick 202 2-door sedan is lowest-priced model, is one of few still carrying Comet name. Overall length is 195.9 inches. Caliente 4-door shows styling influence of big Merc in its new grille. Models in this deluxe series are 203.5 inches.

HERE'S MERCURY'S CANDIDATE for NEW CAR HONORS – THE CYCLONE

With a fresh new slant on styling, the '68 Cyclone fastback could well take all the marbles in the intermediate car scramble. Coupled with new performance options, it'll be hard to beat.

MOTORCADE test drivers put Cyclone GT through torture test and it survived. Car handled well on corners and was white streak on straightaways.

Cyclone fastback has swift look, even when standing still. New 302-cubic-inch V-8 is offered in '68.

Rear end of Cyclone fastback features chopped-off look; side reflectors are standard safety item for '68.

Cyclone fastback attracts crowd wherever it goes; most favorable comment has been how well it carries full fastback theme.

Mercury introduced a new line of cars (rather, a new name for the old Comet line) in '68 — Montego — and in that line was a car that just may be the sleeper of the year. It's the '68 Cyclone fastback, and it's really the first big car to effectively carry the full fastback design. Along with its cousin, the '68 Ford Fairlane fastback, Cyclone threatens to run away with the year's styling awards, and so it is only right that Cyclone be included in MOTORCADE's list of 10 outstanding cars.

Mercury's intermediate fastback comes in two models (actually one model with an expensive and less-expensive version): the Cyclone and the Cyclone GT. MOTORCADE editors who put the Cyclone — GT equipped with the 390-cubic-inch V-8 — through its paces were impressed with the ride and handling qualities of the car. Although it's definitely not a sports car, it has a decidedly sporty flavor about it which makes it a ball to drive. With the big 390 nestled under the hood, there's no lack of horsepower; however, for those who want to buy new tires every 3000 miles, there's the optional 427-cubic-inch V-8 to rip the competition.

Stylewise, the fastback Cyclone is one of the best-appearing American intermediates on the road today. Its fastback roof has an action flair that's hard to match. If only Detroit would get off the striping kick, or at least tone it down a little. The quickest way to tell the Cyclone from the Cyclone GT is to look for those unsightly broad stripes running the length of the car. When they are that broad, they do nothing to enhance the beauty of the car; in fact, they seriously detract from it. Nevertheless, the Cyclone GT is a fine-looking automobile which is raring to go the minute you close the door and buckle the seat belt.

Interiors on the Cyclone line are well laid-out; everything is located in front of the driver so that nothing distracts him from the driving chore. Bucket seats are comfortable, yet firm enough to provide support and contain the upper part of the legs on long trips. Rear seat leg room is only fair, but it seems that way on most American cars today. There is ample head room in the rear seat if one does not sit too tall; fastbacks are not noted for this feature.

All-in-all, the '68 Cyclone is a pleasant surprise in a year of few surprises in the automotive industry. Its fresh new styling and new high-performance options should make an attractive package to the new car buyer in '68.

Can Mercury's Daytona Image Maker Deliver?
428 STREET CYCLONE

GREAT TORQUE and tremendous traction of Goodyear's new Polyglas tires made Cyclone fastback clear winner in dragstrip competition with 427-cid Cougar. Cougar had no limited-slip axle, and wasted much of its torque spinning right rear tire. Cyclone bit and pulled to quarter-mile times in low 14-sec. bracket.

PHOTOS BY PAUL E. HANSEN

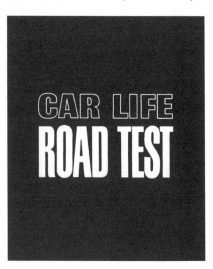

CAR LIFE
ROAD TEST

MERCURY HAD A PERFORMANCE image, once, back in the dear dead days of the flathead V-8. Then came limbo, the middle-aged Merc.

But now, with Mercury stock car racers winning the Daytona 500 and the Atlanta 500, look who's got a new performance image. For the salesmen, it's great, but the question remains: Do Mercurys off the showroom floor benefit from the Mercurys in NASCAR racing?

Sometimes they do, and sometimes they don't. The street Cyclone, starting point for the stock car racers, gains in performance as well as performance image. Equipped with the latest version of the 428-cid V-8, the handling package that comes with the engine, a beefed-up automatic transmission and disc front brakes, the Cyclone, got it.

The engine, advertised as the Cobra Jet, is the key to the Cyclone's performance. For a while, Mercury had two big engines, a 428 cid that was just a humdrum production engine made bigger, and a 427 cid, the genuine racing engine tamed down. Neither was quite the answer on the production line or in daily use. The Cobra Jet is a mixture of the two; the regular, mass-production 428 block and internals, with the race-bred 427 cylinder heads and manifolding, topped by a huge four-barrel carburetor. The 427 used at Daytona is no longer being built for production cars.

The Cyclone is a big, heavy car, but the Cobra Jet is more than enough for the job. Quarter-mile runs were in the low or mid-14s, in the Supercar class, and trap speed at the end of the quarter was in the high 90s. The Cyclone would reach 60 in 6.2 seconds. The 428 Cyclone is one of the quickest full-size production cars on the market today.

In anticipation of complaints from owners of other Supercars, the Cyclone had a few little advantages. The test car was fitted with a 3.91:1 rear axle ratio. The 428 was turning close to peak revs by the end of the traps, which means the gearing was close to ideal—for the dragstrip. Other places, it's a nuisance. The extra low gearing means the engine is running fast all the time. The driver with a sensitive ear or an eye for the tachometer will reach for the console-mounted gearshift almost automatically, to make sure that the car is in top gear, not second. It will be in high; the transmission doesn't make mistakes. But the gearing is so low that top gear sounds like second.

There are some practical disadvantages, too. High engine speeds equal low gas mileage, even with a light foot on the throttle. True, the man who buys a big-engine, high-performance car, and doesn't flinch at the $306 tag on the Cobra Jet package, isn't likely to be worried about the gas bill.

But engine life might be involved, if the car were run hard enough, long enough. High ratio gearing was one of the reasons the first imports went through engines like Sherman through Georgia. They weren't designed for open American roads, and the handcrafted little gems just ate their tiny hearts out. The 428 is a strong engine, but even NASCAR racers take unplanned lunch breaks. At 70, the engine was turning almost 4000 rpm. A lower numerical gearset would be worth the slight loss in acceleration.

The Cyclone was also aided by its tires, Goodyear's new Polyglas, a combination of bias plies and a fiberglass belt under the tread. Goodyear claims that the use of cross plies and a tread belt gives the advantages of standard and radial tires, at the same time. They certainly worked on the Cyclone.

Horsepower at the flywheel makes for nice advertising, but in real life the power is delivered to the pavement. If the tires won't deliver, the car won't go. The Polyglas tires delivered all the horsepower, right from the start.

That's not an attempt to damn with faint praise. All the traction in the world won't help a weak engine. The Cyclone is one of the few cars that comes with tires to match power. Some Supercars would look better in acceleration tests if full power didn't go up in tire smoke. It might be fairer to say that other cars are handicapped, rather than that the Cyclone's tires give it an advantage.

Stronger springs and shock absorbers are part of the Cobra Jet package, and the handling kit would almost be worth the price without the engine. The 428 is heavy, as all big V-8s are; it sits between the front wheels, as all American V-8s do; and the Cyclone understeers, with more steering lock required to keep the car on course, as all domestic, front engine cars do. But someone, or some design group, knows what handling is, and the Cyclone has it. The understeer can be quickly corrected, either by simply turning the wheel, or by applying more power. The Cyclone can be balanced, and kept balanced, at cornering forces far beyond what normal driving could demand. In terms of cornering power, predictability and controllability, the Cyclone rates very high for a full size car, and higher than at least one Ponycar.

Braking, with power assisted discs in front and drums in back, was very good, embarrassingly so. When the Cyclone was first delivered, the brakes worked fine, but the rear axle leaped and bounded uncontrollably. Bolts attaching the axle housing to the rear springs were loose. The bolts were tightened and the test resumed with a

CYCLONE'S SUPERIORITY carried over from dragstrip to road course. Cyclone, with handling package that accompanies Cobra Jet engine, displayed near-neutral handling, high cornering power and almost perfect controllability during all-out, maximum-effort cornering tests: Race car handling in a street car—a fine accomplishment.

COBRA JET 428-cid engine gave Cyclone plenty of pizazz. This package replaced no-longer-produced 427-cid street engine. Cobra Jet engine has same speed-producing components as race-sired 427, but uses cheaper standard block.

CYCLONE

Mercury engineer as a passenger. On the first stop, the decelerometer registered 30 ft./sec.², close to one G and much higher than can be reached by most cars.

Stop after stop, the Cyclone dug in

and shut down. All four tires stayed on the ground, and the car came to a halt in a straight line. The Cyclone has braking power to go with the engine. That's praise few cars have earned.

The Cobra Jet's automatic transmission *could* do with some refinement. Shifts at full throttle are quick and sharp, as they should be, but the transmission doesn't know when to ease up. Ordinary starts in traffic have that same snap. Unnecessary, if not exactly unpleasant.

Driving the Cyclone in everyday traffic was pleasant, with several minor drawbacks. The dragstrip gearing was one, but the extra noise and impression of busyness soon wears off. More of a bother as the miles roll by is the throttle. It feels like early power steering, that is, as if the foot pedal is connected to some mysterious gadget, which in turn attaches to something else, which finally gets the message to the carburetor. Not so much just plain stiff as stiff, springy and vague. The Cyclone needs a heavy foot, literally. For full power, when merging into traffic on the expressway, the driver plants his foot on the pedal, braces himself against the seatback, and stomps. When the slack has been taken up and the spring or whatever stretched out, the car surges ahead, right into

---

1968 MERCURY
CYCLONE

DIMENSIONS

Wheelbase, in.	116.0
Track, f/r, in.	59.0/59.0
Overall length. in.	203.5
width	73.8
height	54.5
Front seat hip room, in.	26.0 x 2
shoulder room	58.0
head room	38.1
pedal-seatback, max.	40.5
Rear seat hip room, in.	58.0
shoulder room	58.3
leg room	34.1
head room	36.8
Door opening width, in.	42.5
Trunk liftover height, in.	33

PRICES

List, FOB factory	$2918
Equipped as tested	$3875

Options included: 428 Cobra Jet V-8; Handling package, power assisted disc brakes, steering; limited-slip dif.. GT package, Polyglas tires, Select-Shift trans.

CAPACITIES

No. of passengers	5
Luggage space, cu. ft.	17.1
Fuel tank, gal.	20.0
Crankcase, qt.	4
Transmission/dif., pt.	26/5
Radiator coolant, qt.	20.5

CHASSIS/SUSPENSION

Frame type: Unitized.
Front suspension type: Independent by s.l.a., telescopic shock absorbers and coil springs.

ride rate at wheel, lb./in.	119
antiroll bar dia., in.	0.85

Rear suspension type: Hotchkiss live axle, multileaf, telescopic shock absorbers.

ride rate at wheel, lb./in.	146

Steering system: Recirculating ball gear, linkage boost power assist, parallelogram linkage behind front wheels.

overall ratio	21.6:1
turns, lock to lock	3.5
turning circle, ft. curb-curb.	41.5
Curb weight, lb.	3740
Test weight	4060

Distribution (driver),

% f/r	55.2/44.7

BRAKES

Type: Disc front, duo-servo drums rear.
Front rotor, dia. x width,

in.	11.37 x 1.84
Rear drum, dia. x width	10.0 x 2.0
total swept area, sq. in.	361.0

Power assist: Integral vacuum.

line psi at 100 lb. pedal	1200

WHEELS/TIRES

Wheel rim size	14 x 5.5J
optional size	none
bolt no./circle dia. in.	5/4.5

Tires: Goodyear Polyglas.

size	F70-14
normal inflation, psi f/r	28/28
Capacity @ psi	5600 @ 28

ENGINE

Type, no. of cyl	ohv 90° V-8
Bore x stroke, in.	4.13 x 3.98
Displacement, cu. in.	428
Compression ratio	10.7:1
Fuel required	premium
Rated bhp @ rpm	335 @ 5600
equivalent mph	109
Rated torque @ rpm	445 @ 3400
equivalent mph	66

Carburetion: Holley 1x4.

throttle dia., pri./sec.	1.52/1.56

Valve train: Hydraulic lifters, pushrods and overhead rocker arms.
cam timing

deg., int./exh.	18-72/82-28
duration, int./exh.	270/290

Exhaust system: Dual with branched headers.

pipe dia., exh./tail	2.25/2.25
Normal oil press.@ rpm. 40-60 @ 5500	
Electrical supply, V./amp.	12/42
Battery, plates/amp. hr.	78/80

DRIVE TRAIN

Transmission type: Three-speed automatic with torque converter

Gear ratio 3rd (1.00:1) overall	3.91:1
2nd (1.46:1)	5.71:1
1st (2.46:1)	9.62:1
1st x t. c. stall (2.10:1)	21.8:1

Shift lever location: Console.
Differential type: Hypoid.

axle ratio	3.91:1

that hole in the traffic. About as soon as the car begins to go, the driver must be ready to back off; once underway, the Cyclone picks up speed at a great rate. The sound keeps the drivers in front of the Cyclone alert, though.

Stability at highway speeds is quite good. With a crosswind, the car hunts slightly. The fastback shape is known to be good and clean, so this may be tire feel. Pure radials feel squirmy, at first, and the belted bias ply may have the same characteristic. It isn't really unstable, simply an illusion caused by the sidewalls flexing on the tread.

Engine quirks aren't there. Many high horsepower engines, even the big-inch ones, trade power and smoothness at idle and low speed for more horsepower at high speed. The Cobra Jet is strong all the time. The idle has just enough rump-rump to make the guy in the other lane respectful. There is so much torque at low speed, in fact, that with the Cyclone in gear at 800 rpm idle, the brake must be held down or the car moves smartly away.

Interior appointments are contemporary extra-cost options. Two soft separate seats in front (not genuine buckets because they provide no lateral support) are comfortable for hours at a time. The seatbacks rake enough to put the driver a nice distance from

CYCLONE INTERIOR scored high marks for comfort and functionality. Instruments were readable, though lack of oil pressure and water temperature gauges with high-performance engine was discomforting and potentially dangerous.

the wheel without losing touch with the pedals. The test Cyclone did not have a tilting or adjustable wheel, and it wasn't missed. The rear seat will fit for only a short trip. Small people might be able to last all day, but when

they emerged, they'd likely be wedge shaped.

The instrument panel is attractive, and furnishes all the information the driver needs. The panel is covered with real test-tube wood. Even tree

---

CAR LIFE ROAD TEST

CALCULATED DATA

Lb./bhp (test weight)...........12.1
Cu. ft./ton mile...............42.0
Mph/1000 rpm (high gear).....19.5
Engine revs/mile (60 mph).....3040
Piston travel, ft./mile........2030
CAR LIFE wear index............61.1
Frontal area, sq. ft...........22.4

SPEEDOMETER ERROR

30 mph, actual..................29.4
40 mph.........................40.4
50 mph.........................50.6
60 mph.........................60.97
70 mph.........................71.71
80 mph.........................82.11
90 mph.........................92.87

MAINTENANCE

Engine oil, miles/days.....6000/180
oil filter, miles/days.....6000/180
Chassis lubrication, miles.....36,000
Antismog servicing, type/miles . .
  change PCV valve/12,000, clean
  air pump lines/12,000, check
  engine tune/12,000
Air cleaner, miles. . . .replace/36,000
Spark plugs: Autolite.
  gap, (in.)............0.032-0.036
Basic timing, deg./rpm. 6/600
  max. cent. adv.,
  deg./rpm..........24-29/4000
  max. vac. adv.,
  deg./in. Hg.........16-22/16
Ignition point gap, in....0.014-0.018
  cam dwell angle, deg.......26-31
  arm tension, oz.........17-21
Tappet clearance, int./exh......0/0
Fuel pressure at idle, psi..........5
Radiator cap relief press., psi......15

PERFORMANCE

Top speed (6000), mph.........117
Test shift points (rpm) @ mph
  2nd to 3rd (5800)............77.6
  1st to 2nd (5800)............46.0

ACCELERATION

0-30 mph, sec..................2.7
0-40 mph........................4.0
0-50 mph........................4.8
0-60 mph........................6.2
0-70 mph........................7.7
0-80 mph........................9.7
0-90 mph.......................12.1
0-100 mph......................14.6
Standing ¼-mile, sec..........14.4
  speed at end, mph..........99.44
Passing, 30-70 mph, sec..........5

BRAKING

Max. deceleration rate from 80 mph
  ft./sec.² 30
No. of stops from 80 mph (60-sec. intervals) before 20% loss in deceleration rate..................8
Control loss? None.
Overall brake performance.very good

FUEL CONSUMPTION

Test conditions, mpg...........10.2
Normal cond., mpg............10-13
Cruising range, miles.......200-260

ACCELERATION & COASTING

ELAPSED TIME IN SECONDS

MPH — 5 10 15 20 25 30 35

(Graph: QUARTER MILE, 2nd-3rd, 1st-2nd)

BEST ELAPSED time for Cyclone was 14.18 sec., with two people and full test gear aboard. Deep gearing (3.91:1 rear axle) was perfect for quarter-mile work. Cobra Jet was turning around 5300 rpm through the traps. Maximum engine speed was 5600-5800 rpm, and strong powerplant was still pulling hard at these lofty speeds.

CYCLONE

wood is spurious decoration and the laboratory substitute looks as good without the bother. The tachometer is located in plain sight, for once, and it's the proper size, with legible numbers. The fuel gauge is the only other instrument. It's too big, or at least bigger than it needs to be. The condition of everything else—engine temperature, oil pressure—is signalled by a small set of warning lights. That's an assumption. None of the lights came on during the test, and nothing caught fire or fell off, so presumably the warning lights would warn if called upon to do so.

Driving over rough roads produced no worse than the thump of tires in chuckholes. The Cyclone is solid, and quality control is thorough. Again, all cars should come that way from the factory, but they all don't. Fords, in particular, have been prone to rattles this model year, but Mercurys aren't, for reasons unknown.

The fastback body attracts comments, almost all favorable. Styling a big fastback is quite a challenge. There

may be more than mere good looks involved. Mercury's fling at racing was as sudden as it was successful. Before the season started, parent Ford Motor Co. announced that Ford Division would compete in stock car races, and Mercury would run at the dragstrips. The intent, presumably, was to avoid last season's intramural battles, in which brotherhood was forgotten and Ford and Mercury teams ran each other into the ground.

Then came Daytona, and Mercury arrived with top-flight drivers and cars that were more than competitive. Something had happened. Those who know won't say, but one group of those who do say claims that Mercury Division heads felt they needed some wins in the big time and persuaded the corporate powers. Another version is that the Mercury body shell, in particular the front fenders and hood, has a cleaner aerodynamic shape at racing speeds than Ford fronts and that the Mercury shape was needed to keep the prizes in the family. FoMoCo has been experimenting with aerodynamics for several years, and it might even be that streamlining was the reason for

that attractive roofline, and that the good looks were an accident. Unlikely, but it's possible.

The claim that racing improves the breed is as old as racing. In the Cyclone's case, there's merit to it. The engine parts were tested on the idol of the age, the computer. They ran in races and broke. The engineers put the racing experience to use, and the engines don't break any more. Some of the exotic parts were changed, but there's a lot of racing engine in the Cobra Jet.

The suspension, too, is a big improvement over Mercury systems of pre-racing days. The work could have been done on the proving grounds, but it could also be no one would have bothered. The body shape, as noted, may be based on past races, and adopted for this season's races.

Added up they make the Cyclone good. If the Cyclone owner's neighbor wanders up, as one of ours did during the test, and asks, "Is that the car that won the Daytona 500?," the owner can say, as the tester did, "Sure did."

Photos by Pat Brollier

Test by Eric Dahlquist **Cyclone Cobra Jet**

ere come the jets like a bat out of hell, someone gets in their way someone don't feel too well."*

"This car has only two speeds, fast and stop," said Don Long. And he should know. We're out on Western Ave. in Gardena nearing escape velocity and the C6 automatic has just walloped into second to the accompaniment of this solid "chirp" from the tires and Don Long, the guy who builds 220-mph dragsters for other guys like Don Prudhomme doesn't believe that the Montego Cyclone GT he's driving is actually putting away the entire world in one run. He stops and tries it again and it is the same — it is always the same. You mash the accelerator pedal and the Merc leaps away from the mark like you had backed into a big coil spring. Wham! Chirp! That beautifully positive transmission socks you right between the shoulder blades and the wide F-70x14 Goodyear Polyglas tires let out a yell. Wham! Chirp! There it goes again and the speedometer looks like it's spring loaded as it sweeps past 100 mph. Up ahead you just know there's got to be a couple of pairs of eyes wondering what the hell happened to their radar outfit.

This isn't an automobile, it's a club Mercury is going to use to beat into oblivion the idea that their cars were ever considered "stones." Like it was a big paradox, brother. Here was a division of the Total Performance company that was getting cut down on the street by everything but VWs. Not on the track, mind you. "Dyno Don" Nicholson and Eddie Schartman were having a field day at the nation's drag strips in Comets — the division's cars almost never lost. At the same time, Comet sales sank to new lows. Obviously, said the central accounting department, racing doesn't sell cars. But, of course, we know better. Mercury's trouble, as well as Ford's, was that their production cars were about as inspiring as 9-day-old porridge. It wasn't that they lacked the hardware or knowhow, just the will to get all the right stuff into a single package.

The Cobra Jet Cyclone GT is one of the packages. When you first lay eyes on the car, the Cyclone seems as if it just drove out of Wide World of Sports' Daytona coverage — or maybe it was Victory Lane at Atlanta. It's that wild — Calypso Coral paint, stripes, Cragar mags, fat rubber and slight forward rake, man. Someone has finally made his street product look almost like his NASCAR Grand National product. Put on number 21 and you turn into Cale Yarborough. Zoomie styling or whatever, this wouldn't work very well if the machine weren't the hottest thing since the Chicago fire. But it is, so it's okay.

Other things have changed at Mercury, too. For years, about the only car you could count on being properly prepared for a performance test — any test — was a Pontiac and the competition screamed foul. Mercury finally saw that this was the plan so the Cyclone we received was right on. The sole item in the GT that could be faulted for sloppy detail was the driver-side door lock which rattled occasionally. Everything worked properly, the body panels fit well and the door latches sounded as secure as the vault at the Bank of America. Even the speedometer was calibrated correctly at all speeds, a first of some kind or other. Although it really isn't a part of the detailing, this was the only intermediate-sized Detroit car we tested in which the front seats went back further than our 6-foot 3-inch frame required. Unfortunately, we couldn't say much for the rear bench, which, though comfortable, didn't provide what could be called generous knee room.

Driving the 428 Cyclone GT will warm the hearts of the combined drag- and road-race fraternity and probably others as well. The machine is so nimble in any traffic situation it's in a class by itself. The power reserve on tap is in the proportion of the Grand Coulee Dam, and if you're worried about stopping, forget it. The great disc/drum combinations will halt the car on a plumb-line from 60 mph in an abbreviated 124 feet.

As far as handling goes, this is one of the best Mercs to ever come down the road, making it around all the corners at speed along the way. It's like the first well-balanced sports car you ever drove, only probably better. That 428 up there is not aluminum, which means there is a natural understeer but the gobs of horsepower can turn this to oversteer by pressing down on the throttle. It's all so neat. You set up in a gentle, controlled drift — and suddenly you're Dan Gurney at Riverside winning the Motor Trend 500. Heavy-duty springs, shocks and a robust stabilizer bar truly work wonders.

Mind blowing, brute acceleration is the 428 Cyclone's long suit. Right off the street it ran 14.39 at 98 mph through Orange County Raceway clocks. A few more passes to shoot out the carbon and it was pinching 14.12s at 99 and change. Removing the power steering belt improved this to 13.95 at 100.5 and a set of BF-32 spark plugs were good for 13.86/101.69, a clean half-second fleeter than the best of the intermediate supercars. How about a string of 0-60s like this: 6.1, 6.2, 6.0, 6.2, 6.2 seconds? Or the 0-40 mph in 3.3 seconds or 50-70 in 3.5? Out of sight.

The generating station producing such phenomenal performance turns out to be nothing more exotic than a garden variety 428-cu.-in. engine with 1963½-type cylinder heads (2.06-inch intake valves and 1.625-inch exhausts), 390-type hydraulic-lifter cam, Police Interceptor manifold, Holley 735 dual-feed carburetor and free-flowing cast iron exhaust headers. To make sure

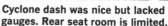

Cyclone dash was nice but lacked gauges. Rear seat room is limited.

To stop a 3880-pound car from 60 mph in just 124 feet takes a lot of moxie in the anchor department — like 214-sq.-in. of swept brake area. But you'd expect that from a car Cale Yarborough would drive, right? And bags of horsepower and neat styling too, right? Lucky for you, the C.J. Cyclone's got it all. C.J.? That's short for Cobra Jet which is street eliminator abbreviated.

Puff, the magic draggin' Mercury stops arrow-straight on every pass.

Cyclone

the 4.13 bore x 3.98-inch stroke engine lives past the first 435 Corvette encounter, a high-volume oil pump is part of the deal. The engine will not rev much beyond 5500 rpm and it doesn't need to because its 445 lbs.-ft. of torque comes way before that at 3400. If this were two years ago, the advertising gang would have come busting into the scene and demanded one of those awe-inspiring 500 hp numbers but sliding scale insurance rates penalizing high-powered machines has caused a complete about face. So the Cobra Jet is rated at an ultra-conservative 335 ponies, sufficiently low to cause the National Hot Rod Asso. to factor this figure up some for stock classing.

As hard as Mercury tried, which was plenty hard, there are a few rather obvious hangups in the Cyclone GT. The price of pure fastback styling is a pronounced blind-spot in the rear quarters big enough to conceal a Mayflower Van, or a couple of imports, depending on your luck. Cale (Yarborough) uses a Wink wide-angle rear-view mirror and we can see why. The interior was finished very tastefully in black vinyl but a low roofline precludes stovepipe hats or even styled hair. One of these years someone will

come along with a better instrument layout than the Pontiac GTO; we're still waiting. Idiot lights in a supercar don't make it, baby. Especially when you've got a temperature gauge that indicates red when it's cold and red when it's hot. It wasn't supposed to work that way but it did occasionally. Mercury probably thought they were being very clever and very different by using an imitation wood-grain dash panel resembling a walnut-patterned plastic rifle stock and that's just what it looks like — a plastic rifle stock.

One thing supercars never are is cheap. By the time you get everything you want, the window sticker has a little "continued on opposite door" on the bottom. Four grand is about the going tab these days, except for the Road Runner. In this respect the Montego Cyclone GT doesn't look all that bad, pricing out at a measly $3700 f.o.b. Detroit, less the Cragar mags. Gas mileage is a rather dismal 11.5 mpg on the highway and 8.5 to 10 in town, but that's the penalty for never being beaten on the street and a 4.11 final gear ratio. Mercury dealers aren't really going to have to sell this car. One run through the gears will do that. Wham! Chirp! Next.   /MT

CYCLONE COBRA JET

PERFORMANCE

Acceleration: (2 aboard)

0 mph	2.7 secs.
5 mph	4.2 secs.
0 mph	6.1 secs.
5 mph	8.5 secs.

Standing Start ¼-mile:

94.69 mph ....13.86 secs

Passing Speeds:

60 mph	3.3 secs. 241.5 ft.
70 mph	3.5 secs. 308 ft.

Speeds in Gears:

	42 mph @ 5500 rpm
	72 mph @ 5500 rpm
	105 mph @ 5500 rpm

MPH per 1000 RPM: 20 mph

Stopping Distances:

from 30 mph	30.1 ft.
from 60 mph	124 ft.

Mileage:

Range: 8.5-11.5 mpg
Average: 10.5 mpg

SPECIFICATIONS

Engine: 8 cyl. V-8 ohv. **Bore & Stroke:** 4.13 x 3.98 in. **Displacement:** 428 cu. in. **Horsepower:** 335 @ 5600 rpm. **Torque:** 445 lbs.-ft. @ 3400 rpm. **Compression Ratio:** 10.7:1. **Carburetion:** 735 Holley 4-bbl. **Transmission:** 3-speed automatic. **Final Drive Ratio:** 4.11:1. **Steering Type:** Recirculating ball & nut, power-assisted. **Turning Diameter:** 41.45 ft. curb-to-curb, 3.5 turns, lock-to-lock. **Tires:** F-70 x 15 Goodyear Polyglas. **Brakes:** Disc front, drum rear. Swept area 214 sq. in. **Suspension:** Front: Independent coil. Rear: Parallel leaf. **Body/Frame Construction:** Partially unitized frame. **Dimensions, Weights, Capacities:** Overall Length: 206.1 ins. Overall Width: 74.1 ins. Overall Height: 53.5 in. Wheelbase: 116 ins. Front Track: 58.53 ins. Rear Track: 58.53 ins. Curb Weight: 3880 lbs. Fuel Capacity: 20 gals. Oil Capacity 5 qts. with filter.

OPTIONS & PRICES

Manufacturer's suggested retail price, f.o.b. Detroit $3703. Factory-installed options: Disc brakes, $64.85; Power Steering, $95.00; GT package (upper body stripe, lower body stripe, insignia, heavy-duty springs, shocks, front stabilizer, bucket seats), $168.40; Cobra Jet engine, $287.60; Automatic Transmission, $226.10; Traction-Lok Differential, $63.50; 4.11:1 axle ratio, $6.55; Goodyear Polyglas tires, $45.40.

(1) The entire world will come to recognize this engine — the 428 Cobra Jet — at the pop of a hood. (2) The big hang-up with the company's engines was breathing, or rather lack of it. 2.06-inch intakes and 1.625-inch exhausts took care of a lot. (3) Manifold is police interceptor-type. Stocker is cast iron, but a few aluminum jobs are around. (4) Manifolds are free-flowing. (5) Pistons are aluminum with reliefs cut for valves. Standard compression is 10.75:1 with escalation to 11.50 possible

Heavy-duty suspension is part of the CJ package. Fiberglass-belted tires are also standard, and they contribute greatly to handling.

428 CYCLONE CJ

Mercury hops on the supercar bandwagon with a 428-inch Cyclone that's whipping up a storm in street circles

MERCURY HAS come up fast in the performance field over the last few years, spurred on mostly by NASCAR victories and the funny-car dragstrip exploits of "Dyno" Don Nicholson. But until this year, Mercury didn't have a real, full-fledged, bona-fide supercar. Now they do. It's the Cyclone CJ, a package based on Ford's very successful 428 Cobra Jet street engine. It should be enough to do the job on the street and strip this year.

The Cyclone CJ comes only one way—a two-door fastback. In the car, as standard equipment, is a whole load of goodies, and the list of options is even longer. Standard equipment for the CJ includes the CJ 428 engine, an engine dress-up kit, four-speed manual transmission, 3.50 rear axle ratio, low-restriction dual exhausts, wide-tread fiberglass-belted F70-14 tires, a competition handling package including staggered rear shocks on the stick shift cars, a matte-black front grille, a non-functional hood scoop with matte-black racing stripe, all vinyl bench seat interior and wood-grained instrument panel.

Options include ram-air induction with a functional hood scoop, exposed NASCAR-type hood locking pins, a tachometer, SelectShift automatic transmission, Traction-Lok limited-slip dif-

ferential, high-performance axle ratios (3.91 and 4.30), styled-steel wheels, dual upper body stripes, power front disc brakes, power steering, bucket seats, console, tinted glass, and the usual radio and convenience options.

Our test car had all of these items, including the 3.91 rear axle ratio and the automatic transmission. And they turned our Cyclone CJ into a rather plush street machine—a street machine that was very comfortable to drive, yet one that was capable of holding its own in both standing-start stoplight digs and top end goes.

We're not saying that our Cyclone CJ was strictly a street racer. It wasn't. But it was a groovy street machine that felt much stronger on the street than strip times proved it to be. For instance, we could run equal with, or take, most other supercars we came across on the street. Yet, at the drag strip, our car could do no better than 14.40 elapsed times with trap speeds not quite breaking 100 mph. Best quarter-mile speed was 99.44. This is good performance, make no mistake about it. But most of the supercars now roaming the strips can turn low-13-second times with no sweat, and they're over 100 through the traps every time. Guess the Cyclone CJ's thing is the street.

Stronger springs and shocks are part

of the CJ package, and the handling would probably be worth the price of the whole package itself. The 428 is a pretty heavy engine and the car understeers naturally. You have to crank on more steering lock to keep the car on course. But the understeer can be quickly corrected in the Cyclone CJ, either by turning the wheel a little more, or by applying more power via the throttle. In other words, you can balance off the understeer in the CJ, and keep it balanced at cornering speeds far beyond what normal humans are capable of.

The stiffer springs and shocks also give the Cyclone CJ a tight, responsive, maneuverable feeling that is missing in many other intermediate-size cars, even with handling packages tacked on. It sort of makes you feel like you can do anything with the Cyclone CJ and come out alive.

Braking power on our Cyclone CJ was very good. The car had the optional power-assisted front disc/rear drum setup, and we couldn't find anything wrong with it much as we tried. After about five panic stops from 80 mph, we gave up. The main thing we liked about the braking performance is that every stop was straight. There was no swerving or skidding, mainly because there was no rear wheel lockup. And the discs resist fade beautifully. There was some

With 3.91 gears and C-6 SelectShift automatic, our test car couldn't break 100 mph on the strip. Best elapsed time was 14.40 seconds.

Test car weighed in at 3798 pounds. With 335 horsepower, performance on the street was excellent, but gas consumption averaged 9 mpg.

slight fade after the fifth panic stop, but who makes five panic stops in a row from 80 mph?

One thing we really like on the Cyclone CJ is the SelectShift three-speed automatic. Our car was fitted with the optional buckets and console. The selecter lever was mounted in the console and became very convenient to use. We found ourselves downshifting for engine braking, even in normal everyday driving. We used the gearbox every opportunity we got, and it always performed beautifully.

Combined with the 3.91 rear axle ratio, the torque converter of the automatic transmission provides all kinds of breakaway torque coming off the line at the drag strip. With the F70-14 Goodyear Polyglas tires, we found that we got our best times by torque-loading the automatic to about 1,500 rpm, then flooring the throttle on the green. This gave us a lot of tire smoke, but also the best times. Sort of weird to find a car that has to come off the line like a double-A fuel dragster to record good drag strip times.

We also found that manually shifting the automatic gave us better times too. Full-throttle automatic shifts come on strong at 5,500 rpm. We shifted manually at six grand, and cut about .3 seconds off our et. The shifts were very strong and positive, no matter if they were automatic or manual. You can't hardly beat the SelectShift.

We had great fun on the street with the SelectShift, throwing manual shifts and making everyone think we had a manual transmission. You can't tell the difference on the street because a full-throttle manual shift will break the rear tires loose for about 25 feet the same as throwing a full-bore power-shift would.

We liked the interior very much on the Cyclone. One thing we didn't care for, though, was the wood-grained steering wheel with the rim-blow horn. The wheel itself is pretty keen, and it's just the right diameter for fast spinning. But we found ourselves blowing the horn every time we cranked the wheel in a tight corner. Finally, we had to consciously handle the wheel with kid gloves to avoid blowing the horn unnecessarily. We're sure Mercury's engineers can come up with something better than this.

We didn't like the rim-blow horn for another reason. You don't have something to punch at when a rotten driver cuts you off. Like, who ever heard of squeezing the steering wheel when you get pee-ohed?

The wood instrument panel was very

Heavy-duty cooling and electrical system are both standard on CJ.

Beefed suspension, normally a $30 option, is part of the CJ package.

Wood-grained instrument panel has room for optional 6000-rpm tachometer next to speedo.

The CJ package features a long list of performance, comfort and dress-up goodies

nice to the eye, even though it's fake wood. Our test car had the optional tachometer which is built right into the instrument panel next to the speedometer. It's round and very readable, but it only goes to 6,000 rpm in 500-rpm increments. Since it's very easy to wind the engine higher than six grand, why don't the Mercury stylists design an 8,000-rpm tach? It would seem like the sensible thing to do.

The seats in our test car were very comfortable, but they didn't give any lateral support. We really had to buckle up tight to remain in an upright position during our handling tests. The buckets in the Cyclone CJ are not true buckets in that they're almost flat. Yet, you do sink into them since they're very soft and flexible. We found the wheel and pedals to be in just the right relationship to each other so that we were always in a good driving position.

If you're looking for economy, look elsewhere. Our test car could do no better than 10.5 miles per gallon on a 200-mile turnpike trip. Around town and during our acceleration tests, the mileage dropped down to 7 mpg.

The buyer who wants economy should steer away from CJ. Standard is the 428-cube engine.

Cyclone sits on 116-inch wheelbase. Functional cold-air hood scoop is an optional item.

There are no other engine options in the Cyclone CJ, other than the functional Ram Air induction package which our test car had. The cold-air package doesn't raise the horsepower rating, though. It remains 335 at 5,200 rpm.

If you want a lower horsepower engine or an engine with smaller displacement, Mercury's got you covered. You can get a Six, a 302 V-8, a 351 V-8 with either a two- or four-barrel carb, and a 390 four-barrel V-8. However, if you want the Cyclone CJ, only the 428 engine is available. You'll have to order one of the lower series lines like the Montego or Comet.

Mercury's ads say "Cyclone CJ leads the way." They're not far from wrong.

76

CYCLONE CJ

ENGINE

Displacement, cu in	428
Compression ratio	10.6-to-1
Bhp @ rpm	335 @ 5200
Torque @ rpm, lb-ft	440 @ 3400
Carburetion	1 Holley

TRANSMISSION

Type	C-6 SelectShift
Control	Console-mounted

REAR END

Type	HD limited slip
Final drive ratio	3.91-to-1

BRAKES

Type front/rear	Power disc/drum
Size front/rear, in	11.3/10

SUSPENSION

Front	HD coils, shocks, stab.
Rear	HD leafs, shocks
Steering	
Type	Power
Ratio	21.6-to-1
Wheels	Styled steel
Rim size, in	6
Tires	F70-14 f-belted

GENERAL

Test weight, lb	3798
Wheelbase, in	116
Overall length, in	203.2

PERFORMANCE

0 to 60 mph, sec	6.2
SS 1/4 mile, mph	99.44
SS 1/4 mile, sec	14.40
Top speed, mph	120
Fuel consumption, mpg	7/11

OPTIONS

Base price of Cyclone CJ 2-dr hardtop: $3207.00

Optional engines, cu in/hp		Tachometer	48.00
428/335	STD.	Gauge package	N/A
428/335 Ram Air	138.60	Mag-styled wheels	STD.
Automatic transmission	42.00	Bucket seats	110.10
4-speed manual transmission	STD.	Transmission console	55.70
Optional rear axle ratios		Wood-style steering wheel	STD.
3.50, 3.91, 4.30	6.50	Tinted glass	35.00
Limited-slip differential	63.50	AM radio	60.90
Power steering	94.60	AM-FM radio	185.30
Power disc brakes	64.80	Air conditioning	375.70
Heavy-duty suspension	STD.	Vinyl roof	N/A
Fiberglass-belted tires	STD.		

CYCLONE CJ

Top image car in the Mercury's Montego models for '69 is the Cyclone CJ, a formidable entry in the supercar field. Features include clean sides with no chrome; blacked-out grille; functional hood air scoop on the ram air version; the CJ 428-cubic-inch engine, and F70 x 14 belted tires. Horsepower of the 428 is 335 at 5600 rpm. A four-speed manual transmission is standard and Select-Shift automatic is optional.

Ford's Traction-Lok differential has been improved. The limited slip unit tends to lock both axles together more positively as power is added—the locking force actually increasing in proportion to the amount of driving torque applied.

The Cyclone's racy fastback lines are further enhanced by optional racing-type outside rearview mirrors for left and right sides of the car. Front bucket seats with vinyl upholstery are optional on the Cyclone CJ hardtop and convertible models. A center console option is also available with bucket seats. Wheelbase of the Cyclone is 116 inches.

Mercury Cyclone two-door fastback has racy lines further enhanced by optional racing-type outside rearview mirrors.

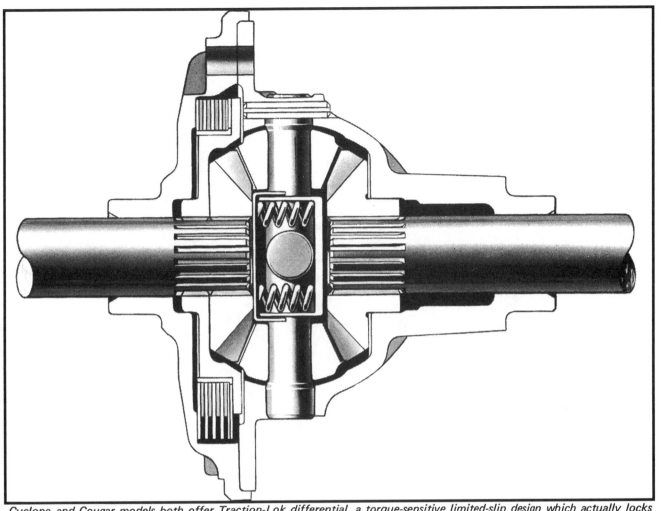

Cyclone and Cougar models both offer Traction-Lok differential, a torque-sensitive limited-slip design which actually locks both rear axles together more positively as power is added.

by John Raffa

Cee-Jay is Mercury's new '69 slogan for politely sayin' they'll blow your doors off!

"MERCURY'S GOT IT!" That's the Lincoln-Mercury Division's claim for 1969, and after a first, extensive look and preliminary tests of Merc's offerings for the new model year, we're inclined to agree.

Although Don Nicholson and Eddie Schartman have done their utmost to bring the Mercury name plate to a place of prominence in the eyes of the performance-minded over the past few years, the products themselves have left something to be desired at Christmas tree countdown time. With the '69 line-up, however, you've got a whole new bunch to choose from — here we'll stick to those models specified for high performance — our kind of cars. We were lucky enough to enlist the aid of long time Mercury adherent Don Nicholson to help evaluate these hot packages.

Montego — no doubts here. This class, introduced last year, will be aimed directly at the medium priced performance market. In '68, Montegos were responsible for the largest sales gain among all L-M Division car lines, and the marketing people are expecting even further gains in '69. Biggest news will revolve around the high-performance 428 Cobra Jet engine which will be standard equipment on the MONTEGO CYCLONE CJ, and will be optional in this series on the standard CYCLONE and the COMET, not to mention Cougar, but hang on.

You won't see too much ink devoted to the Comet this year, as L-M is apparently phasing out this series, but with its relatively low price ($200 less than the Cyclone) and high horsepower to weight ratio, the Comet could be the sleeper of the year. Available only as a two door hardtop, we'll be surprised if

we don't see a whole gaggle of Comets in drag race country in '69.

Standard engine for all Montego class models, except the Cyclones, is a big, new six-cylinder of 250 cubes. Like its 200 CID predecessor, the 250 features a seven-main-bearing crankshaft and should be desirable for performance building in lower classes of drag racing.

The V-8 lineup includes a worked-over 302, with two-barrel carburetion, standard on the Cyclone; optional two- and four-barrel versions of the brand new 351 mill (more on this later); the 390 four-barrel engine and the high performance 428 with four-barrel, standard on the Cyclone CJ. A ram-air version of the 428 CJ will be optional. Most of the Montego powerplants can be coupled with either three- or four-speed manuals or with the Select-Shift automatic trans.

Good news comes in rear gears available; in the big numbers you can choose a 3.50, 3.90 or 4.30 ring and pinion, the latter obviously aimed at the street and strip performance gang. Traction-Lok is worthy of special mention, as it is a greatly improved limited-slip unit which tends to lock the axles together more positively the harder you push on the "loud" pedal — the more torque applied, the more positive the locking force. And coupled up with the new fiberglass tires, you'll have the best off-the-line performance seen in a strictly stock Merc in a long time. We'll talk more about these tires in future new car previews, but for now, take our word for it — these tires do everything the manufacturers say they will, and then some.

For drag racers, the Cyclone CJ is of course the "in thing." Priced right, the "Cee Jay" is the top image car in the Merc lineup for '69. With cleanly styled sides, no chrome, blacked out grille, functional hood air scoop on the ram-air version and the honkin' 428 engine, the Cyclone CJ is living proof of the effect performance-minded drivers have had on Ralph Peters' Product Planning staff. By the way, remember Mr. Peters' name; you'll be hearing a lot more of it in '69 when performance

John Raffa compares notes with "Dyno" Don during testing at new car preview. The veteran "funny" pilot had a ball helping put the Mercurys through their paces.

Merc Cyclone dash features five instrument cluster, including big tach, set in attractive teakwood applique panel. Three spoked woodgrain finish wheel is option.

cars at L-M are mentioned. He's attuned to the desires of the performance market and has many more new performance features planned.

When you purchase your Cyclone CJ, you might as well make it a point to get the optional ram-air package while your salesman is making out the order. Included in the package are the functional scoop, F70/WSW wide tread fiberglass belted bias tires and hood lock pins. And, since there's no sense in doing half the job, make sure you get a tach and Traction-Lok differential with your choice of the gear ratios listed above.

We had the good fortune to test a new Ram Air CJ during L-M's long-lead press preview and, along with "Dyno" Don, we were able to give it a pretty good wringing out, even though traction was spotty due to rain showers. Our model was equipped with automatic, the 3.90 rear, power steering and power brakes. The power steering is up to you, but if we had our way, every high-perf car ordered would have the optional power front discs and drum rears. They really get the job done in a hurry! As a matter of fact, we'd have no objection if legislation were passed making the discs mandatory on *all* cars, *(continued on following page)*

Photos by Pat Brollier and Bob Swoim

Our test Cyclone had the CJ 428 mill, automatic, 3.90 gears, power steering, and power disc/drum brakes, had no trouble cutting 14.0's and 100+ mph. Goodyear Polyglas tires gave plenty of traction. All hood scoops are functional, as only Ram Airs have 'em.

'69 DRAG STOCKS

Continued from page 81

period. If you haven't tried 'em yet, you'll see what we mean the first time you ease on the brake pedal. We made a series of passes in our test "CJ" that showed us where to get 14.0-second performances "just like she comes," and tried to "use up" the brakes in stopping from the 100+ mph blasts, but all the discs seemed to do was to get better the harder we tried!

In usual "performance nut" fashion, we've talked about the CJ's power teams first, but now let's take a look at some of the other features that are going to appeal to folks who want more than just bland transportation and, if we don't miss our guess, to a lot of people outside the most publicized segment of the overall '69 auto market. That's right, even "old people" (all those over 25) are going to get a kick out of many of the Cyclone CJ's features.

Inside, for instance, bench seats are standard – and our test model was so equipped – but bucket seats are optional, along with a sports console. Adjustable head restraints are optional, along with either the buckets or bench; these restraints will be mandatory after January 1, 1969.

The instrument panel on all Cyclones is designed for max safety and convenience. Five dials, including tach and speedometer, are set in a simulated teakwood panel that not only looks smart but is placed so that the driver can really read them! The teakwood applique also covers the lower dash and you can really set off the entire interior by adding an optional three-spoke simulated woodgrain steering wheel with the new Rim-Blow horn (just squeeze the rim at any point to blow the horn).

Stylingwise, the choice is up to you in the option department: deluxe wheel covers, tape stripes, two-tone paint, GT decals, the list goes on and on. The body itself is of unitized construction providing "guard-rail" safety for driver and passengers. Here, the underbody, cowl, side panels, roof, front end, wheel housings and back panel are all welded together into a single unit, making for functional rigidity and controlled flexibility.

If we've gone to some length in describing the new Cyclone CJ, it's only because we're excited about L-M's latest entry in the performance field. Drivers like Cale Yarborough, on the NASCAR circuit, and Wayne Gapp, Top Gas Funny at the recent AHRA Spring Nationals in a Cougar, have already proved that Merc's can run with the best of 'em; now you can take a shot at some of the gold.

MERC MAKES THE MUSCLECAR SCENE

with a striped and scooped Comet Cyclone GT that doubles in durability

BY MARTYN L. SCHORR

COMET TEST Continued from page 52

Once underway on the open road we found the Cyclone to be a rather stable car even at speeds over 100 mph. The compromise suspension worked well and the tires, Firestone 500's, seemed to hold up even though we were averaging well over normal highway speeds. We felt that power steering was not really needed in this car, as we missed the normal feel of the road afforded by the manual setup. One thing that really impressed us, however, was the head-turning ability of our test car. The combination of bright red paint, rallye stripes, chrome wheel covers and the purr of the dual pipes, attracted young and old alike. The clean, sleek lines and the massive forward styling tie all the goodies into one neat image car package.

Equipped with 335 horses under the hood and a close ratio four-speed and 3.90-to-1 limited slip cogs between the rails, the GT proved to be an excellent performer. Even with the good gears it did not pack the punch of a tri-carbed GTO or a "semi-hemi" Chevelle. We were, however, able to walk away from most of the average stoplight drag racers. Shifting was exceptionally smooth except for the small uncomfortable-shaped shift knob. Running around town upshifts were made around 3000-3500 rpm, which coincidentally is when maximum torque comes in with the hot hydraulic lifter cam. Engine flexibility rates high, as no trouble was encounted lugging the engine down to 1000 rpm in top cog or winding past the 5500 rpm mark.

In the past we have had very few kind things to say about Detroit brakes in general and supercar brakes in particular. Most of the manufacturers use one set of brakes for six, standard eight, and ultra quick supercars. Some list optional linings and drums, but dealers knew little or nothing about their whereabouts. Our test Comet was fitted with 10-inch finned drums and metallic linings to cope with the extra horses up front. Heat dissipation is good with the finned drums and the metallic linings help combat against fade during repeated panic stops. They are not as good as drums in the fade

department, but discs will not be available on the Comet until 1967 so there is little choice. Five or six panic stops from 85 mph managed to fade the binders, but they would not fade under average or above average stopping conditions.

As far as all-out performance went we were a bit disappointed with the GT. The compromise suspension worked out just fine on the street and road, but left a lot to be desired for maximum strip performance. We were plagued with wheel hop and axle windup throughout our quarter mile testing, even though the car was factory fitted with the special suspension. Our best run through the eyes netted us with a 98 mph, 14.95-second time slip and that was after 12 attempts. Most runs were well into the 15's. Performance could be improved by the simple addition of adjustable Air Lifts (C60Z-5A589-A, $49.50) available through any FoMoCo dealer. With the air bags in place the chassis can be properly preloaded to compensate for track conditions, engine tune or various suspension settings. For more serious competition good lift or traction bars would be a wise investment.

After adding 500 miles to the already racked up 8000-plus miles we felt that the Cyclone GT is a very competitive package in the supercar sweepstakes. It may not be as quick as a good running tri-carb GTO or handle as well as an Olds 442, but it sure has a lot going for it. It has image written all over it, lots of performance packed under the hood and between the rails, and man, is it ever durable. And just think next year limited models will be available with the 427 wedge, disc brakes and a maximum performance suspension that allows you to use all of those 425 ponies.

MONTEGO SPOILER

The Cyclones from Mercury should really stir things up for the high-performance-minded driver

After wandering around for a couple of years in search of a personality, the Montego is now at least getting a foothold in the U.S. auto scene, which is certainly not in need of further proliferation. Mercury's performance-character cars in their intermediate branch have received the Cyclone title. There's the regular Cyclone, the Cyclone GT, and the Cyclone Spoiler. All are very good-looking cars, coming off better in appearance than the Ford Division counterpart. There's no fastback offering on the '70 Cyclones, which may nullify the cars' use in Grand National racing. We wouldn't bet on that right now. The NASCAR-born 429 HO engine is very much alive in the Cyclone option list. The Cyclone and the Cyclone Spoiler can be had only with 429-cubic-inch engines, in various power ratings, while the Cyclone GT comes with the newly designed 351-cubic-inch V8 in two-barrel carburetor form. Upgrading to the 4-bbl 351 is possible with the GT. The Cyclone and Cyclone Spoiler get the passenger car 429 V8 in base form. The 10.5:1 com-

pression, 4-bbl Cobra Jet engine is the first option, and then the Ram-Air CJ, with a through-the-hood shaker air scoop, is the next step. Top of the list is the better-be-ready-for-action NASCAR 429, complete with aluminum heads, O-ring combustion chamber sealing, and a price tag which will most likely discourage all but the serious. Four-speed transmission cars get Hurst shifters, though not the linkage arms for the trans. That's not hard to change, and most likely will be done by knowledgeable owners. Suspensions equal the engines, with the Competition package standard on Cyclone and Spoiler versions. A positive locking axle design is on the option list, and bias-ply fiberglass-belted tires are standard rigging for all Montegos.

Spoiler models are quite easily spotted by their front and rear air spoilers, and they have recessed instruments (tach, oil, temperature, and ammeter) in the center dash area. The gauges are optional for all 429 4V-engined cars.

The Cyclone may be a rel-

MONTEGO CYCLONE, GT, & SPOILER

Wheelbase	117.0 in.
Tread: Front	60.5 in.
Rear	60.0 in.
Height	52.4 in.
Length	209.9 in.
Width	77.3 in.
Standard Engines	351-2V, Cyclone; 429-4V, GT & Spoiler
Optional Engines	429 CJ, CJ Ram-Air, and 429 NASCAR V8
Body Style	2-dr. hardtop

atively big car, but it sure doesn't act like one. The tail end stayed well-glued to the asphalt during our sessions around the Dearborn ride and handling course; and front-end tire roll, while always evident, didn't get past the point of steering loss. The car will tilt and the tires will emit their peculiar noise, but if the throttle is used judiciously, there's no problem in negotiating tight turns. The 429 CJ engine held up under hours of this kind of treat-

ment, though the tires did get a bit rounded. Hydraulic lifters are specified for all the 429's, including the NASCAR engine, but that may change by showroom introduction date.

Rear shocks are staggered, right ahead and left behind the axle, on 4-speed cars. The 3:50:1 axle in the Cyclone we guided around the test track was suitable for road coursing, but barely got the car to the 100-mph mark in the quarter. That's not bad for a big car, yet the optional 4.30:1 with Traction-Lok holds a lot of promise. Rear-wheel bounce was not evident on acceleration or deceleration.

Appearancewise and performancewise, there are very few shortcomings in Lincoln-Mercury Division's most recent Montego. ■■

'70 MONTEGO

WHAT'S NEW: Greater front and rear differentiation from Torino although center sheetmetal is shared . . . 4-door hardtop added . . . All models longer, lower, more rakish . . . All-new 351-cubic-inch V-8.

INTERMEDIATE

The Mercury people outdid themselves in lengthening their intermediates for 1970. Since you can't stretch the existing basic structure, the extra inches were tacked on in front in the form of a gunsight grille but then, Mercury stylists found out that this protrusion prevented use of those portable headlight aimers favored by police for roadside inspections. So, engineers had to hinge the grille so it could be lifted up and out of the way for headlight aiming.

Assuming that the hinges and extra assembly work cost about $2 per car, you can see, in an average 100,000-model run for the series, what a "little" mistake like that can count to. But, it would have cost much more to redesign two different grilles at the last moment, so Mercury's taking its bath.

Big body news is the addition of a 4-door hardtop to the premium Montego Brougham series. This puts Mercury in a position to compete for the first time on an even basis with Cutlass, Skylark, Tempest and Chevelle and ahead of Chrysler Corp. which lacks this style in its intermediate lines. On the other hand, Mercury dropped its Montego convertible, reasoning that anyone who wants to spend this kind of money might as well be upgraded a slight step further into a Cougar ragtop.

The greenhouses of both coupes and sedans feature a lower roofline, resulting in a lower overall height of up to almost an inch in some models. The wheelbase on all models is lengthened 1 inch to a total of 117 inches — 114 inches on wagons. Overall length has been increased by 3.7 inches on sedans and hardtops to a total of 209.9 inches — 7.8 inches on station wagons to a total of 211.8 inches.

Grille availability is a little complicated. Montego and Montego MX's have exposed dual headlights in a grille composed of horizontal bars. The Montego Broughams have the same design but with hidden headlights. Cyclones and Cyclone Spoilers have exposed lights, Cyclone GT's hidden, and there's a special center section that looks like a gunsight flanked by two vertical parking lights. Obviously a Cyclone grille will fit a Montego or vice versa, but the factory won't interchange them for you.

Oddly enough, the big 429 4-barrel-

1. Montego Cyclone GT is combination luxury and performance model with standard 429 4-barrel V-8. Dual racing mirrors and styled steel wheels are optional extras.

2. Top-of-the-wagon-train Montego Villager has standard "wood" sides, but unlike American Motors' equivalent models, you pay extra for the built-in luggage rack.

3, 4. Living up to its boldly emblazoned name fore and aft, the Cyclone Spoiler greets the aerodynamic age going and coming with high-speed functional appendages.

5. Montego MX Brougham's side marker lights flash with turn signals, day or night.

6. Brougham headlights are hidden, as are windshield wipers (on all models). Vent windows are retained, but flow-through ventilation is optionally available.

carb engine is standard on the basic Cyclone, while the more expensive Cyclone GT starts out with the 351 2-barrel. The 351 in 4-barrel form is the new choice of Mercury engineers for their personal cars — replacing the old 2-barrel 390 in their favor — and is available in any Mercury intermediate. It's an all-new design of what's known as the NASCAR family even though its displacement is coincidentally the same as a previous offering.

The Cyclone Spoiler has the 429 CJ (Cobra Jet), the top regular production performance option, and it comes equipped with ram-air plus a functional hood scoop to complement the spoilers fore and aft from which this model derives its name. Unlike the Charger Daytona, the Cyclone rear spoiler adds nothing appreciable to directional stability and it's not adjustable unless you bend it. The front spoiler is hidden under the bumper and of course all of this is strictly an homologation gambit. These aerodynamic niceties do nothing for a car at legal speeds — except, perhaps, the exaggerated devices used on the Daytona model.

FoMoCo's fine 3-speed automatic transmission is optional on any engine but the NASCAR 429, and with the 350 4-barrel and up, you can buy a 4-speed manual with Hurst linkage. If you order power assist for brakes, front discs come with the package. Power steering is available on any model but you can't combine that with air conditioning in conjunction with the 429 V-8. We don't think we'd want to live in the Rockies and own an air-conditioned 429 Cyclone with manual steering, although the Unser family admittedly does pretty well with the non-cooled variations on Pikes Peak hillclimbs.

Because of its generally higher retail prices, model for model, Mercury adds little extras that Ford Division can't afford. One you can't see is superior standards of sound deadening, perhaps 50 pounds' worth. Another are the rubber-cushioned torque boxes that isolate longitudinal wheel movements from the chassis or body structure. An interesting one that you can see, at night anyway, is hooking the side marker lights up to the turn signals so as to make your turning intentions evident from a few more angles.

Mercury also offers an optional instrumentation pack on any model equipped with a 429 engine. The new ignition lock is a 3-way unit, securing the transmission as well as electrics and steering. There are "Up-Beat" trim options and colors available but thankfully, they've made no attempt to name the latter. Interiors in general are more luxurious than Ford counterparts and there is more lavish use of simulated wood veneer.

New high-back bucket seats are standard on the Cyclone GT and Spoiler, optional in other hardtops both formal and fastback. In fact, no other style bucket seats are available. The extension amounts to about 8 inches and doesn't block vision to the extent that a separate raised head restraint does.

4

5

6

MONTEGO/MX/BROUGHAM/ CYCLONE/GT/SPOILER

ENGINES/ 250 cu ins (150 hp). 302 cu ins (220 hp). 351 cu ins (250, 300 hp). 429 cu ins (375 hp).
TRANSMISSIONS/ 3-spd manual std, 4-spd manual opt, 3-spd auto opt.
STEERING/ Manual std, power opt, curb-to-curb 41.5 ft.
TIRES/ 78-series std, 70-series opt.

BRAKES/ Drums std, power front discs opt.

FUEL CAPACITY/ 22 gals.

DIMENSIONS/ Wheelbase 114 (wgns)-117.0 ins. Track 60.5 ins front, 60.0 ins rear. Width 77.3 ins. Length 209.9-211.8 ins. Height 52.4 ins. Weight n/a. Trunk 16.2 cu ft.
BODY STYLES/ 2-dr hdtp, 4-dr sdn, 4-dr hdtp, 2- and 3-seat wgns.

Mercury, the fabled god of eloquence and bearer of messages, has loaned his personality to the Cyclone C-J. The Cyclone message is quick and unmistakable.

WINGED-FOOT STREET ROD

By Steve Kelly ■ If I were a Ford Division engineer assigned to the intermediate car project, I'd make it a point to call up my cohorts down the street at the Lincoln-Mercury Division from time to time and set them up for lunch. While they were eating, I'd be picking their brains, because the L-M guys are doing a lot of good on the Montego. They're making it less of a Ford and more of a Mercury. The L-M Division is a separate entity within the Ford corporate structure; but engines, running gear and major components are common to those used in the Ford Division models. Most people are aware of this, so you have to give potential customers a very good reason for buying a Mercury over a Ford. That reason is shaping up in good quality and good design.

Montego Cyclones have a 351 engine as their base powerplant. But the 429 V8 is what turns them into supercars. In Cyclones, Cyclone GTs and Cyclone Spoiler Mercurys, there is a choice of C-J 429s. One is a non-ram-air version. Then there's the ram-air variety, and finally a Super Cobra Jet design that is part of the Drag Pack option. The Super C-J has mechanical valve train, 4-bolt bottom end, forged aluminum pistons and remote oil cooler, and is supplied with either a 3.91:1 limited-slip axle or a 4.30:1 Detroit Locker-equipped rear cog. All the C-J engines offer either a four-speed stick or three-speed automatic. There is also a limited-production option containing the NASCAR crescent-head 429 in street-operable form. In street form, the engine isn't at its peak, and the limited-production restraint causes it to have a rather high price tag. It is offered as much to qualify it for use in stock car racing as it is to be sold. Most, if not all, NASCAR 429-powered Cyclones will wind up on some type of race track.

Our Cyclone hardtop carried the ram-air 429 C-J, a 3.50:1 limited-action rear axle and a three-speed Cruise-O-Matic.

A hydraulic cam and valve lifter arrangement is used, and it is a good one. It compares almost equally to the mechanical cam, which has a 300-degree valve-opening duration and .515-inch lift. The hydraulic stick has .500-inch lift, 282° intake and 296° exhaust duration. The Super C-J has 10.5:1 rated compression, while the hydraulic action 429s have 11.3. Because of the closeness in performance, using an aftermarket-available mechanical cam might prove more valuable. Trouble here is that the Super C-J has a lot of other features, such as four-bolt mains and forged aluminum pistons. For a car that will see the majority of its use on the street, the hydraulic-lifter C-J is nothing that will ever require apologies.

A lower ratio, like a 3.91:1, would help drag strip times, though the 3.50:1 is a good worker and a fuel saver for highway use. Our first pass at Orange County International Raceway netted a 14.44 e.t. and a speed of 100.00 mph flat.

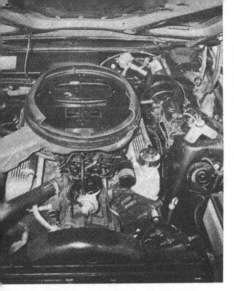

TOP LEFT — Extended nose and fender edges contribute to Cyclone's upgraded appearance. CENTER — Interior arrangement is made better when optional gauges are included. Discomfort isn't a part of sustained driving. ABOVE — Removing the air-inlet flapper valve pan lowers e.t. Spring/shock towers hurt engine room access, although plugs are at least visible.
FAR LEFT — Carrying height is decent; ride is stiff. Side trim is not part of Cyclone styling, much to the benefit of appearance and the endangerment of paint.
LEFT — Trunk liftover distance is a little on the high side. Vertical bumper guards would go far in protecting tail end metal.

photography: Eric Rickman

This was with the selector in "Drive" and all stock pieces attached. With a full fuel load, the Cyclone weighed 3980 pounds. Front tires were pumped to 45 psi, and rears stayed at 35. The transmission shifted itself at 5800 rpm, and attempts at shifting manually couldn't prove a better shift point. The air filter element and the vacuum-operated flapper door were removed for the next step in testing. Before running in this mode, the power steering drive belt was taken off, even though it also turns the water pump. Lots of engines don't mind running for short bursts without the water pump spinning, but a 429 FoMoCo isn't one of them. Within 100 feet of startup, the radiator began spitting boiling water out the overflow tube. So the belt was replaced and the engine given a thorough cooldown. Cobra Jets respond kindly to cool temperatures, and merely by cooling it down and removing air-inlet restriction, the Cyclone dropped two-tenths of a second. First

pass here was a 14.23 seconds and a speed of 101.12 mph. Each succeeding run became slower, mostly because they were back to back and the engine temperature began climbing.

Stall speed is around 1100 rpm, and the most engine speed you can use off the line is 1200 rpm. The rear brakes won't hold effectively against torque build-up past this point. A stick shift car would work better off the line, because the Quadrajet carb, used by Ford as a method of getting 429 hydraulic-lifter C-Js to pass emission laws, doesn't kick in with the secondaries soon enough. Even with the primaries doing all the work, rear wheel spin can be excessive in no time at all. Hooked up to a good set of rear tires, the Cyclone should be able to use more carburetor opening and quicken its time through the quarter. Attaining 14.0 times, or slightly less, is possible, providing the stock car uses sticky rear tires.

The Cyclone shows the greatest amount of spirit as a road car, especially on a twisting road. Competition handling suspension is standard with Cyclones, and ride height is relatively low. Spring rates are relatively high, particularly in the rear. Gabriel tubular shocks (1.125-inch piston diameter) are part of the package, and the Cyclone over-the-road behavior puts you in mind of a sensation not unlike that of being strapped into the same seat occupied by a Yarbrough or a Pearson and running for the pole spot at Daytona. To say the car is agile is accurate; to say it is altogether comfortable on the street is less than accurate. Only a person who appreciates stiff suspension and truly predictable behavior can get along with the Cyclone's ride habit. The front end has a slight taste of oversteer, and this may be a fault of the power steering. The manual steering is far too slow for general super-car consumption, but the power steering gears will fit the manual steering box, since they are the same item. Ford design uses a linkage booster rather than an integral assist. Swapping the gears might prove tiresome for slow-speed turning, but it would definitely aid medium- and high-speed maneuverability.

Braking offers no drawbacks, and trying to get the car to lock up to the point of control loss is near to impossible. Internal valving is used to control front to rear brake effectiveness, and while this isn't exactly an anti-skid device, under most braking conditions it works like one.

Overall quality showed up well on the Cyclone: no rattles, and everything worked. Interior noise is low, but the flow-through ventilation doesn't work too well with the windows sealed tight. If you want fresh-air flow, a window has to be rolled down a bit from its topmost position. The optional instru-

ments are recessed in the center of the padded dash panel, and they are good ones. The large-face tachometer has a problem with reflections from its glass covering. Automatic seat-back releases were on the Cyclone we tested, and they carry our full endorsement. When the door is opened, the seat-back lock is released by a solenoid. This works at all times, whether the key is in the ignition or not.

Cyclones have a style all their own, which is good. The extended nose could be a vulnerable part in a parking lot. Mercury is doing the right thing with sheet metal shapes, despite their making one part of it damage-prone. That's the case with most cars, unfortunately. It will be interesting to see how L-M creates future Cyclone supercars. If they use their '70 model as a guide, the car can't help but get better. And the Mercury product planners will be getting a lot of free lunches. ∎∎

VEHICLE . . . Montego Cyclone

PRICE . . . Base, $3238.00; As tested, $4061.90

ENGINE . . . Ohv V8, 429-cu.-in. Cobra Jet. 4.362-in. bore, 3.590-in. stroke. 370 hp @ 5400 rpm; 450 lbs.-ft. torque @ 3400 rpm. 11.3:1 compression.

CARBURETION . . . Single 4-bbl Rochester Quadrajet. 1.38-in. primary bore; 2:25-in. secondary

VALVE TRAIN . . . Hydraulic lifters, 1.75:1 rocker arm ratio. Intake valve: opens 32° BTC, closes 70° ABC, 282° duration. Exhaust valve: opens 90° BBC, closes 26° ATC, 296° duration. Overlap: 58°. Valve head diameter: 2.248-in. intake, 1.728-in. exhaust. Intake lift: .500-in.; exhaust lift: .500-in.

DRIVE TRAIN . . . 3-speed automatic. Torque converter with planetary gears. 2.05:1 maximum ratio at stall. Gear ratios: 1st, 2.46:1; 2nd, 1.46:1; 3rd, 1.00:1. Limited-slip rear axle. 3.50:1 ratio. 9-inch-dia. ring gear

BRAKES . . . Front caliper disc, rear drum, with Bendix tandem integral dual master cylinder power boost. 11.3-in.-dia. front disc, 11.0-in.-dia. rear drum. 40.6-sq.-in. effective lining area. Pressure differential controlled valving for front to rear brake effectiveness

WHEELS & TIRES . . . G70-14 belted bias wide-pattern tires. 14-in. x 7-in. wheels

SUSPENSION . . . Front: Independent, short-long-arm type. Coil spring and tube shock mounted above upper control arm. Spring rate: 500 lb. per in.; 151 lb. per in. at wheel. .95-in.-dia. stabilizer bar. Rear: Hotchkiss-type rear suspension. 58-in. x 2.5-in. semi-elliptic leaf springs, four leaves. Spring rate: 210 lb. per in.; rate at wheel: 190 lb. per in.

STEERING . . . Recirculating ball and nut with Bendix power-assist, linkage booster. 3.5 turns lock to lock. 20.64:1 overall ratio; 16.1:1 gear ratio. 15-in. x 15.5-in.-dia. semi-oval steering wheel. 42.33-ft. turning diameter, curb to curb

PERFORMANCE . . . Quarter-mile (best): 14.23 sec., 101.12 mph

DIMENSIONS . . . Wheelbase: 117.0 in.; front track: 60.5 in.; rear track: 60.0 in.; overall height: 52.3 in.; overall width: 77.3 in.; overall length: 209.9 in.; test weight: 3980 lb.; shipping weight: 3615 lb.; body frame construction: unitized; fuel tank capacity: 22 gal.

MERCURY CYCLONE GT
Mercury Division whips up a stormer

When it's time to go racing, Mercury takes the Cyclone off the trailer. This is the 'performance' model of the intermediate sized 117 in. wheelbase Mercurys (the Montego is the corresponding 'luxury' series). The Cyclones come in three versions, all available only in a two-door hardtop fastback body style which is shared with the Ford Torino.

The basic Cyclone, with standard 429 cu. in. engine, is in the traditional Muscle Car concept of large high power engine mated with minimum trim and optional accessories.

The super performance oriented Spoiler, billed as the hottest and toughest Cyclone this side of sanctioned racing, goes all out for performance with a CJ 429-4V standard engine and front anti-lift and rear deck body spoilers plus a substantial number of performance and appearance items as standard equipment.

ROAD TEST selected the Cyclone GT for a full test evaluation. It offers the most sophisticated appearance and trim options while still retaining the wide choice of power teams which will permit obtaining performance comparable to the Spoiler.

After a very successful 1969, the intermediate Mercurys have been extensively restyled for 1970 with sharply prowed grilles, new and lower roof lines and new rear-end treatments. Ventless side glass is standard now. With certain reservations, we feel that the Cyclone is an excellent appearing, well styled car. Our test car was finished in a mustard brown color which will be familiar to anyone who has had small children, and set off by a black vinyl roof.

The lower rocker panels, below the center line of the wheels, are finished with matte black which is also carried around the wheel cutouts. The black is separated from the basic color by a slender chrome strip. Both front and rear overhang have been kept reasonably short, and it all adds up to a very pleasing profile. The restyled rear end has the fenders and lower body canting inwards from the bumper which establishes the maximum width at the rear. Two sets of three horizontal lights are set into a matte black panel which is relieved in the center by a small rear grille.

The front end styling does not measure up to the balance of the car, and in fact actually appears to detract from the performance image sought in the Cyclone concept. Two of our least favorite features on General Motors cars, the vertical 'knife' front fenders of the Oldsmobile and the massive prow configuration radiator grille accentuated by hood lines featured on the Pontiac have been transplanted to the Cyclone but they don't sit well.

Drive train

A wide variety of power train combinations permit the Cyclone buyer to select virtually any desired degree of performance potential. No less than seven engines ranging from 351 to 429 cu. in. and from 250 to 375 hp are available. To most of these, either a three speed automatic, a three speed manual or a Hurst-shifted four speed manual transmission can be mated. Rear end ratios range from 3.00 to 4.30.

The standard team for the Cyclone is the 429-4V with either four-speed or automatic and 3.25 rear end. The Spoiler comes with the ram induction CJ 429-4V, and the same transmission and rear end as the Cyclone unless ordered otherwise. The standard setup for the Cyclone GT is the 351-2V with three-speed manual transmission in an obvious price-advertising ploy. We can't imagine many Cyclones being delivered with this power team.

Our test car was fitted with the optional ram air induction CJ 429-4V, Select-shift automatic and 3.50 Traction-Loc rear end. Induction is through a single four barrel Rochester carburetor. An 11.3 to 1 compression ratio is used, requiring premium fuel. The 429 cu. in. displacement is obtained by the use of a well oversquare 4.36 in. bore and 3.59 in. stroke. The valves are canted in the head and actuated by hydraulic lifters. Cast iron headers exhaust into highly

Traction-Lok differential and an engine oil cooler. There is also a Super Drag Pak which includes a 4.30 rear axle, available only with a Detroit Locker differential, and an engine oil cooler.

For those with fat enough wallets who desire a still higher level of performance there is also a series of bolt on performance kits featuring different headers, manifolds, heads, pistons, valve train, and cam.

Power and performance

After reading of the formidable selection of performance options offered for the Cyclone GT, we almost wondered whether the GT with nothing more than the Ram induction 429-4V and 3.50 axle would even be worth testing on the dragstrip. The dreaded *editor* said, "Go anyway!", so go we did to Lions Dragstrip. It didn't take long before we all decided that we were glad we had come.

Plainly, the CJ 429 went a lot better than anticipated. The 450 lb./ft. of torque was more than enough to spin the wheels for a long time, including a

resonant dual mufflers. The result is an exhaust note which is a solid pleasant roar reminiscent of a NASCAR stocker and highly pleasing from the outside or with the windows down, but almost inaudible with the windows up due to an excellent job of sound insulation.

Engine starting is immediate, with a quick warmup settling down to a ragged vibratory idle at 600-800 rpm. Accessibility for service is reasonable, although the high mounting points for the front springs and shocks encroach somewhat

on the middle sparkplugs on each bank. The plugs are high enough, though, to be easily reached from above the engine on top, and other accessories aré well within reach.

In addition to the power team choices mentioned there are also a pair of drag racing packages available for the Super CJ 429 4-V engine (the solid lifter, Holley carburetor version of the engine in our test car, which produces five more horsepower at 5600 rpm). The Drag Pack includes a 3.91 rear axle with

Competition handling package minimizes body roll but handling is characterized by plenty of understeer. It takes a good poke on the throttle to bring the rear end around in a hurry.

Interior is luxurious beyond anticipation for a Muscle Car. Houndstooth fabric on seats makes pleasing combination with leather textured door liners and seat material. Brake pedal is a long foot lift up from accelerator, but other controls are well placed.

Special instrument package is standard feature on GT and Spoiler Cyclone. Upshifts occur at 5600 rpm during full throttle acceleration runs. Calibrations on oil pressure gauge are unusual to say the least.

loud chirp when the Select-Shift caught second gear. Unfortunately, wheelspin, while lots of fun to watch, doesn't produce the best e.t. and the best we were able to record while standing on the loud pedal all the way through the quarter mile was 15.19 sec. at 98.25 mph. After a little experimenting with just enough foot lifting to let the fat Firestones get a good honest bite we chopped half a second off the e.t., finally settling for a 14.61 at 99.22 mph. Although this was quicker than we expected to go in the first place, we came away from the strip feeling that a little

more practice would get us under 14.5 seconds and over 100 mph.

Engine performance on the strip was quite satisfactory. Allowing the Select-Shift to select its own shift points, we noticed that upshifts were accomplished quite crisply at an indicated 5600 rpm on the dashmounted tach. Since this is the point we would have selected for manual shifting of the automatic transmission, we didn't even bother with any manual shifts. Using this shift point second gear came up rather early and third gear rather late, with the 429 pulling about 4800 rpm in third gear through the traps and indicating 100-105 mph on the speedometer.

Roadability and handling

A conventional suspension is used on the Cyclone — A-arms, coil springs, and tube shocks in front; leaf springs and tube shocks in back. Our test car had the Competition Handling Package — beefed up springs and shocks plus a front anti-roll bar — installed as standard equipment.

With the Competition Handling Package a firm ride is obtained under all conditions. This is not to say an unpleasant ride, as minor bumps are well damped, and the car does not drum over the road. Body lean during normal cornering is greatly reduced.

We took a short comparison ride in a Mercury Marquis sedan which had the standard soft Detroit suspension. The Marquis ride provided complete isolation from the road, and in fact the world around — not unpleasant, and fully consistent with the concept of the car. The

Front brakes lock up first, but directional stability remains excellent. It takes about 150 feet to stop from 60 mph.

Cyclone GT ride, however, provided complete awareness of the road.

Really hard cornering works out almost to a standoff between the massive cornering power generated by the seven inch wide tread on the glass belted Firestone Wide Ovals and the tendency towards terminal understeer associated with having 60 percent of the 4000 pounds carried by the front wheels. As expected, the glass belted $G70\times14$'s squeal in agony until they give up and allow the front end to plow magnificently off course.

The remedy for such handling requires considerable coordination. The steering wheel can't be turned fast enough by twisting at the rim, but since the power assisted steering requires no input effort to speak of it's easy to get full lock in a hurry by spinning two fingers against a spoke. This immediately breaks the front wheels loose but does serve to get them pointed in the desired direction in a hurry. At the same time, the rear wheels can be broken loose by a brisk application of power which is maintained until the tail swings around and the car is headed in the intended direction, at which time the throttle is backed off and the wheel returned to amidships. This technique is lots of fun but hard as the dickens on both tires and peace officer's composure, so it is not recommended for everyday use. In less exigent circumstances the steering returns little road feel, but is quick and precise with no play.

Brakes and safety

With some 4000 pounds to bring to a halt, the Cyclone GT's brakes have their work cut out. A combination of 11.3 in. diameter ventilated front discs and 10.0 in. rear drums is used, with 232 sq. in. of

swept area. In a very hard stop they halt the car in about 150 feet from 60 mph with lots of assistance from the tires. Directional stability is good right until lockup occurs. Fade resistance is fair. We made several runs through the quarter mile in quick succession, pulling the car to the quickest stop possible from over 100 mph without locking up the brakes. On the third such effort both pedal effort and stopping distance increased.

The seat belt arrangement on the Cyclone is among the best we have seen on an American car. The inboard segment is short and fixed in length, with a receptacle when not in use. The outboard end has an inertia reel which automatically adjusts the belt to the right length when it is released after being buckled. And, best of all, the shoulder harness can be snapped into an eye in the end of the outboard segment, and left permanently attached so that it is automatically fastened whenever the lap belt is fastened.

Comfort and convenience

Surprise is the reaction to looking inside the Cyclone GT. The interior is just too nice for a Muscle Car. The vinyl upholstery material on the door liners and seats almost seems closer in color and texture to leather than the real thing. This material is tastefully relieved by inserts of houndstooth fabric on the seats and seatbacks.

Entry to both front and rear seats is convenient. Once seated there's plenty of room in front, with visibility to all directions, save the rear quarters, excellent. A comfortable steering position is readily achieved but it could be greatly improved by providing more slant and lateral support in the seatbacks.

Rear seat legroom is commodious even with the front seat all the way back, but head room is marginal for even an average sized adult. There's enough hip and leg room in back for adults on long trips, though.

Our test car had an excellent AM-FM stereo radio. It was difficult to enjoy it, however, since the wind noise at freeway speed with the windows down was too great, and heat radiation through the firewall almost required that windows be kept open.

A standard Mercury instrument cluster comprised of gas gauge, speedometer, and clock is mounted directly ahead of the steering wheel. Four gauges. inclined toward the driver for visibility, are set into the dash in a horizontal row to the right of the instrument cluster. From the left these are tachometer, oil pressure, temperature, and an ammeter. The calibrations on the

oil pressure gauge are the wildest thing we have ever seen. Would you believe 0-7-38-78 and 90 psi?

Visibility is good for all instruments except that the driver's head has to be turned too far away from the road to look at the gauges on the right.

Controls are clustered below the dash in front of the driver, with the gear selector conveniently located on the center console. The pedals would be more conveniently usable if the brake pedal were lower and if a rest were provided for the left foot.

Economy

A discussion of the subject begins with first cost and the base price of our test car came to $3226 which is certainly in the ball park. However, there were options totaling $1567 loaded on our Cyclone GT, some of them very heavy and performance stealing. Looking over the list we found at least $575 worth of items (clock, power windows, vinyl roof etc.) that could be deleted which would add to the Muscle without upsetting comfort. For an all out racer we could easily drop a few more pleasure producers such as automatic and power disc brakes and decrease both weight and cost. The racing fraternity undoubtedly will.

Maintenance intervals are extended and their costs should be fairly low. Gas mileage works out to a shade over 10 miles per gallon when a little restraint on the use of the right foot is practiced, so operating costs are within reason.

Summary

With good points overlapping bad points, the Cyclone GT/CJ 429 is almost an anachronism. Handsome exterior (save for the execrable front end), luxurious interior, surprisingly brisk performance, and an elevated price tag. Or, good handling — up to the point where the men are separated from the boys, and steady, straight brakes — until the third very hard stop. In all though, the car was fun to drive, and we liked it. ♠

Spare is placed out of way in 16 cu. ft. trunk, promising room for reasonable complement of luggage. Sill is quite high, and it's a long reach to spare.

CJ 429 is a fairly busy fit in engine compartment. Spring and shock mounts are high and close to sides of engine. Hole in grille at lower right is not for crank.

Mercury Cyclone GT

Data in Brief

DIMENSIONS

Overall length (in.)	209.9
Wheelbase (in.)	117.0
Height (in.)	52.5
Width (in.)	77.3
Tread (front, in.)	58.5
Tread (rear, in.)	58.5
Fuel tank capacity (gal.)	22.0
Luggage capacity (cu. ft.)	16.2

ENGINE

Type	OHV V-8
Displacement (cu. in.)	429
Horsepower (at 5400 rpm)	375
Torque (lb./ft. at 3400 rpm)	450

WEIGHT, TIRES, BRAKES

Weight (as tested, lb.)	4000
Tires	Firestone G70 x 14 Wide Ovals
Brakes, front	disc
Brakes, rear	drum

SUSPENSION

Front . . . . . unequal length A-arms, coil springs, tube shocks, locating arm, anti-roll bar

Rear . . . . live axle with leaf springs and tube shocks

PERFORMANCE

Standing start ¼ mile (sec.)	14.61
Speed at end of ¼ mile (mph)	99.22
Braking (from 60 mph, ft.)	150

GT version comes in super-strong thanks to panel painting, hood scoop (non-functional) and striping. It has super-screamer potential.

REMEMBER the good old days? The days when $3000 bought a genuine supercar and all you had to do to run in the 13's was to block up the PCV valve, change plugs and jets and dial in some timing. As the man said, "them days are gone forever." First off, in 1971 you don't get much for $3000 and, if you do happen to be able to hack a $4000 to $4500 super-car tariff, the insurance companies have made it just about impossible for the average guy to do it. Then, to juice up the story, you dial in the smog control timing and modifications and low compression. The net result is a mid-14-second, $4000 to $4500 semi-supercar that you can't afford to insure!

But, there's still hope for the en-thusiast. The slim ray of hope is the compact which can be had with mild V-8 power and built-in basics for re-spectable street performance. To turn one into a supercar requires some imagination and a good under-standing of the hows and whys of per-formance engineering. One such compact is the Comet, Mercury's idea of what a well-dressed Maverick should look like! It can be had in stan-dard or GT trim and with a choice of V-8 or Six power with three-speed automatic or stick transmissions. The popular four-speed is not yet available in this package. It's been blessed with an acceptable rating from the insurance industry and with an acceptable tariff (approxi-mately $3000 with basic acces-sories). The GT trim package adds a approximately $180 to the list sticker and includes buckets which are far more comfortable than the stock bench setup and a decorative scoop, stripes and other status-add-ing pieces.

In stock showroom form, the Comet GT with 302 V-8 power is not the kind of machine that will auto-matically light your fire. Exciting it's not. However, its appeal lies in

Bucket seat interior is comfortable and spacious. Dash is bargain basement cop-out!

the fact that potential for greater things is built-in. It's not a startling performer or a super handler despite HD suspension with staggered rear shocks. It is, however, a two-barrel hydraulic lifter engine package backed up by either a three-speed stick or a three-speed auto and by 2.76-to-1 gearing. The three-speed stick is a go-nowhere setup and the automatic supplied with this package is not the bang-shifting C-6, but rather the cushioned C-4 which was designed for the *supermarket sweepstakes* and not performance applications.

While the idea of stuffing 302 cubes into the Comet perked up ears in the enthusiast fraternity, spirits were immediately dampened when the purchaser had to pay the price in the form of mediocre carburetion, camming, transmission and gearing. Throttle response leaves an awful lot to be desired and the car just doesn't have the punch that you would expect a car of the Comet's size and weight to have with Mustang power. It doesn't really pay to manually shift the C-4 because it doesn't have the beefy snap-shifting qualities of the brawnier C-6 unit. It needs a reworked valve body and increased line pressures to make better use of the torque characteristics of the 302.

Recognizing the fact that the 302 Comet is not a dragstrip package, we made just a few passes against the clocks to get a better feel of the power package under full throttle conditions. Times ran between 17.0 and 17.5 seconds at 78 to 80 mph. The miles-per-hour average was respectable for a car of this type.

We didn't have the opportunity to do any work on this particular car, but it's relatively easy to project improved all-around street and strip performance by just thumbing thru speed equipment catalogs and Autolite's Muscle Parts books. The basic 302 engine is very similar to the small-block Chevrolet. You're only limited by your imagination and bank balance. By simply junking the stock intake and exhaust manifolds, carburetor and ignition and by replacing them with an aluminum high-riser with a good Holley quad (low cfm rating for increased low-end performance), tuned tube headers and a dual-point performance-oriented ignition system with correct timing, you can turn a showroom stock stroker into a supercar. And, your insurance company need never know! Then add a beefed-up automatic or swap from a three to

four-speed stick and add more reasonable gearing. To top it off, install good high-performance shocks, a rear sway bar and a set of traction bars. The complete conversion can run into mucho bucks, but the project can be stretched out over a long period of time and you'll really appreciate the power output after you have put yourself into the picture. It's just like the good old pre-supercar days.

So much for power. Basically, the Comet is put together very well. The Comet makes sense because you can seat four adults into the 103-inch wheelbase and the trunk holds a respectable amount of luggage. Our test car was tight, waterproof and the overall finish was in line with the maker's more expensive full-size models. The interior noise level and comfort level were acceptable by all standards. The dash layout leaves a

lot to be desired as we've become accustomed to full instrumentation. The dash is a throwback to the stagnant early Sixties. The driving position is good and there's plenty of leg-room in the bucket seat GT version.

When it comes down to ride and handling the Comet GT is neither here nor there. You can't get it with disc brakes and you can't get it with a rear sway bar. The power assisted steering is acceptable, but it's not of the variable ratio type and it feels considerably heavier than the power setups on bigger Mercury products. Under power, the GT understeers and leans, but the car can be controlled and the effects are rather predictable. Once the going gets a bit rough, as it is around the New York City area, an obvious harshness is detectable in the suspension. This is especially true at the rear. It seemed

Engine compartment can handle bigger cube small-block mills. Stock 302 needs a shot in the arm for super street performance. Wheels and tires are also a budget cop-out.

Fat wheels and tires would do wonders for the Comet. Lines are pleasing and quality is good.

Trunk space is nothing to write home about, but you can shoehorn in enough luggage for a trip.

like even ordinary dips in the road surface caused the rear to bottom out. A good set of shocks, rear sway bar and some decent tires should do the trick. Our test car was shod with old-fashioned-looking D-70X14-inch tires mounted on skinny 4½-inch steel wheels. While discs aren't available, Ford did a good job on choosing the right drums for the V-8 power. The car doesn't stop like a power disc-equipped car, but the 10-inch binders get the job done. Size-wise, the brakes are oversize for a car of the Comet's wheelbase and weight.

The most exciting part of the Comet GT is something you can't see or feel. It's called potential. To be completely subjective, we think that the above-mentioned power modifications and suspension modifications, the opening up of the decorative hood scoop, the addition of fat Polyglas shoes on slotted aluminum wheels and an instrumentation transformation could turn the GT into one of the most exciting cars on the market. With close ratio four-speed cogs and Mustang suspension goodies, you could reap all the benefits of the early Hi-Per Mustangs plus room for four adults, luggage and affordable insurance. If you want to make it happen you have to do it for yourself, because it ain't never going to happen in Dearborn!

1971 MERCURY
302 COMET GT
SPECIFICATIONS

ENGINE

Type	OHV V-8
Displacement	302 cubic inches
Compression Ratio	9.0-to-1
Carburetion	Autolite two-barrel
Camshaft	Hydraulic
Horsepower	210 @ 4600
Torque	296 foot/pounds @ 2600
Exhaust	Single
Ignition	Single point

TRANSMISSION

Type	C-4 Cruise-O-Matic
Control	Console

REAR END

Type	Stock
Ratio	2.76-to-1

BRAKES

Type	10-inch drums, front & rear, Power
Area	267.2 square inches

SUSPENSION

Front	H.D, Independent
Rear	H.D, leaf spring
Steering	Power
Overall Ratio	16.0-to-1

GENERAL

List Price	$2500
Price As Tested	$3195
Weight	3086 pounds
Wheelbase	103 inches
Overall Length	181.7 inches
Tires	D-70X14

PERFORMANCE

0 to 30 mph	6.0 seconds
0 to 60 mph	9.4 seconds
Standing ¼ mile	79 mph
Elapsed Time	17.25 seconds
Top Speed	108 mph
Fuel Consumption	16 mph

MERCURY COMET

● Suppose Tiffany's opened a bargain basement. Would the climbers burn their Gimbel's credit cards and henceforth buy all of their stainless steel dinner forks on 5th Avenue? Lincoln-Mercury hopes that human nature works that way. And it will soon find out. In the new model year L-M will be selling the nationally advertised Maverick under its own "Comet" brand name and for very little more money than the real thing.

All of this is a part of the revitalization of the Lincoln-Mercury Division. It used to be that dealers could amass handsome fortunes selling big, expensive automobiles, but that market shows signs of drying up now and L-M doesn't want to wither with it. So it's doing the same thing all beleaguered businesses do—it's diversifying. Already it's wider than the Ford Division and it is still spreading. Not only does its line of wares cover the whole American market from the premium Continental Mark III to the compact Comet but it also has imports. The British/German-built Capri made its debut last spring and the De Tomaso Pantera, a mid-engine coupe, is expected any minute now. Whether the car buying public can adjust to this general store approach remains to be seen but L-M is ready.

The Comet is ready too. It's probably as close to the mark as anything in the Mercury stable. Obviously it is a Maverick—no discerning observer will be fooled by the sheet-metal tune-up—but the Mercury stylists have managed to make it seem decidedly more elegant. Naturally it "features a forward-thrusting power-dome hood" and a horizontal bar grille like all of the big Mercurys. And the taillight treatment strongly suggests a Montego, right down to the bright crosshairs on the lenses. All together it's a Maverick that looks like a Mercury, which is exactly the kind of deception that the car business thrives on.

And like the Maverick, the Comet is available in the original 2-door body style as well as the new stretched 4-door. You get an extra 6.9 inches of wheelbase in the 4-door along with wider rear roof pillars and a more squared-off deck lid. The extra room all goes into the rear seat although the leg room back there increased by only 4.4 inches rather than the full amount of the stretch—the rest seems to have mysteriously disappeared. Even so, the result is a sensibly sized family car that will certainly make inroads into the intermediate market, particularly since the Ford and Mercury intermediates have grown to be what the full-size cars were a few years ago.

All of the dimensions we've been discussing apply to both the Comet and the Maverick but the Comet has one significant exclusive—an optional 302 cubic inch, 2-bbl. V-8. There have been rumblings about a V-8 Maverick since its introduction but Mercury obviously has enough clout in the company to get it first. The 302 is not a high performance engine by any means but it does eliminate the sluggishness many drivers object to and makes the Comet even more competitive with the intermediates.

But in all of this talk of utility and function we shouldn't overlook the mini-muscle car, the Comet GT. It's much in the Maverick Grabber tradition. With a bulging hood scoop, tape stripes and D70-14 tires on 6-inch wide wheels, it looks like a pavement-ripping drag racer and at least it has a V-8 to back up its pretensions. They are still pretensions however, although they will pass for advantages when it comes time to fill out your insurance form. With more than 11 pounds for every horsepower, the GT will escape most "high performance" surcharges.

What Mercury is hoping, of course, is that all of the Comets will help it escape the sales drought in its traditional marketing area. And if it doesn't, the bargain basement may be pushing a set of forward-thrusting, domed-hood Pintos next year.

Dimensions	1971
Wheelbase	109.9 in.
Track, F/R	56.5/56.5 in.
Length	188.6 in.
Width	70.7 in.
Engine	
Standard engine	170 cu. in., 105 hp. Six
Compression ratio	8.7 to one
Max. option	302 cu. in., 220 hp. V-8
Compression ratio	9.0 to one
Tires	
Standard	6.45-14
Max. option	D70-14

photos by Joe Farkas

'71 COMET GT

Maverick too slow and austere? Try Mercury's souped-up luxury version.

In an era of fast-changing tastes, it isn't often that an automaker comes up with a substantially different offering which appears in advance to have all the earmarks of a sure-fire sales success. Feats like that don't come easy in the acutely competitive U.S. auto industry despite the fact that much top talent is constantly searching for that elusive model which will substantially boost production volume—and profits.

An up-to-the-minute example of an apparent winner is a car Ford Motor Company has been planning for over two years to spring at an opportune time on the motoring public. This is Lincoln-Mercury Division's V-8 powered version of the Maverick, introduced last fall as a '71 model called the Comet.

How far and well Ford executives have been able to peer into the usually dimly seen future is illustrated by the V-8 Comet's beginning. The story begins way back in 1967, which is ancient history as car models go,

when Maverick began to take shape on engineering and styling drawing boards. One basic design requirement was that the auto, while planned to have an in-line six-cylinder powerplant, had to also be capable of accepting a small V-8 engine such as the 302-cubic-inch, 210-horsepower plant it gets in the Comet. And this was to be without significant cost-adding modifications to frame, front-end, suspension or body.

Big reason for this not-easy to attain (in a small car) engine compartment design was a general agreement that if the Maverick with six-cylinder power did well, it would surely do even better if a V-8 were added to the availability list. It is hardly necessary to record that Maverick, the first of the import fighters, was a solid success and ran Mustang a very close race to cop first-year sales honors.

Thus a V-8 fast became a forgone conclusion for the car, and was preducted in the February, 1970, issue of *Road Test*. The big question was when. Only surprise, and a small one, was that the car getting the V-8 mill would be called Comet and be produced exclusively by the Lincoln-Mercury Division.

Analysis of early Comet sales

quickly shows that Ford hadn't guessed wrong on the impact V-8 availability would have on volume. Nationally, nearly half (46.2%) of all Comet buyers have specified the engine. In the Los Angeles, Calif., sales district, the preference was even greater—an impressive 61.8%. If the Comet with V-8 power posts that kind of sales performance for many months, executives at Ford Division will almost surely raise a loud cry for the same engine to be made optional in the Maverick.

The reason why so many Comet buyers pass over the three six-cylinder engines available for the 302 V-8 is explained in a quick test drive. The performance is just a lot livelier under all driving conditions. With 210 horsepower pushing an auto with curb weight of only 2,953 pounds (*Road Test*'s car) you have a one horse for just slightly over every 14 pounds. That makes for a lot more urge than is normally expected from a compact car basically in the economy class.

The GT package costs a tidy $178.80 (manufacturer's suggested tab). For that you get plenty: "blackout" grille treatment, back panel "blackout," color-matched dual racing mirrors, wheel trim rings, dual body tape stripes, deluxe door trim panels, black instrument panel, nonfunctional hood scoop and bright window frames. In addition, you get bucket seats which are a $100 option

Tough but flexible suspension of Comet GT adjusts to hard handling, keeps tires in full contact with roadway. Handling was helped by optional tires.

by themselves. Tires were optional white sidewall D70×14 belted wide ovals which cost $98.90 extra. They replace the standard 6.45×14's. Other extras (and suggested prices) on the test car included power steering ($95.40), AM radio ($60.80), tinted glass ($37.00) and a heavy duty battery ($12.00 extra).

Two other options had what might be called bargain prices. The floor mounted transmission selector replaced the standard column mounted stick. It costs but $13.10 extra. And the handling suspension package, which includes heavy-duty springs and shocks and a heftier (larger diameter) front sway bar, sells for a trifling $12.00 extra.

What gave our Comet GT its go was the optional 302-cubuc-inch, two-bbl V-8 with 210 horsepower at 4,600 rpm. Certainly no stranger to most buyers of Ford-built autos, this thin-wall block powerplant has at one time or another served as the base V-8 for nearly every Ford Division model and most Mercury cars as well. With excellent power-to-weight ratio, this modern, light, tough basic block, in various cubic-inch and horsepower ratings since introduced in 1963, has been adequate enough to delight many an owner of FoMoCo interme-

diates and pony cars, as any driver of the "Boss" 302 Mustang will verify. In the tamer, two-barrel configuration which powers the Comet GT, the 302 develops 296 ft.-lbs. of torque at 2,600 rpm.

Standard transmission is a three-speed manual with column-mounted shifter. The same box with floor shifter plus a three-speed automatic are optional. Other engines in the Comet stable parallel those available with the '71 Maverick. These are the six-cylinder mills of 170, 200 and 250-cubic-inch displacement. The three-speed manual transmission is standard, with 3-speed automatic optional with the 200-cubic-inch version. Manual three-speed is the only box available with the 170, while the 250 uses the automatic exclusively. All Comet six-cylinder engines are equipped with single-barrel carburetors.

Rear-end ratios are limited to 2.79-to-1 for all models except the 200-cubic-inch six with manual shift plus the 250-cubic-inch six and all air-conditioned Comets.

Rear-end ratios are limited to 2.79-to-1 for all models except the 200-cubic-inch six with manual shift plus the 250-cubic-inch six and all air-conditioned Comets. These vehicles come with a 3.00-to-1 axle.

Our test car was fitted with the optional floor shifter which, in spite of long throws between all gears, is fairly positive, and surer than the standard column mounted lever. There's moderate spring loading to go

Bucket seats, with woven vinyl and wall-to-wall carpet are extra touches for the Comet GT. Floor mounted stick is well worth small extra cost.

into reverse or 1st, which is helpful. But, until the driver gets used to that feature he may find himself going into high gear when 1st was intended. This, of course, damages nothing, but results in a second or two being lost in a situation where top performance may have been desired. The tunnel-mounted stick appears most suitable to the GT character and it will probably be preferred by most buyers.

Although the 2V 302 engine, equipped with three-speed manual transmission and a single exhaust, is a relatively straight forward, domes-

Maximum deceleration shows some front end dive, though not much, and a bit of rear-end rise. Rear wheels are here very close to lockup and one may be virtually stationary.

Although the Comet GT is a small car, it carries off feeling of muscularity. Black-out feature of grille helps in presenting this image.

ticated power team, it presents an intriguing performance package wedged into a Comet. Design engineers did leave room for the 302, but they obviously were not wasting inches, and of course they couldn't since this is a compact car. To say the 302 fits snugly under the hood would be an understatement. There is some room between the radiator and the engine, but getting to the plugs is going to require the proper tools and skill—and a cold engine. With air conditioning the Comet V-8 must be one busy automobile up front. The GT tested also included the non-functional hood scoop, which is part of the package. It can easily be made functional.

To many auto enthusiasts, the Comet characteristic which will most stand out is the solid, tight-knit quality of the whole car both at rest and in motion. This feeling of ruggedness and integrated design was first noted by *Road Test* in checks of the first six prototype Mavericks built (January, 1969). It left a lasting impression. It was again noted in evaluating assembly line versions of the Maverick, including the "Grabber."

The Comet, like the Maverick, rides and handles like a heavier car than it is, and like one with a longer wheelbase than it has. All this provides a "feel" at turnpike speeds which produces a confidence level you don't get in most smaller-than-intermediate size autos.

On modern freeways, the exemplary "whole car" feeling of Comet makes the cruising speed, particularly in the 60 to 80 mph range, seem less than it is. This no doubt results in part from the V-8's low vibration level, and the fact that even at near maximum rpm it is still not strained, pushing a car weighing less than 1½ tons. (After all, the 302 has been a base engine for full size Mercury cars, which weigh a great deal more).

In traffic and in parking, the Comet is agile as only small cars can be. Handling is made even easier with the optional power steering. Considering the short wheelbase (103 inches) and

not so wide track (56.5 inches front and rear) the Comet corners exceedingly well. While pronounced drift can be induced by fast directional changes, the point where the rear tires begin to lose significant traction (on good surfaces) is not abrupt and can be corrected easily. The quicker ratio provided with power steering helps here, too. It is 3.7 wheel turns, compared to 5.2 for manual steering.

Some understeer can be induced, especially in cornering in 2nd gear with a heavy foot on the accelerator pedal, but that's to be expected from just about any auto with the favorable power-to-weight ratio found here. To a large extent, the roadability and handling of our test Comet was helped by the optional handling package.

Even with a 2.79-to-1 axle ratio, Comet exhibits the personality of a high-powered light truck being driven

rpm sooner than the 302 (1,600 compared to 2,600 rpm) and the torque difference isn't huge—240 lb.-ft. for the 250 and 296 for the 302.

Even with the non-performance axle ratio of 2.70 to 1, it was easy to burn the Comet's optional oversize rear tires in 1st. It was to the suspension's credit that there's no power-hop even under maximum acceleration from standstill.

Passing performance of the 302 Comet (exclusively in high gear) has to be considered somewhat close to sparkling. A number of tests were run both directions on the same road (to adjust for a slight grade and for wind) and then averaged. Technique was to establish a steady-state speed, then floor the accelerator. For 30 to 60 mph and for 40 to 70 mph, elapsed time was identical at just under 9

In hard cornering, what camera sees of Comet GT in action is somewhat more spectacular than what the driver feels. Even when punished, car is both docile and forgiving in it's handling qualities.

empty. It really comes on strong in all gears when you depress the accelerator. This, of course, provides broad flexibility in 3rd gear. It is possible to operate there down to about 18 mph and move off quickly—and smoothly—without changing gears. In all-out driving the optional ($13.10) floor mounted transmission selector was appreciated, despite slightly longer throw distances than competition shifters have.

Extracting full performance capability from the 302 engine in a Comet without floating the valves or other damage requires studied familiarity. One reason is that there's no tachometer, and one isn't optionally available. If much lusty driving is planned, a dealer-added tach would be a "must" investment.

Since acceleration is given on the specification page, we won't report it here. For the quarter-mile run, Ford's electrically-timed strip at the Dearborn, Mich., test facility was used. Running due west we were helped by a variable (10-20 mph) wind coming out of the southeast. The first run, interestingly, was the best of the five, with an elapsed time of 16.630 seconds and a terminal speed of 75.44 mph. Times on two other west-bound trips with speed through the finish light: 17.101 sec. (80.71 mph) and 17.071 sec. (80.71 mph). Two eastward tries (into the wind) produced 17.593 sec. (78.39 mph) and 17.641 sec. (78.05 mph). All runs were with a passenger for a total

Comet's trunk will hold a few suitcases, and there's more room forward than shows in photo, for small handbags. Spare tire takes up quite a bit of space, however.

occupant weight of 365 lbs, plus a ¾-tank of fuel.

Elapsed times, especially the best one, compare very favorably with the '70 Maverick "Grabber" tested earlier (August, 1970 issue). That car, with the 250-cubic-inch, 155-horsepower six-cylinder plant, ran the quarter mile in 17.94 seconds, taking 1.31 seconds longer than the 302-powered Comet. This is in part significant because the 250 engine gets its maximum torque a full 1,000

seconds. Generally, it won't be necessary to downshift the 302-powered Comet in most passing situations.

With the V-8, Comet weight is up 194 pounds over the smallest six, producing a different set of brake requirements. There was no pennypinching to meet them. Instead of the 9-inch drums all around for the two small six-cylinder engines, the 302 gets 10-inch drums (as does the 250 six when fitted with the bigger D70×14 tires)

Like most smaller cars, the Comet performs well in stopping, to an appreciable extent because there's less mass involved. However, with under 100 miles on the odometer when checked, the brake system friction surfaces on our test car lacked the burnishing necessary for full effectiveness. Best maximum deceleration stop from 60 mph was 171.4 feet.

Minor instability was noted in hard stops but was corrected with under three inches of steering wheel movement. The quicker ratio of the power steering was appreciated here. Disc brakes on the front would contribute much to arrow-straight stops but are not (at this writing, at least) available for the car. For all normal braking they really aren't needed, considering the auto's low total weight.

Reel-type front safety belts were appreciated, but it was found that the belt end is best grasped before the door is closed. If it isn't, there's barely enough clearance between the seat and door to reach the end. That's something which illustrates how

In hard acceleration Comet GT's front end raises up, rear squats under power of 302 engine.

closely some parts of the Comet fit to one another—in non-important places. The contribution to safety of the dual outside mirrors must also be mentioned. So too should the better than average (for a small sedan) rear visibility.

Basically, the Comet is a straightforward derivative of Ford Division's Maverick. But it's also a Mercury. That means the car is overall more extensively trimmed-out. This justifies the L-M nameplate and the slightly higher cost. The GT (and two- and four-door Comet sedans) provide carpeting, front and rear armrests and vinyl door liners which are features not found on all Mavericks. Standard Comet seating is cloth-and-vinyl covered benches for the sedans, and a choice of cloth-and-vinyl or woven-vinyl buckets with the GT package.

In earlier Maverick tests, we alerted readers to the surprising roominess of the Maverick front seat, but this bears repeating with respect to Comet. These cars actually offer more leg room than a couple of luxury automobiles we know. Combine this overall

front-seat space with the excellent high-back optional bucket seats and you have a most pleasant driving environment. Although we were pleased with the Comet's deference to body comfort (at least for the front-seat occupants), the most significant impression of the car was total solidness, as mentioned earlier.

The dash area, as might be expected in what is still an "economy" compact, is on the austere side. Instruments are large and easy to read, but oil-pressure and coolant temperature gauges would be welcome options for the GT. So would a tachometer. An electric clock is available for the Comet in a mini-console, dubbed "consolette" by Mercury, which can be had as an option only with column-shift models.

Hinged rear windows are a feature which will be appreciated. While the flow-through ventilation is adequate under normal conditions, popping open the back panes really produces a volume air flow.

Comet's dash board incorporates an open storage shelf. Even with the half-inch retainer lip at the edge of this compartment, a fast getaway can often put much of the tray's contents into the laps of front-seat passengers.

The 302 cu. in. V-8 just fits in under the hood. With air conditioning, space would really be at a premium. Clearance between engine and wheelwells is just enough for powerplant motion under high torque conditions.

And, as we experienced during testing, it's possible to have loose papers blow out the window if left in this area.

Visibility in the Comet is superior to that of many full-size and intermediate vehicles. The support posts are trimmed down considerably from the wide beams currently considered stylish. The GT package also includes color-matched dual racing mirrors which contribute much to exterior appearance, and even more to safe driving.

The Comet GT as tested was not exactly head-on competition for some of the price-leader imports, or even the U.S.-built compact cars. The total posted price ($2,940.50) didn't include dealer preparation, transportation charges or state and local taxes. With a few other options like air conditioning and vinyl roof you can have a car in the $3,500 range. That's quite a ways from the original Maverick, which everyone must recall, listed at $1,995.

Yet, for someone who wants quite lively, comfortable transportation in an auto smaller than an intermediate, and not of the "pony" class, the Comet GT is one strong contender. It plugs still another gap in the model line-up between U.S. compacts (Gremlin, Pinto and Vega) and the intermediates. There's no completely parallel competitive offering. For this reason, and particularly with the V-8 engine, Comet—an all-around fine little auto—ought to do very well in the market place. Tony Grey

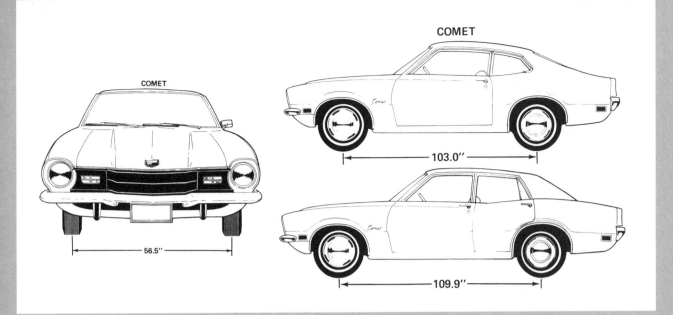

COMET

COMET

103.0"

109.9"

56.5"

COMET GT 2-DOOR SEDAN

PERFORMANCE AND MAINTENANCE

Acceleration: Gears:
  0-30 mph . . . . .3.0 secs.—I
  0-45 mph . . . . .5.5 secs.—I, II
  0-60 mph . . . . .9.0 secs.—I, II
  0-75 mph . . . . .15.0 secs.—I, II, III
  0-¼ mile . . . . .16.6 secs. @ 75 mph
Ideal cruise . . . . .67 mph
Top speed (est.) . . . . .117 mph
Stop from 60 mph . . . . .171.4 ft.
Average economy (city) . . . . .15.1 mpg
Average economy (country) . . . . .22.2 mpg
Fuel required . . . . .Regular
Oil change (mos./miles) 6/ 6000
Lubrication (mos./miles) 12/12000
Warranty (mos./miles) 12/12000
Type tools required . . . . .SAE
U.S. dealers . . . . .2689 total

SPECIFICATIONS AS TESTED

Engine . . . . .302 cu. in., ohv V-8
Bore & stroke . . . . .4.002 x 3.00 ins.
Compression ratio . . . . .9.0 to one
Horsepower . . . . .210 (SAE gross) @ 4600 rpm
Torque . . . . .296 lbs.-ft. @ 2600 rpm
Transmission . . . . .3-speed, manual
Steering* . . . . .3.7 turns, lock to lock
                       36.9 ft., curb to curb
Brakes . . . . .drum front, drum rear
Suspension . . . .coil front, semi-elliptical leaf rear
Tires . . . . .D70 x 14, 4 PR belted
Dimensions (ins.):
  Wheelbase . . . .103.0 Front track . . . 56.5
  Length . . . . . .181.7 Rear track 56.5
  Width . . . . 70.6 Weight . . . .2961 lbs.
  Height . . . . . . 53.0 Ground clearance 6.1
Capacities: Fuel . . . . .15 gals. Oil . . . . .4.0 qts.
  Coolant . . . .8.9 qts. Trunk . . . .10.0 cu. ft.

*Power-assisted as tested.

RATING

	Excellent (90-100)	Good (80-90)	Fair (70-80)	Poor (60-70)
Brakes		85		
Comfort		88		
Cornering	91			
Details		82		
Finish	92			
Instruments . . .			78	
Luggage		85		
Performance . . .	93			
Quietness		81		
Ride	94			
Room	95			
Steering	96			
Visibility		89		
Overall		88.4		

n/a — not available

BASE PRICE OF CAR

(Excludes state and local taxes, license, dealer preparation and domestic transportation): $2380 at Detroit.
Plus desirable options:
$ 12.00 Handling/Suspension Package
$ 13.10 Floor Shift
$ 178.80 GT Package
$ 98.90 D70 x 14 Tires
$ 60.80 AM Radio
$ 95.40 Power Steering
$2839.00 TOTAL
$.81 per lb. (base price).

ANTICIPATED DEPRECIATION

(Based on current Kelley Blue Book, previous equivalent model): $ n/a 1st yr. + $ n/a 2nd yr.

N/A — not applicable

MERCURY
COMET

The Comet nameplate disappeared briefly during the period when Detroit's former compacts grew into intermediate-sized luxury or performance models, so it was logical to revive it for Lincoln-Mercury Division's new Maverick-based offering. With the 2-door on a 103.0-inch wheelbase and the 4-door on a 109.9, size is now back in true compact perspective.

The addition of a "power dome" hood and grille, following the Division's policy of being imitative of Lincoln, does wonders for the car's appearance. So, too, do the typical Mercury twin-pod taillights and touches of extra chrome on the body sides. These items, however, constitute the only real exterior differences from Maverick.

Inside, Comet retains the Maverick instrument panel with its full-width package shelf but the trim, whether in base or decor-group form, is generally more luxurious. The GT version of the 2-door has the usual "racing-type" outside mirrors, body stripes and blacked-out panels surrounding the taillights and instruments. Bucket seats and vinyl upholstery are standard in this. Plain Comets are normally supplied with a bench front seat and a combination of vinyl and cloth upholstery.

The standard Comet engine is a 170-cubic-inch 6 of 100 hp. Since this

has only four main bearings, it would be wiser for the purchaser to opt for either the 200- or 250-cubic-inch 6, each of which has a sturdier 7-main-bearing construction and 115 and 145 hp, respectively. The latter engine is simply a stroked (0.780-inch greater) version of the first option, and all including the V-8 run on regular gas.

When Maverick was first introduced in April, 1969, it was obvious that the engine compartment was deliberately designed to accept a V-8 but no one anticipated that this option was to be reserved for the Comet. The engine selected was the 302-cubic-inch, 210-hp unit that forms the base for the famous Boss Mustangs and Cougar Eliminators. Naturally, the parts are readily available to upgrade the Comet version to about 300 hp, although the factory has no intention of cataloging a hot rod Comet.

The standard transmission with all engines except the largest 6 is a 3-speed manual box with column shift that is synchronous in all forward gears, a feature that the competitive Hornet lacks. A floor shift is optional on any body style at a very small additional cost. If automatic shifting is your preference, it's standard on the 250-inch 6, optional on the 200-inch 6 and V-8 but not available with the smallest engine. It, too, may be floor shifted if you so choose. The semi-automatic box offered on early Mavericks is not listed.

Comet suspension is carried over from Maverick. It consists of McPherson-type, tower-mounted coil springs in front and leaf springs at the rear. A new feature for 1971 is the adoption of staggered shock absorber mountings at the rear to control wheel hop during acceleration and braking. In keeping with Comet's intended image, no handling package is offered—which is too bad because past Mavericks, at

least, have displayed rather sloppy ride and handling characteristics. Wide-oval, D-70 series tires are optional, however.

Power steering is offered but there is no power assist for the brakes. These brakes are normally 9-inch drums with 106 square inches of effective lining area, but when options specified such as air conditioning and vinyl top total to a certain amount of weight, 10-inch drums (flared and finned at front) are provided.

Easy serviceability is another feature inherited from Maverick, complete with a do-it-yourself section in the owner's manual. Front fenders bolt on to the body structure, the grille is quickly removable as are the instruments, and the headlights may be adjusted for aim without removing the bezels. While the V-8 crowds the engine compartment a bit, the 6's leave plenty of working room.

Internal dimensions are identical with Maverick and therefore larger in most cases than will be found in the Mustang or Cougar. The new 4-door style passes back most of its 6.9-inch-greater wheelbase in the form of leg room for the rear seat occupants. This dimension measures 36.7 inches, compared with 31.9 inches in the 2-door. Front head room at 37.9 inches is more than adequate, as is the 41.3 inches of leg room there.

The unitized bodies were designed too early in time to incorporate guard rails in the doors but they do have a form of roll bar construction at each end of the roof. They also lack the flush door handles now favored by safety officials. Other legislated add-ons include evaporative emission control for all cars and nitrous-oxide suppression for California-bound cars.

Price-wise, the Comet should fit in a range $150 to $400 higher than Maverick's $1997 base, depending up-

on major options ordered that are available on one and not the other. Obviously, we're relating to 1970 prices here as no one knows what increases will be required from the impending labor negotiations this fall. •

COMET/GT

ENGINES: 170 cu ins (100 hp) 200 cu ins (115 hp). 250 cu ins (145 hp). 302 cu ins (210 hp).

TRANSMISSIONS: 3-spd manual std, 3-spd auto opt.

SUSPENSION: Coil front, leaf rear.

STEERING: Manual std, power opt, curb-to-curb 35.6-37.7 ft.

BRAKES: Drums std.

FUEL CAPACITY: 15.5 gals.

DIMENSIONS: Wheelbase 103-109.9 ins. Track 56.5 ins front and rear. Width 70.6-70.7 ins. Length 181.7-188.6 ins. Height 52.6-53 ins. Weight 2596-2689 lbs. Trunk 10-10.4 cu ft.

BODY STYLES: 2-dr sdn, 4-dr sdn.

MERCURY
MONTEGO CYCLONE

This L-M Division grouping was almost totally revamped for the 1970 season so consequently, no major changes have been made for the coming year. The convertible was dropped and a 4-door hardtop added at that time also to bring offerings in line with public preferences. This leaves the 2-door hardtop in formal and "SportsRoof" form, 4-door sedans and hardtops, and a pair of wagons, the top model of the latter resurrecting the name "Villager."

As before, Montegos and Cyclones are distinguished by their different grilles. For '71 the Cyclone continues its "gunsight" theme as well as covered headlights and as before, it has the better looking front end of the two. All Montego models have a rather gross checkerboard pattern for their grilles and the dual headlights are exposed. In 1970, it will be remembered, top-line Montegos featured covered lights and a full-width, horizontal grille. At the rear, the taillights retain the same pod theme with two pairs designating lower-line models and three pairs, the top Montego MX and Broughams.

Engine choices remain the same with the 250-cubic-inch, 145-hp 6 being standard for all Montego models including wagons. This one would be quite marginal in a 3-seat wagon, especially if it were equipped with an automatic transmission. Optional Montego engines include a 302-cubic-inch, 210-hp V-8 and a pair of 351 V-8's that give 240 or 285 hp depending upon whether they have a 2- or 4-barrel carburetor.

Cyclone choices are a little odd as you'd logically think that a Cyclone GT designation would mean more car than plain Cyclone. This, however, is not true. The 302 V-8 is standard in the GT, whereas the 351 4-barrel will be found in the Cyclone. The Cyclone Spoiler then reverts back to logic with a standard 429-cubic-inch, 370-hp V-8 with or without ram-air. This engine is an option on any other Cyclone but not for Montegos.

The standard 3-speed manual transmission with column shift can't be had past the 302 V-8. The 3-speed automatic box is a mandatory option with the 2-barrel 351 but you can't get it with 429's. The Hurst-shifted 4-speed box starts with the 4-barrel 351 and is a mandatory option of 429's. Apparently, L-M studied customer preferences in the recent past and decided to eliminate some combinations that didn't sell. Some people, however, may

CYCLONE SPOILER

not appreciate being forced to pay extra for a transmission they don't particularly want as in the case of the 2-barrel 351 and automatic combination. Also, elimination of automatics coupled to 429's won't do Mercury any good on the drag strips.

Buyers of 4-door sedans and hardtops will appreciate a new provision for a half-inch greater rear-wheel jounce clearance at design load. These models in the past have been a bit prone to bottoming on rough roads. Then, there are two types of heavy-duty suspensions, a cross-country package and a competition handling package. The latter is standard on all cars with 429 engines and not available on others. Again, this is arbitrary as some buyers might like a 4-barrel 351 Cyclone or Montego with the stiffer of the two suspensions.

In common with all the company cars, the intermediate Mercurys feature a new method of retaining the side-door glass on 2-door models. The glass is mechanically retained by bolts through holes in the bottom of the glass. The nylon bushings and washers are installed over the bolts to prevent direct metal contact with the glass. The main purpose here is easier removal.

Also new to the intermediate line is an AM/FM stereo radio option with integrated circuitry, electronics jargon for combining elements such as transistors, diodes and capacitors into one component with external connections. Compared to radios of the recent past it cuts individual components from 31 to 2. It makes diagnosis easier in the field, but you have to replace half the radio if any single component fails.

Progress of intermediates of any make on the 1971 marketplace will be interesting to watch as only Dodge and Plymouth are fielding all-new cars. At the present point, they represent the second most popular line for all makers, having supplanted the compacts in that respect. However, Maverick is fast catching up to Torino, and the Nova is nudging Chevelle. So the question is, what will the new Comet do to the Montego and Cyclone? •

MONTEGO

MONTEGO MX

MONTEGO MX BROUGHAM

ACCELERATION standing ¼ mile, seconds

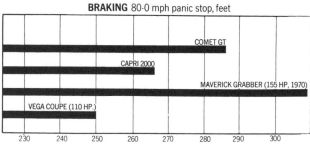

COMET GT
CAPRI 2000
MAVERICK GRABBER (155 HP, 1970)
VEGA COUPE (110 HP.)

13 14 15 16 17 18 19 20

BRAKING 80-0 mph panic stop, feet

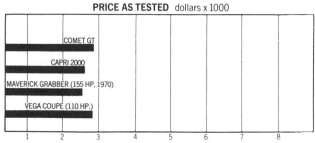

COMET GT
CAPRI 2000
MAVERICK GRABBER (155 HP, 1970)
VEGA COUPE (110 HP.)

230 240 250 260 270 280 290 300

FUEL ECONOMY RANGE mpg

COMET GT
CAPRI 2000
Maverick not available
VEGA COUPE (110 HP.)

6 10 14 18 22 26 30 34

PRICE AS TESTED dollars x 1000

COMET GT
CAPRI 2000
MAVERICK GRABBER (155 HP, 1970)
VEGA COUPE (110 HP.)

1 2 3 4 5 6 7 8

MERCURY COMET GT

Manufacturer: Lincoln-Mercury Division
Ford Motor Company
3000 Schafer Road
Dearborn, Michigan 48121

Vehicle type: Front engine, rear-wheel-drive,
5-passenger coupe

Price as tested: $2859.20
(Manufacturer's suggested retail price, including all options listed below, Federal excise tax, dealer preparation and delivery charges, does not include state and local taxes, license or freight charges)

Options on test car: Comet 2-door V-8, $2387.00; heavy duty battery, $12.00; floor shift, $13.10; handling package, $12.00; GT package, $178.80; power steering, $95.40; AM radio, $60.80; D70-14 white stripe tires, $110.10.

ENGINE
Type: V-8, water-cooled, cast iron block and heads, 5 main bearings
Bore x stroke . . . . .4.00 x 3.00 in, 101.6 x 76.2 mm
Displacement . . . . .302 cu in, 4950 cc
Compression ratio . . . . .9.0 to one
Carburetion . . . . .1 x 2 bbl Autolite
Valve gear . . . . .Pushrod operated overhead valves, hydraulic lifters

Power (SAE) . . . . .210 bhp @ 4600 rpm
Torque (SAE) . . . . .296 lbs/ft @ 2600 rpm
Specific power output . . . . . . .0.70 bhp/cu in, 42.5 bhp/liter

DRIVE TRAIN
Transmission . . . . .3-speed, all-synchro
Final drive ratio . . . . .2.79 to one

Gear	Ratio	Mph/1000rpm	Max. test speed
I	2.99	8.9	45 mph (5100 rpm)
II	1.75	15.1	77 mph (5100 rpm)
III	1.00	26.5	100 mph (3800 rpm)

DIMENSIONS AND CAPACITIES
Wheelbase . . . . .103.0 in
Track, F/R . . . . .57.0/57.0 in
Length . . . . .181.7 in
Width . . . . .70.6 in
Height . . . . .52.6 in
Ground clearance . . . . .6.1 in
Curb weight . . . . .2935 lbs
Weight distribution, F/R 56.8/43.2%
Battery capacity . . . . .12 volts, 55 amp/hr
Generator/Alternator capacity . . . . .456 watts
Fuel capacity . . . . .15.0 gal
Oil capacity . . . . .4.0 qts
Water capacity . . . . .13.5 qts

SUSPENSION
F: Ind., unequal length control arms, coil springs, anti-sway bar
R: Rigid axle, semi-elliptic leaf springs

STEERING
Type . . . . .Recirculating ball, linkage booster
Turns lock-to-lock 3.9
Turning circle curb-to-curb . . . . .35.6 ft

BRAKES
F: . . . . .9.00 x 2.25-in cast iron drum
R: . . . . .9.00 x 1.50-in cast iron drum

WHEELS AND TIRES
Wheel size . . . . .14 x 6.0-in
Wheel type . . . . .Stamped steel, 5-bolt
Tire make and size .Goodyear D70-14
Tire type . . . . .Bias-belted, tubeless
Test inflation pressures, F/R . . . . .24/26 psi
Tire load rating . . . . .1320 lbs per tire @ 32 psi

PERFORMANCE
Zero to	Seconds
30 mph	2.5
40 mph	3.8
50 mph	5.8
60 mph	8.2
70 mph	10.9
80 mph	14.5
90 mph	19.5
100 mph	26.8

Standing 1/4-mile . . . . .84.2 sec @ 16.3 mph
Top speed (estimated) . . . . .115 mph
80-0mph . . . . .286 ft (0.75 G)
Fuel mileage . . . . .13-17 mpg on regular fuel
Cruising range . . . . .195-225 mi

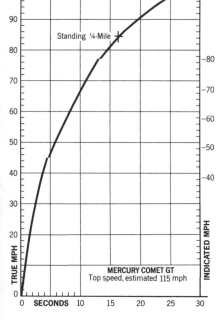

Standing ¼-Mile

MERCURY COMET GT
Top speed, estimated 115 mph

TRUE MPH
INDICATED MPH
SECONDS

ROAD TEST

MERCURY COMET GT

The "big motor" Maverick gets a Comet nameplate.

D oes anyone remember when a Maverick was just a Maverick, with narrow-rim, 13-inch wheels and skinny tires, a cast-iron Six for an engine and all the luxury touches and furbelows of an A.P.C. Probably someone, somewhere, does—but not the guys at Ford Motor Company who seem to have forgotten the whole affair. They will, if you get really insistent about it, still build you that kind of car, but the fact is that all the buyer insistence is aimed off in the other direction. Make a car and offer options that will make it go faster or look better and people will just wear out that options list every time. And in that manner the option list attached to the Maverick has been extended and the Maverick itself has become a real automobile and a thing pleasant to own and drive.

What we have here is a *Mercury* Maverick, which has prompted that division to resurrect the name "Comet" and which is distinguished from the Ford product by the nameplate and small differences in the sheetmetal around its nose and hood—and the optional 302 cu.in. V-8 rated at 220 hp—which was 65 hp better than Ford's best until Dearborn's policy makers loosened up in midyear and gave Ford division the same optional engine. And, like its near identical cousin from Ford, the Comet carries an enticing base price and from there you grab up the options list and build your own vehicle—like clipping cutout clothes for a paper doll. It is your basic Barbie marketing technique. The only substantive difference between the car and the doll is that some of the stuff you clip-on goes inside the car, and of course the selection process gets to be a lot more expensive. You start the game, if you care anything about performance, by ordering the V-8 engined version of the basic Comet and that raises the ante to $2387. A heavy duty battery only costs an extra $12, and as it gives you a 55 ampere/hour capacity, or 10 over standard, you go for that. The floor shift goes for $13—if you opt for the 3-speed manual transmission we had in our test car (you can't get the car with a 4-speeder, worse luck)—and you'll go for the power steering at $95.40 just because that reduces the number of turns, lock-to-lock, from a stem-winder 5.2 to 3.7. Then, because you want to keep current on the downtrend in acid rock and upturn in acid indigestion, you specify a radio for $60.80 and a chap would be a fool not to get some decent rubber between himself and the pavement, so it's a set of D70-14 tires (with zippy stripes) for another $110.10—which would be a lot of money for a set of tires, except that these come on a set of wide-rim wheels (6.0-in., as compared to the standard 4.5-in.). Finally, having spent big bucks for wheels and tires, you are certain to decide on Mercury's $12 suspension package, which is, like the others of its kind, a real bargain.

The suspension package? There isn't a thing in it that you don't get on any Comet, but while all the same parts are there, the parts themselves are somewhat different. The front stabilizer bar, for instance, has an 0.69-in. diameter as standard, while the one you get with the heavy duty suspension package (in this context, "heavy-duty" means handling) has a diameter of 0.850 in. Similarly, the wire diameter of the front suspension's coil springs is larger with the suspension package, which raises the spring rate from 255 lb.-in. to 280 lb.-in. At the rear axle, which is clamped to asymmetrical leaf springs, the rate is stiffened from 77 lb.-in. to 120 lb.-in.

Having gone this far, you might as well go all the way and shell out the $178.80 Mercury is asking for the GT package. It is a lot more money than the suspension package, but then the GT stuff is right out there where your friends and neighbors can see it and marvel. Let us quote to you directly from Mercury's 'brag-book': "In front, a color-keyed hood scoop and blacked-out grille impart the appearance of performance. From the sides, the 'competition car' look is stressed by dual racing mirrors finished in body color, a special wide body-side tape stripe, and bright metal wheel trim rings. Bright metal window frames also are included on the Comet GT. The back panel continues the performance appearance with a blacked-out treatment around the twin pod taillights."

How could anyone resist such marvels? All those stripes and brightwork and mirrors and such—not to mention that big hood scoop, even though all the scoop scoops is a large chunk out of the driver's field of vision. The scoop just sits up there atop the hood hoping no one will notice that unless air will filter down through solid sheet metal, that 2-barrel (1.56-in. throttle bore) carburetor down below will simply have to do the best it can on warm underhood air. The whole thing is a visual hype.

We could do without the stripes and the hood and all the rest of the jazz that, collectively, "impart the appearance of performance." But we're for ordering the GT package anyhow, because unless you do that you don't get the GT seats. The standard Comet, and all the rest lacking the GT package, comes with a bench-type front seat. Benches are fine things, in a park, surrounded by strutting pigeons and anointed with bright sun and warm air; we just don't think they are the best possible perch for the driver of an automobile. A driver isn't so much interested in feeding pigeons as in avoiding hitting them (especially the ones in human form) and one of the requirements for being able to do the driving job well is to be more or less securely positioned behind the wheel. Also, even if the driver is *not* firmly positioned behind the wheel, he will still have to stay there to drive, which means that even if the front seat is as spacious as Louis XIV's canopied bed, it doesn't confer any benefits on said driver. In consequence, the only seat that makes any sense is one of those most often called 'buckets' that will hold one firmly in place. And that's what you get with the GT package.

The holding aspect is rather important when your Comet has the fat tires, wide-rim wheels and suspension package, because with the little bit of help you get from *those* friends the car will get around corners quite quickly and you'd be sliding all over a bench seat. The only thing that spoils the Comet as a sports car is that all the controls are so full of elasticity, lash and gollywobbles that you get awfully busy trying to make the car steer a smooth course into, around and out of a corner. The steering is quick enough to satisfy the demands of such situations, but too imprecise for those little midflight corrections one must make. The

text continued on page 118

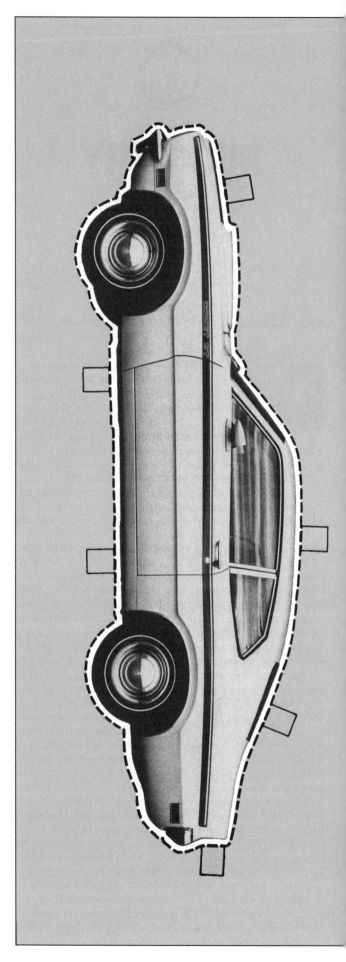

Just like clipping clothes for a paper doll, you can build your own car from the option list.

Comet

COMET GT

The first Comet was a Falcon-based compact Mercury built from 1960 to 1966. The name has been dormant since then until a year ago when it was revived and attached to Lincoln-Mercury's version of the Ford Maverick. Right from the start, the Comet had the advantage of two body styles (2-door and 4-door sedans), a comprehensive power team lineup, and a list of other options. There are no extensive changes in the 1972 Comet, but many refinements and minor improvements have been made on the car.

For 1972, the Comet is offered in two series, the base series, which includes the 2- and 4-door models, and the Comet GT—a sporty 2-door model. A major difference between the models is their body profiles—the 4-door has a traditional sedan silhouette with a formal roofline, but the 2-door sports a low, fastback styling. Overall dimensions of the two series are unchanged for '72.

The Comet's base engine is the same 170-cu.-in. unit that is used in the Maverick, with an all synchromesh 3-speed transmission as standard. The Select-Shift 3-speed automatic is available with the two optional larger 6-cylinder engines and the 302-in. V-8.

Column-mounted shift levers are standard with both transmissions. However, the optional floor-mounted selector can be ordered for the 3-speed manual transmission with the 200 and 302 engines, and for the SelectShift automatic transmission with the GT option. Comet's semi-oval shaped steering wheel provides extra high clearance, and the optional power steering reduces the number of turns from 5.2 to 4.0 lock-to-lock.

A driver can easily adjust the Comet's brakes by stepping on the brake pedal while the car is moving backwards. This maintains proper pedal height for quicker braking.

COMET 2-DOOR SEDAN

COMET 4-DOOR SEDAN

As is the case with the Maverick, the Comet has no disc or power brake option. The drum brakes have fairly high fade resistance, but side pull is not eliminated. Front/rear brake balance is easily upset, and premature rear wheel locking can jeopardize the stability of the car under heavy braking. The V-8 Comet in particular deserves front disc brakes and an anti-lock brake system.

Comet interiors are neutral; they're neither drab, nor cheerful. The standard front bench seats on the Comet are mounted on ball bearing seat tracks and can be adjusted 5 ins. front to rear. The 2-door model has folding front seat backs that self-lock in an upright position; a lever on the side of the seat back releases the lock. The Comet GT features highback bucket seats; the latching handle is located in the center of the seat back—easily accessible for rear passenger exit and convenient for one-hand entrance.

In the 4-door sedan, front and rear head room is almost the same as in the intermediate-size cars, and rear leg room equals or exceeds most cars in the Comet price class.

Illuminated heater controls, windshield wiper and light switch are conveniently located to the left of the instrument pods! To the right, concealed behind a pull-out door, are the cigarette lighter and ash tray. Below the instrument panel, which is covered with a padded hood, there is a wide stowage tray. (Like the Maverick, the Comet has no glove compartment.)

Fresh air ventilation is provided by ducts located behind the instrument panel stowage tray. The 2-door sedan features front-hinged, rear quarter windows which exhaust stale air. The heater features a 3-speed blower for convenient operation.

Comet's size offers easy handling and parking maneuverability. Its efficient powerplants offer economy with adequate power, and the many "do-it-your-self" features reduce maintenance costs. These features, plus its contemporary styling, make Comet a value much appreciated by a growing clientele. 🔧

COMET/GT

ENGINES: 170 cu. ins. (94 hp), 200 cu. ins. (100 hp), 250 cu. ins. (113 hp), 302 cu. ins. (130 hp). (Est.)

TRANSMISSIONS: 3-spd. manual std., 3-spd. auto opt.

SUSPENSION: Coil front, leaf rear.

STEERING: Manual std., power opt., curb-to-curb 36.9-37.7 ft.

BRAKES: Drums std.

FUEL CAPACITY: 15 gals.

DIMENSIONS: Wheelbase 103-109.9 ins. Track 56.5 ins. front, 56.5 ins. rear. Width 70.6-70.7 ins. Length 181.7-188.6 ins. Height 52.6-53 ins. Weight 2691-2786 lbs. Trunk 15 cu. ft.

BODY STYLES: 2-dr. sdn., 4-dr. sdn.

ACCELERATION standing ¼ mile, seconds

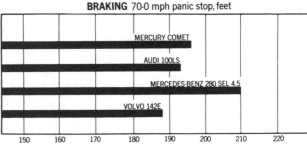

MERCURY COMET	
AUDI 100LS	
MERCEDES-BENZ 280 SEL 4.5	
VOLVO 142E	

13 14 15 16 17 18 19 20

BRAKING 70-0 mph panic stop, feet

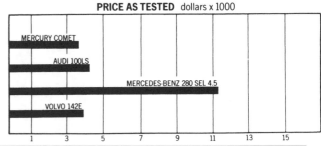

MERCURY COMET	
AUDI 100LS	
MERCEDES-BENZ 280 SEL 4.5	
VOLVO 142E	

150 160 170 180 190 200 210 220

FUEL ECONOMY RANGE mpg

MERCURY COMET	
AUDI 100LS	
MERCEDES-BENZ 280 SEL 4.5	
VOLVO 142E	

6 10 14 18 22 26 30 34

PRICE AS TESTED dollars x 1000

MERCURY COMET	
AUDI 100LS	
MERCEDES-BENZ 280 SEL 4.5	
VOLVO 142E	

1 3 5 7 9 11 13 15

Mercury Comet

Manufacturer: Lincoln-Mercury Division
Ford Motor Company
Rotunda Drive
Dearborn, Michigan 48121

Vehicle type: Front engine, rear-wheel-drive, 5-passenger
4-door sedan

Price as tested: $3689.71
(Manufacturer's suggested retail price, including all options
listed below, dealer preparation and delivery charges, does
not include state and local taxes, license or freight charges)

Options on test car: Base sedan, $2448.00; Glamour
paint, $34.66; Automatic transmission, $177.96; Power
steering, $92.45; Air conditioning, $359.59; Rear defogger,
$27.73; AM radio, $58.94; Custom interior, $151.00; Custom exterior, $240.00; Tinted glass, $35.83; Heavy-duty
battery, $11.55; Handling package, $11.55; Consollette
and clock, $40.45

ENGINE
Type: V-8, water-cooled, cast iron block and heads, 5 main
bearings
Bore x stroke . . . . 4.00 x 3.00 in, 101.5 x 76.0mm
Displacement . . . . .302 cu in, 4940cc
Compression ratio . . . . .8.5 to one
Carburetion . . . . .1x2-bbl Motorcraft
Valve gear . . . . .Pushrod-operated overhead valves, hydraulic
lifters
Power (SAE net) . . . . .143 bhp @ 4200 rpm
Torque (SAE net) . . . . .242 lb.-ft @ 2000 rpm
Specific power output . . . . . . .0.47 bhp/cu in, 29.0 bhp/liter

DRIVE TRAIN
Transmission . . . . .3-speed, automatic
Max Torque converter . . . . .2.01 to one
Final drive ratio . . . . .3.00 to one

Gear	Ratio	Mph/1000 rpm	Max. test speed
I	2.46	9.9	42 mph (4250 rpm)
II	1.46	16.7	75 mph (4500 rpm)
III	1.00	24.4	103 mph (4200 rpm)

DIMENSIONS AND CAPACITIES
Wheelbase . . . . .109.9 in
Track, F/R . . . . .56.5/56.5 in
Length . . . . .188.6 in
Width . . . . .70.6 in
Height . . . . .53.1 in
Ground clearance . . . . .5.0 in
Curb weight . . . . .3230 lbs
Weight distribution, F/R 57.8/42.2%
Battery capacity . . . . .12 volts, 55 amp-hr
Alternator capacity . . . . .670 watts
Fuel capacity . . . . .15.0 gal
Oil capacity . . . . .5.0 qts
Water capacity . . . . .14.2 qts

SUSPENSION
F: Ind., unequal-length control arms, coil springs, anti-sway
bar
R: Rigid axle, semi-elliptic leaf springs

STEERING
Type . . . . .Recirculating ball
Turns lock-to-lock 3.8
Turning circle curb-to-curb . . . . .38.8 ft

BRAKES
F: . . . . .10.0 x 2.2-in, cast-iron drum
R: . . . . .10.0 x 1.8-in, cast-iron drum

WHEELS AND TIRES
Wheel size . . . . .6.0 x 14-in
Wheel type .Stamped steel, 5-bolt
Tire make and size . . . . .Firestone Radial, DR78-14
Tire type . . . . .Tubeless, radial
Test inflation pressures, F/R . . . . .24/26 psi
Tire load rating . . . . .1320 lbs per tire @ 32 psi

PERFORMANCE

Zero to	Seconds
30 mph	3.2
40 mph	4.9
50 mph	7.2
60 mph	9.7
70 mph	12.5
80 mph	16.6
90 mph	22.5
100 mph	35.0

Standing ¼-mile . . . . .17.2 sec @ 81.0 mph
Top speed (observed) . . . . .103 mph
70-0 mph . . . . .196 ft (0.83G)
Fuel mileage . . . . .11.0-13.0 mpg on 91-octane fuel
Cruising range . . . . .165-200 mi

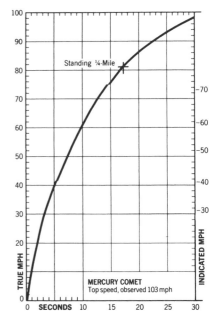

MERCURY COMET
Top speed, observed 103 mph

Mercury Comet

Luxury in a miniature package,
a blatant violation of Detroit's
favorite rule of thumb

• Yet another coffin nail has been firmly driven to prepare the final resting place for Detroit's fading mainstay—the full-size sedan. In this instance, the unlikely arm behind the hammer belongs to Ford's Lincoln-Mercury Division, and while the act reeks of overt masochism, there's no denying its logic. Even though hulking luxury-mobiles are still Detroit's bread and butter, Mercury dispatched its smallest and cheapest sedan, the Comet, to the sound labs, the interior studios, and past fabric designers who had been support troops for the Mark IVs and Continentals. Out of those shops emerged instant luxury in a miniature package, a blatant violation of Detroit's favorite rule of thumb: comfort is proportional to bulk. No longer will you need a warehouse to store your passport to sumptuous motoring. And if you demand more from driving than a silver lining, the attendant virtues of the trim Comet package are truly in your best interests.

As a basis for such endeavors, the Comet 4-door sedan stands as one of the most sensible cars offered by any arm of the Ford conglomerate. It's only 19 inches longer than a Chevy Vega, and in that extra length, you'll receive a genuine big-car interior. From the meager beginnings of the skinny-tired, starkly-finished, six-cylinder only, slope-backed Maverick, the Comet has mastered a transition into a full-strength automobile. The Mercury packaging artists have restrained their natural impulses and kept the wheelbase to a reasonable 109.9 inches for the 4-door, while careful contouring has eliminated every vestige of the 2-door's graceless profile. Add the necessary fillips to make a Ford a Mercury—like four gunsight taillamps from the Montego in place of the Maverick's glowing beer cans, plus a muscular nose courtesy of the Lincoln-Mercury stylists, and the Comet looms stylistically as one of America's most pleasing sedans.

Introduction-year anemia in the Maverick, caused by a shortage of cylinders, caught the Mercury product planners' eyes last year, and they specified the 302 two-barrel V-8 as an option for the Comet's engine room right at the start. Stunning acceleration is not the attraction, but the 242 lbs.-ft. of torque on hand assures tractability with the 3-speed automatic transmission. This combination excels at never intruding on the driver's consciousness, and with 17.2 seconds at 81.0 mph quarter-mile acceleration, ensures peace of mind for freeway on-ramps. On top of it all, even flat-out acceleration is so reserved that not a single patrolman's eyebrow need be raised in the direction of a ticket book.

The options list does not offer any sources of additional power, but within the myriad of codes and equipment groups lies the path to motoring success with the Comet. Only a hemorrhoid sufferer could bypass the Heavy Duty Suspension option at $11.55. For that token sum you'll receive not a single additional anti-sway bar, but all the important suspension design parameters are adjusted in the direction of more capable handling at minimal deterioration in the standard version's marshmallow ride. For an enthusiast, it is the bare minimum, not an option. The conventional ball joint, unequal-length control arm front suspension benefits from higher-rate (19%) coil springs, a stiffer anti-sway bar, and shock absorbers with more control. No anti-sway bar is provided at the rear, but the semi-elliptic leaf springs are 34% stiffer and again, the shocks have additional control. Still, even with the optional Firestone steel-belt radials, handling suffers from overly-generous helpings of understeer. But in comparison with full-size sedans, the 3230 lb. Comet is eminently more at home on a surpentine stretch than those heavyweights. Don't expect sport sedan performance, however. Any attempts to encourage a drifting tail via power applications will be met with increasing understeer, leaving the driver no choice as to cornering attitude. The front tires *always* reach their cornering limit well in advance of the rears, as the Ford Motor Co. considers this the safest way to travel.

However, Ford's logic is reversed when the brakes are applied. Pedal effort distribution is such that the rears will always reach their limit of adhesion first. Unfortunately, in the lightly-loaded condition, the front tires have barely begun their contribution to stopping the car before the rear tires cease turn-

PHOTOGRAPHY: HOWARD KOBEY

Even the padded vinyl
body side moldings are
color-coordinated, framed
in polished steel as if
they deserve to be exhibited
at the Whitney Annual

9

ing. And at the instant both rear wheels lock up, all directional stability is cast to the wind. Fortunately, the all-drum un-assisted brake system in the Comet does offer excellent modulation characteristics and amazing resistance to fade—but short stopping distances will never happen. And there is no relief within the options list. Engineers claim that minimal room under the hood disallows use of the vacuum booster necessary with disc brakes. But non-assisted disc/drum systems have been successfully applied to the heavier intermediate models, so the drum-only situation is likely one of pure economics—the expected sales volume won't support the engineering costs. No matter if the stopping power comes from discs, drums, or wooden blocks, better proportioning is necessary for acceptable braking performance.

The Comet's ultimate salvation is that while the car is not earth-shaking to drive, it is a genuinely excellent conveyance to ride in. Through the magic of two checkmarks on the option sheet, the low-line Mercury can be transformed from a price-leader hair shirt special into a hedonist's dream. Discretion in this instance will deliver bona fide enhancements, in contrast to the cardboard consoles and tacky trim previously dominating all luxury packages destined for a compact. The interior group is the best buy at $151. For a starter, it features reclining bucket seats. The internal reclining machinery is similar to that in Capri seats, and offers 15 backrest positions for about 60° of travel. Within the broad cushion is a heart of dense foam. Unfortunately, there's absolutely no lateral restraint, so any hard cornering is limited by personal suspension require-

Continued on next page

Continued from previous page

ments as well as the car's. The subtle tanned-manilla hues of the seat covers continue through the headliner, door panels, and instrument panel padding in the same soft expanded vinyl. Beneath it all is carpeting—the likes of which has never graced an under-$6000 car. The pile is dense, long, and the ends are sheared to length rather than looped back as in carpeting reserved for the working class. Only if your feet have grown used to the caresses of Gucci loafers will they be prepared for such regal treatment.

In a serious attempt to match the comfort virtues familiar in European sedans, the Comet benefits from arm rests with an integral door close handle ("Audi-type" in Lincoln-Mercury argot) and Capri-style door release handles. The package shelf below the instrument panel has been with the Comet/Maverick since its inception, but also has origins distant from Dearborn. With the optional interior, a shag lining graces the shelf and guarantees compatibility with the carpeting. Sadly lacking is a lockable compartment for those reluctant to display their Nikon on the utility shelf. The $40.55 "consollette" (with a clock carefully masked from the driver's eyes), has hardly enough room for three pieces of bubble gum.

A more subtle and perhaps most beneficial feature of the Luxury Interior option is the deluxe sound package. The barely adequate pads, absorbers and coatings of the standard Comet body insulation have been nearly doubled in size, weight and effectiveness, and additional pads are used under the hood and in the trunk. In addition, for relief from road harshness, there's a rubber isolator under the front coils and quieter bushings for the rear leaf springs. As a result, the Comet is the quietest car we've tested under full throttle acceleration to 70 mph, and generates slightly less noise (73.5 dbA) than the slippery Citroën SM while cruising at 70 mph. A pleasant sound environment is a prime requirement for a comfortable car, and in the Comet, not a murmur has eluded the sound engineers' influence.

The ride is markedly improved over the standard Comet, but the well-damped poise that guarantees a wide following for many European sedans is still a goal to be reached. Expansion joints are especially prominent, and at suggested tire pressures the Comet's ride is much too harsh for a luxury car.

The combination of radial tires, a short wheelbase, and the absence of ponderous masses is a new situation for the Lincoln-Mercury ride engineers. Recalibration of their sensitivities may be necessary to fine-tune the shock absorbers, but their efforts could be well applied to the Comet if they desire to bring the car's ride quality into line with its other specifications. Those serious about the possibilities of replacing their longer, lower, wider behemoth with something of more reasonable dimensions, should not overlook the Luxury Exterior option. At $240, the package may not seem like much of a bargain, but it includes Firestone DR78-14 steel-belted, white sidewall radial tires in addition to the visual wonders. Their 40,000-mile guarantee and better cornering abilities are well worth the expense and slight ride harshness penalties involved. The vinyl roof, on the other hand, will appear with no penalty at all. It's the latest science in elegant roof coverings and features a grain so coarse, it would be welcome on the back of an armadillo. What's more, a stainless steel molding graciously frames this provoking material on the B-pillar as if it deserves to be displayed at the Whitney Annual.

The stylists with color-coordinated shoelaces and underwear have been granted a free hand with the Luxury Exterior package and they've carried their sense of order to extreme ends. The color and texture of the vinyl roof matches a wide, full length body side molding and also front and rear bumper guards. Whether or not you're offended is a matter of taste (as are the color coordinated wheel covers), but the protection is invaluable in parking lots. An assortment of chrome-plated stainless steel trim moldings completes the package, and they are thankfully held in tasteful reserve like quality picture frames.

A firm dialogue will be necessary, but the Lincoln-Mercury product planners should have some success in convincing the world that their Comet is a competitor to the imported sedans. No Mercedes owner will stamp into Lincoln-Mercury dealers demanding a trade, but for the first time, comfort and convenience exist simultaneously under a single American nameplate. Most lacking right now is a strong identity to correlate the array of options into a single distinctive package not to be confused with any other Comet or Mercury. Without a doubt, it's proof that less can be more.●

Continued from page 110

clutch and brake pedals have very long throws—and the throttle is not linear with regard to pedal-in/power-out. The net result is that you can get around a road course fairly quickly, but it takes a lot of the old flailing of arms and stomping of feet to make it happen. Then, as one of our number so cleverly put it, "If you don't get your feet caught in the package shelf, or step on one of your hands, you can go pretty fast in this thing."

And indeed you *can* go pretty fast in the Comet. Its 302 cu.in. V-8 only makes 210 hp, but it does deliver a whacking 296 lb.-ft. of torque and that's a *lot* when you have a car that weighs 2935 lbs., with a full tank of gas. It is worth mentioning too, that the torque is delivered over an astonishing engine speed range, and one gets the impression that the car would perform entirely satisfactorily with a 2-speed transmission.

Curiously, the long-legged drive ratio doesn't seem to do a lot for fuel economy. A very gingerly placed foot on the throttle will get you about 17 miles-per-gallon, and lashing away at it makes the Comet eat gas like it is trying to put on fat for a hard winter. But, while the fuel economy is nothing to boast about, the car's braking capability is something you'll never want to mention at all. With the Comet, you get a sturdy cast-iron drum at each wheel, and about the best thing you can say about these is that they increase the scrap value of the car after you're through with it.

However, such mundane considerations as fuel economy and braking power aside, the Comet is a good car—and it *could* be a really great car. It is, for one thing, just about the size an American four-seater should be, and it is a very solid piece of structure around its four seats. The overall finish is a trifle stark (stripes and chrome-strips notwithstanding) but it is also very well done. The panels all fit together and the paint hasn't any built-in blemishes, and the carpeting has a quality look.

In short, the Comet has its flaws, but these are outweighed in our view by its good points—not the least of these being the price, $2859.20, complete; which not only is a friendly price for a V-8 equipped car of the Comet's dimensions, but gives you the mental satisfaction of having sorted through the option list and come up with something out of the mainstream plus the added fillip of having foiled the insurance surchargers. Because, at least at the time this is written, the V-8 Comet with its 3-speed manual transmission just nicks into that safe area populated mostly by cars an enthusiast wouldn't touch. ●

MERCURY

Comet

Both Maverick and Comet are testing to the ultimate the new-to-Detroit theory that economy-oriented cars will maintain if not increase their sales from year to year without the annual model change as we once knew it. The average Comet, like most any other modern car, will serve its first owner for perhaps 100,000 miles without incurring burdensome maintenance expenses, so the problem is either depending entirely on so-called "conquest" sales or serving up just enough that is new and different to entice the present owner into trading prematurely.

Nova, operating in the same marketing area, has rather successfully combined keeping the same basic bodies for now five years, with superficial appearance changes that do bespeak a new model. They also were quick enough to jump in with a new body style, or rather an adaptation of an old one, at what seems to be the right point in time. This is the hatchback coupe described elsewhere in this book. Hornet, too, has approached the problem in the same manner. First there was the 5-door Sportabout sedan and then the hatchback. Either of these might induce the owner of an original 1970 Hornet to trade. Equally enticing were the Plymouth Duster and Dodge Demon to owners of more mundane Valiants and Darts.

In view of the above, we firmly predict the appearance of Maverick and Comet hatchbacks by the early spring of 1973 which, as in the case of the Pinto wagon this last model year, will cost six month's worth of sales. Ford Motor Co. can be and has been a leading innovator on many occasions, but except perhaps for the original, Comet has not been a beneficiary.

The two body styles are continued, with the 4-door sedan on a 109.9-in. wheelbase and the pillar 2-door in plain or GT form on 103.0. The grille insert is the only styling change, with a box texture taking the place of the former horizontal stripes. The side appearance has been enhanced but not restyled by the addition of standard bright window and fender well moldings. That, except for the prominent impact-resistant bumpers, is about it.

As with Maverick, the 200-cu.-in. 6 becomes standard in the Comet, replacing the less durable 170-cube unit used before. Other choices are the 250 6-cylinder and the 302 V-8, the bigger 6 being entirely adequate for every purpose other than trailer towing. The standard 3-speed manual transmission may be obtained with either a column or floor shift, and an automatic is offered with any engine.

Lack of a 4-speed option for the 302, which has long existed for use in Mustangs and Cougars until just recently, is hard to understand. Product planners at least should give Comet a chance to appeal to the enthusiast because adding fundamentals like this could make a nicer package. This even includes adapting the Pinto/Capri 4-speed box to the 6's and providing them with optional disc brakes. For the moment, though, Comet is of interest mainly to those who want something just a bit above basic transportation, Detroit-style.

Mercury nameplates traditionally offer a higher degree of soundproofing than their Ford counterparts, and the Comet is no exception. Already measurably quieter than the Maverick, the '73 Comet adds a molded dash absorber that extends around the cowl sides, a molded cowl top absorber, a full-width hood-to-cowl seal, a molded package tray absorber, and sprayed-on mastic in the quarter panels. All of this will help you appreciate the new AM/FM stereo option. That doesn't, however, include provision for stereo tape, which continues to be illogically combined with the base AM radio.

Comet uses the MacPherson-type front coil suspension with leaf springs at the rear, which is an adequate if uninspired method of connecting compact unitized bodies to

COMET 4-DOOR SEDAN

119

wheels. Refinements for '73 include new front and rear shock absorbers and voided-type rear spring front eye bushings. Sound transmission is reduced by rubber insulators under the front springs, eliminating metal-to-metal contact between the spring and upper control arm.

Like the Maverick, Comet has no glove compartment, although it would seem that there would be space on the extreme right for at least a small one. Both types of transmissions can be ordered with an optional floor mount, but no mention is made of a console that might contain an out-of-sight storage area. Cameras and the like, which you don't want banging about back in the trunk, are the obvious problem, but there's also the little matter of registration slips in those states that require them to be carried in the car. Who wants one's name and address available to any stranger who has temporary access to the car?

We were more enthusiastic about the Comet when it was first introduced as a 1971 model. At that time one could understand why it started out simply as a rather attractive adaptation of the Maverick with the added advantage of having a 4-door sedan in the line. By the next year, though, we expected some imaginative exclusives such as Cougar's XR-7 package but they were not, so far at least, forthcoming. ⊞

COMET / GT

ENGINES: 200 cu. ins. (90 hp), 250 cu. ins. (98 hp), 302 cu. ins. (140 hp). (est.)
TRANSMISSIONS: 3-spd. manual std, 3-spd. auto opt.
SUSPENSION: Coil front, leaf rear.
STEERING: Manual std., power opt., curb-to-curb 36.3-38.8 ft.
BRAKES: Drums std.
FUEL CAPACITY: 15.0 gals.
DIMENSIONS: Wheelbase 103.0-109.9 ins. Track 56.5 ins. front, 56.5 ins. rear. Overall length 185.4-192.3 ins., width 70.5 ins., height 53.0-53.1 ins. Weight 2782-2877 lbs. Trunk 9.5-10.1 cu. ft.
BODY STYLES: 2-dr. sdn., 4-dr. sdn.

COMET 2-DOOR SEDAN

120

SCALED DOWN LUXURY

Those having to give up on big cars quite possibly can find true happiness with the Comet.

The more visible effects of the fuel shortage might have eased somewhat, but indications are that buyers are still turning away from larger cars in droves. Perhaps the $10-plus fill-up is causing as much alarm among full-size car drivers as the time when service stations would only sell them $5 worth of gasoline. Most of these people were driving big cars because they *like* big cars and not, as has been asserted, the auto industry somehow forced the cars upon them. Sure the automakers pushed the big ones because they made more money from them, but the accusation that they were preying on unwilling victims just won't wash.

The big car addict might mention roominess as one of the justifications for his choice, but the typical passenger load for those cars is one or two persons, same as for the smaller cars. Those who mention quietness and general feel as reasons for their preference are being far more objective.

There's good news for those making what they undoubtedly consider a step down, however. It's the Comet. From fairly humble beginnings as a compact at the bottom of the FoMoCo totem pole, it and its Maverick counterpart have emerged as the closest things the company has to big car feel and noise level but with significantly better gas mileage. And what really makes the car feel and sound like the larger ones is a package consisting of acoustic damping and isolation materials, including heavy cut-pile carpeting, with such things as a vinyl roof, reclining bucket seats, steel radial tires, and outside vinyl panel moldings thrown in for good measure. Ordinarily we are on the cool side toward package deals because they

contain so much chaff with a few grains of wheat. This one is different, however, and we recommend it without reservation. The quality of the upholstery and interior trim that comes with the package is second to none and appears to be very durable and easy to keep clean. The seats are comfortable to sit on and give good support over the longer driving stints.

The Comet comes standard with a 200 cubic inch L-6 engine, with a 250 L-6 and a 302 V-8 optional. Our test car had the latter engine coupled to a Selectshift Cruise-O-Matic (C-4) automatic transmission. The combination, it turns out, produces performance almost identical to that of the 2.8 liter Capri V-6 with manual transmission, making the 302 Comet one of the hotter products in Lincoln-Mercury showrooms. It comes on particularly strong at the low end, where you feel it and where you need it for maneuvering in traffic. The engine has an unfettered feel reminiscent of the pre-emissions controls era.

In town and using the air conditioner, which we used a lot on this test for reasons we will explain later, the average fuel economy turned out to be a so-so 11.2 mpg. Not anything to brag about, but a huge improvement over some of the big gas hogs that get 8 or 9 under the same circumstances. Our standard test, which involves highway driving at a maximum of 55 mph and city driving at about a 2 to 1 ratio yielded 14.8 mpg, again using the air conditioner most of the time. Now, this might not seem like such a great feat

to a Honda Civic driver, but to anyone used to averaging 10 or 11 this represents a 34 to 48 percent improvement. A person driving 20,000 miles a year could realize approximately an $800 annual savings with the seemingly small 4.8 mpg improvement.

New this year is a disc brake option that formerly wasn't available. The discs are quite similar in size and design to those used on the full-size Mercurys and Fords and bolster up what was a weak area in the Comet before. Their stopping manners, working with the whitewall steel radials, add a safe and secure feeling that former big car owners will come to like very much.

Handling is something else that drivers who are accustomed to herding about something much longer and wider and maybe 1200-1500 pounds heavier will also learn to love when it comes to parking and maneuvering in close quarters. Handling in the sense of cornering at the limit of adhesion is something few owners will ever try, but be apprised the Comet acquits itself as well as anything in its class in this regard.

The ride won't be a floating nor will the car wallow as much on lane changes etc. as erstwhile full-size car drivers might have experienced, but it isn't harsh in the least. The improved steering response over most big cars is something else a new Comet driver might learn to like.

One thing about the Comet that we feel hardly anyone will like is the lack of a vent position on the air conditioner con-

trols. There are many occasions on sunny days with moderate outside air temperatures that it's desirable to shut off the air conditioner and pull fresh air from the outside through the air conditioning vents. You can't do that with the Comet. It's either open the window and be buffeted by the wind, or run the air conditioner at just about any outside temperature down to the point where you need the heater. We used the air conditioner all the time for the test. Had we had some alternate fresh air system, the gas mileage would have been better.

Whether a full instrument array is necessary or desirable on a car like the Comet, we leave to each individual, but it has only a speedometer/odometer and gas gauge, with the other functions or malfunctions being handled by warning lights. The view is widely held among automotive engi-

122

COMET
PERFORMANCE DATA

Acceleration, sec:
0–30 mph	3.8
0–40 mph	5.7
0–50 mph	8.2
0–60 mph	10.9
0–70 mph	14.8
0–80 mph	20.4
Standing start, ¼ mile	17.84
Speed at end ¼ mile, mph	76.98
Avg accel over ¼ mile, g	0.197

Speeds in gears, mph:
1st (4000 rpm)	42.0
2nd (3800 rpm)	66.0
3rd (3500 rpm)	92.0
Engine revs at 70 mph	2700

Speedometer error:
Electric speedometer	Car speedometer
40 mph	40 mph
50 mph	50 mph
60 mph	60 mph
70 mph	70 mph
80 mph	80 mph

Brakes:
Min stopping distance from 60 mph, ft	167
Avg deceleration rate, g	0.720

Fuel economy (on closed test course):
Overall avg	14.8 mpg
Range on 15.0 gal tank	222 miles
Fuel required	regular

Skid pad:
Max speed on 100-ft rad, mph	31.7
Lateral acceleration, g	0.672

Interior noise, decibels (dBA):
Idle	52
Max 1st gear	76
Steady 40 mph	65
50 mph	67
60 mph	70
70 mph	74

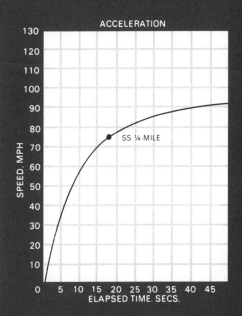

ACCELERATION — SPEED, MPH vs ELAPSED TIME, SECS. SS ¼-MILE

Graph Of Recorded Data Expressed In Percentage of 100 (100 = best possible rating) *

Acceleration
Brakes
Skid Pad
Interior Noise
Tire Reserve
Fuel Economy
Overall Rating
Best Car To Date (overall) — Porsche 914
Worst Car To Date (overall) — Mercedes 240D

SPECIFICATIONS

Engine:
Type	OHV V-8
Displacement, cu in	301.6
Displacement, cc	4942
Bore x stroke, in	4.00 x 3.00
Bore x stroke, mm	101.6 x 76.2
Compression ratio	8.0:1
Hp at rpm, net	140 at 3800 rpm
Torque at rpm, lb-ft, net	230 at 2600 rpm
Carburetion	1 2-V

Emissions, gm/mile:
Hydrocarbons	3.2
Carbon monoxide	39.0
Nitrogen oxides	2.0

Prices:
Factory list, as tested
West Coast	$4553 plus destination chg.
East Coast	$4553 plus destination chg.

Accessories included in price:
$383—air conditioning; $106—power steering; $34—disc brakes; $37—special paint; $212—automatic transmission; $222—AM/FM radio; $38—tinted glass; $30—rear window defogger; $408—custom option package; $24—bumper protection group; plus misc. items

Manufacturer's guarantee and service:
Warranty (mos/miles)	12/12,000
Oil change (mos/miles)	6/6000
Lubrication (mos/miles)	
Tune-up (miles)	
Lubrication (mos/miles)	36/36,000
Tune-up (miles)	
Minor	as needed
Major	as needed

Drive line:
Transmission	3-spd auto
Gear ratios:	
1st	2.46:1
2nd	1.46:1
3rd	1.00:1
Final drive ratio	3.00:1
Driving wheels	rear

Wheels	14 x 6
Tires	DR 78-14 Firestone SBR
Reserve load, front/rear, lb	592/993

General:
Wheelbase, ins	103.0
Overall length, ins	190.0
Width, ins	70.5
Height, ins	53.0
Front track, ins	56.5
Rear track, ins	56.5
Trunk capacity, cu ft	11.3
Curb weight, lbs	3375
Distribution, % front/rear	59/41
Power-to-weight ratio, lbs/hp	24.1

Body and chassis:
Boady/frame construction	unit
Brakes, front/rear	disc/drum
Swept area, sq in	332.4
Swept area, sq in/1000 lb	98.49
Steering	recirculating ball
Ratio	21.3:1
Turns, lock-to-lock	3.7
Turning circle, ft	36.4

Front suspension: short/long arms, coil springs, tubular shocks, anti-sway bar

Rear suspension: live axle, leaf springs, tubular shocks

Test Equipment Used: Testron Fifth Wheel, Esterline-Angus recorder, Ammco decelerometer, General Radio Sound Level Meter

* Acceleration (0-60 mph): 0% = 34.0 secs., 100% = 4.0 secs.; Brakes (60-0 mph): 0% = 220.0 ft., 100% = 140.0 ft.; Skid pad lateral accel.: 0% = 0.3 g, 100% = 0.9 g; Interior noise (70 mph): 0% = 90.0 dBA, 100% = 65.0 dBA; Tire reserve (with passengers): 0% = 0.0 lbs., 100% = 1500 lbs. or more; Fuel economy: 0% = 5 mpg, 100% = 45 mpg or more.

neers that the average driver won't read other gauges anyway.

It seems that domestic cars in general have the most uncomfortable to wear and hard to get in and out of seat belts in the business, but the Comet is a happy exception. They're easy to sort out, and you hardly know you're wearing them. About the only complaint about seating or entrance and egress was the driver's seat release lever which caught the trousers cuff almost without fail whenever we left the seat. It needs to be relocated to a more out of the way spot.

The general controls placement, seating position, visibility etc. are such that anyone used to driving anything made in this country the last 20 years will feel right at home. All the main buttons and knobs are in the standard positions.

The Comet has a more finished appearance around the dash compared to earlier models. It now has a glove box, but some will find that the earlier open shelf was in some ways more useful.

Starting and cold drivability were above average, although the fast idle was so fast that it was necessary to restrain the car with the brake at every traffic signal until the engine warmed up and released the

fast idle mechanism. Hot starts were uneventful.

To sum up, the Comet is typically "American" in general design philosophy, but with the custom interior package (the way most are sold, we understand) it's quieter and plushier than the typical compact. It represents a considerable upgrading of the class, and can compete on the basis of a low noise level and quality of interior fittings with luxury cars of just a few years ago. It's as good an inducement as we've seen to attract big car drop outs and woo them away from lower priced strictly economy cars. ●

Comet

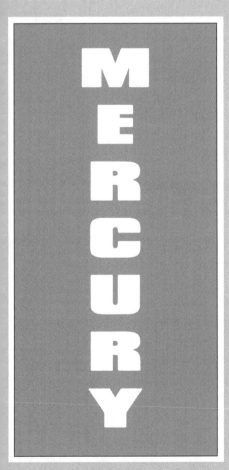

Comet

Comet

With an identical wheelbase of 109.9 inches and within two inches of the overall length of the new Monarch, it is little wonder that the Comet has undergone no physical changes for the new season. Basically the Comet has been an economy mainstay for Mercury since the Ford-Mercury concept several years ago. To upgrade the Comet with frills and power-plants in the face of the upcoming Monarch would be an exercise in tail-chasing. The Comet will remain the economy car it was meant to be, with prices fluctuating only due to economic pressures instead of new tooling expenses and design concepts. This is good to hear in a year when smog devices and safety requirements mean an addition of as much as $600 to an economy car price.

The engine sizes are unchanged, with the 200 cid six-cylinder as the standard powerplant, the 250 cid six-cylinder and the 302 cid V-8 optional. The three-speed transmission is installed with all three engines, and a Select-Shift automatic with a 2.79:1 or 3.00:1 ratio is available.

In a move to maintain their share of the compact market, Mercury has treated the Comet to an electronic ignition system and steel-belted radial ply tires. For comfort, the Comet received more sound-proofing material and a cut-pile carpet.

The Comet GT (two-door model) has upgraded interiors, adding bucket seats which recline and are covered with a new, softer vinyl.

It's ironic that this little gas-saver (19.9 mpg) has offered an optional fuel economy reminder light, but if you are shopping for a low priced, low maintenance car, the Comet at least gives a buyer the chance to make every penny count.

SHOOTING STAR

America's Dazzling Drop Tops

Ford's Falcon proved to be a massive hit, despite its dimunitive size; but could Mercury replicate its success with a ritzier package? **Ben Klemenzson** *finds out ...*

Photography: Mike Key

As we all know by now, compacts were big news at the start of the Sixties, pretty much everyone was getting in on the act, but by far the most successful was Ford's Falcon, which was the most conventional of all the compacts to be offered by the Big Three.

Chevy's Corvair had an air-cooled engine in the back and swing-arm suspension, something which American buyers would happily buy in the funny bug-eyed format of a German Volkswagen (what the Hey! It was 'imported', it was bound to be a bit exotic!), however they were less accepting of such exotica with a Chevy badge on it. And the Valiant? Well, the Valiant's looks were an acquired taste, and not everyone was taken with them.

That left the Falcon, which buyers voted most popular with their hard-earned dollars. Ford had chosen not to push the envelope too much in the styling department, preferring instead to produce what to many looked like a scaled down Galaxie.

Not to be left out, from 1960 Mercury offered the Comet, which was basically a Falcon in a ball gown. To mark it out as the Ford Motor Company's senior compact, the Comet featured dual headlights and was some 4 1/2-inches longer than the Falcon (despite making use of the same 114-inch wheelbase). It also featured a front grille that looked more like the Galaxie's and unusual – though not terribly attractive – slanted tail lights.

Most of the extra length seemed to have been used to give Mercury's little Comet (if a car over 16-feet can be described as 'little') a bigger trunk (26.6.cu.ft.) than its Falcon sibling. Interestingly, Tom McCahill tested the new Comet in the June 1960 issue of *Mechanix Illustrated* and was very impressed with it. He felt its styling was handsome, particularly the Thunderbird-inspired

roofline, and welcomed the ample boot.

What McCahill didn't particularly like about that first 1960 Comet was its performance. Despite being a slightly bigger and heavier car, the running gear was lifted wholesale from the Falcon, a set-up which at the best of times was a bit 'unhurried'. Powered by the 90bhp 144cu.in. straight six, the Comet was capable of 0–60 in around 22 seconds with the soporific two-speed Ford-o-Matic (or 'Merc-o-Matic' as it was called in the Comet), or a slightly sprightlier 17 seconds with the stick shift. However, whereas the Falcon used 3.10 rear axle ratio, the Comet utilised a 3.56,

THE MERCURY COMET GOT A FRONT END TREATMENT ALL OF ITS OWN, BUT THE SWAGE LINE IN THE SIDE GAVE AWAY ITS FALCON ORIGINS

ODDLY, THE ONLY OPTION THIS UPMARKET FALCON HAS IS A POWER HOOD. OBVIOUSLY THE FIRST OWNER LIKED TO POSE!

meaning that what the Ford gained in economy, the Mercury should've made up for off the stoplights.

Like the Falcon, the Comet was built using unitised body construction, something which 'kept it rattle-free and squeak-proof throughout our tests' according to McCahill. Although the puny little 'Thrift-Power' in-line six did seem to struggle when it came to passing, it was good for around 28mpg, a figure unheard of for most standard-sized offerings from the Big Three. Although the biggest of the compacts on offer at the time, the Comet did fit neatly into NASCAR's criteria of what a compact was: an engine of less than 200cu.in. displacement and a sticker price under $2,500 (the Comet was priced just under $2000).

Although the Comet may have started out as one of Mercury's more austere offerings (comprising two- and four-door sedans and wagons initially) back in 1960, as the decade progressed, so did the Comet line-up. For 1961 Mercury pulled the new S-22 coupe out of the hat, a $2,282 two-door Comet coupe that was aimed for the newly emerging sporty compact market.

Like Ford's Falcon Futura, the S-22 emulated its bigger brother the T-bird, with contoured front bucket seats, a console, a sporty steering wheel, deluxe interior trim and carpets, special wheel covers and extra insulation. All in all it was a very nice package, and to add to the whole mini T-bird concept, Ford even offered air-conditioning to the options list for the first time.

Motoring journalists at the time had been unimpressed with the first Comet's 144cu.in. Falcon straight six, so for 1961 Ford offered an enlarged version of the same engine, the 101bhp 170cu.in. This engine (which went on to provide sterling service for Falcons, Comets and Mustangs for many years to come) was claimed to be 11% faster at passing and 22% faster at climbing hills than the old 144cu.in. unit and the general consensus was that it was a vast improvement. Nevertheless, 60mph still took 22 seconds to reach and fuel economy suffered as Comets achieved only around 18mpg (combined).

1962 saw Mercury offering a Fairlane clone, the Meteor, which like its Ford sibling was based on a stretched Falcon/Comet floorpan. Ford was quick to respond to customers who complained that the diminutive Falcons and Comets were too small, whilst the full-size cars were too big. The solution was to produce what to many were America's first generation of mid-size cars; bigger than a compact, but smaller than a full-size car.

By 1963 the Comet line was complete with the addition of a convertible, which was available in just the fancier S-22 line. Other than the usual annual model facelift tweaks and tucks, the '63

FOUR-DOOR SEDAN

TWO-DOOR HARDTOP

TWO-DOOR SEDAN

CONVERTIBLE

STATION WAGON, WITH DI-NOC WOOD TRIM, AS SEEN ON MKI CORTINAS!

model was much the same as the two previous years' cars and for that matter the upcoming '64s. It wasn't until '63 1/2 that the Comet line was finally offered V8 power, in the form of a 260cu.in. small block. It was like the one offered with the Falcon Sprint package, however, on the Comet version was called the Sportster. It was what many had argued the Comet needed; 60mph now only took 11 seconds.

For many people 1964 was the year that the Comet (and it's Ford Sibling, the Falcon) was transformed from ugly duckling to Swan. A major restyle resulted in a handsome Lincoln Continental front style

ABOVE: THE MERCURY COMET GETS THE PILLARLESS HARDTOP LOOK
ABOVE RIGHT: 170CU.IN. SIX MAY NOT BE A MATCH FOR A BIG-BLOCK POWERHOUSE, BUT GUESS WHO HAS THE LAST LAUGH AT THE FILLING STATION?
RIGHT: ONE-PIECE REAR LENSES HAD THREE CHROME-TIPPED CIRCLES MOULDED IN
BELOW RIGHT: ALAN, CAROL AND THEIR 'COMPROMISE CAR'!

grille and a 'full-size' appearance, although it's dimensions remained very much the same. With the rise of racing as a promotional tool, Mercury dispatched a fleet of Comets to Daytona for a 100,000 mile endurance race. The Comets were a great success, breaking over a 100 world endurance records. Spurred on by this success, the '64 Comets competed in the East African Rally and soon became a popular sight at dragstrips across the nation.

Mercury decided to abandon its mid-size Meteor range for 1964, and upgrade the top line Comets, renaming them Comet Calientes and offering even ritzier appointments. It turned out that Mercury had made all the right moves, as 1964 became a banner sales year for the division's compact, selling almost 183,000 cars

One of 9,039 built, the Fernwood Blue Metallic Comet Caliente convertible pictured here belongs to Carol Mardon of Moulton, Lincolnshire. Carol's boyfriend Alan French looks after the car and originally spotted it for sale at Americana almost four years ago. It was Carol and the kids' enthusiastic reaction to the Comet when they saw it that determined the car was the right choice. Unfortunately at the time the Comet owner was asking too much money for the car, but eventually when Alan called back three weeks later, a deal was struck and the Mercury made the long pilgrimage from Bishop Auckland, County Durham down to Lincolnshire, where it now resides.

It's quite a contrast Alan's other Merc, a 429-powered Mercury Grand Marquis, second only to the Lincoln Continental in terms of sheer bulk. As Alan explains, Carol had always been into Consul Capris, and in the Comet they found a vehicle which blended their vehicle tastes nicely.

The car didn't come with a great deal of history, although they know the US dealer who sold the car back in 1990/1991 was Colgan's Auto Sales of Orange Blossom Trail, Florida. The car's first UK owner was located down in Bexhill and it's unclear whether some of the car's restoration work was actually done then and there, or had already been carried out in the United States. Whatever the answer, there can be little doubt that the Comet has been well looked after. With 19,000 miles on the clock (that's probably 119,000 miles) it has been resprayed, but the interior looks factory-fresh and the engine still runs beautifully tight.

Fitted with the 170cu.in. straight-six and a three-speed manual 'box. Alan reckons it's unusual for an American car in that the only thing that's power-operated is the top. That means no servo assistance on the all-round single-circuit drum brakes and no power steering! However, with its single-carburetted straight-six engine, there can be no doubt that fill-up time at the the petrol station must be a welcome change from the thirsty 429 of Alan's old Grand Marquis!

The car was in nice all-round condition when it was first acquired and the ambition has been to keep it this way, whilst getting out and enjoying it as much as possible during the summer. So fingers crossed for a long hot summer – this is one lucky star we'd love to hitch a ride in! ★